Successful Investing in No-Load Funds

Successful Investing in No-Load Funds

Alan Pope

JOHN WILEY & SONS

New York   Chichester   Brisbane   Toronto   Singapore

Library of Congress Cataloging in Publication Data:

Pope, Alan, 1913–
  Successful investing in no-load funds

  Includes index.
  1. Investment trusts—Handbooks, manuals, etc.
2. Individual retirement accounts—Handbooks, manuals,
etc. I. Title. II. Title: No-load funds.

HG4530.P59 1983 332.63'27 82-23856

ISBN 0-471-89773-6

Printed in the United States of America

10 9 8 7 6 5 4 3 2

Preface

This is a book about the best investments I have been able to find in over 40 years of looking: certain no-load (no commission) mutual funds. Their wide diversification, the cash flow they get from investors, and the investor's freedom from legal responsibilities, all coupled with zero costs for buying and selling (they are sold by mail or telephone) give them advantages unavailable in any other investments. They can provide more income now; rapid accumulation for an estate later on; or simply a solid, profitable, low-risk investment requiring minimum watchfulness on your part.

Successful Investing in No-Load Funds gives the story behind and guidance for investing in this relatively new field. It covers in nontechnical language getting started, selecting, buying, holding, switching, selling, registering, pledging, and trusting no-load mutual funds. And if you would like to see what I consider successful, turn to Tables 4.10 and 4.11. They are impressive.

Many times readers of an earlier form of this book wrote to me and gave the ultimate accolade: "Thank you for writing this book." I hope you will say so, too.

Good luck and good investing.

ALAN POPE

Albuquerque, New Mexico
March 1983

Contents

Successful Investing in
No-Load Funds

1

Mutual Funds

1.1. THE NEED FOR INVESTING

Investing is as American as apple pie. Every working person does it, either directly through buying things that offer income or profit or both, or indirectly when his or her employer puts aside money that could go into salaries and invests it in order to provide pensions later on.

All this is part of the American free-enterprise system, the system that has given us dishwashers, clothes washers, clothes dryers, vacuum cleaners, television sets, microwaves, and lots more—most of which are only dreams for hungry people the world around.

After nearly 50 years of "Let the government do it," many of us have forgotten just how people make free enterprise work. It goes like this:

> People work and make things and earn money. They spend most of their money on living expenses and taxes and save what is left over. Employers borrow the savings to buy new tools. These in turn provide new jobs so that more people can work and make things and earn money and save—and so on.

For a number of reasons, possibly peer pressure and advertising and certainly inflation ("It will cost more next year"), American workers in recent years have spent 95 percent of

1

their earnings and saved 5 percent. Japanese workers, for reasons of their own, have spent 75 percent and saved 25. Guess who has the best tools? So saving and investing are not only good for you and the country, they are essential.*

1.2. INFLATION

Compounding the problem of not having enough savings to provide loan money for industry has been the phenomenon of inflation. When prices are going up for everything, there is little or no incentive to save—you'll only pay more next year. For the little lending that takes place, loaners reasonably want enough interest so that what they get back will pay for things they could buy today for the same money.

There was a period when our leaders could get by with placing the blame for inflation on others. The increase in the price of oil was a scapegoat for a number of years. It raised the prices of all the things that come from oil: electric power, gasoline, heating fuels, diesel oil, plastics, and synthetic fibers. But higher oil prices don't cause inflation. Higher prices for a few things simply mean that you buy less of them, or less of something else, provided your money supply is kept constant. It wasn't. Additional money was printed, and prices rose in *all* categories. Milton Friedman linked the increase in money supply to inflation by saying that the average rate of inflation would be the increase in the money supply less the increase in the goods produced (same thing as the gross national product, GNP), all as percentages. If the money supply is increased 10 percent and the GNP goes up 4 percent, then the inflation 2 years later (there is a lag in the system) will be 6 percent. Is it that simple? Just about. Table 1.1 shows the average increase in the money supply for 14 nations over a 20-year period, less their average increase in GNP, thus establishing the expected

---

*Consider the Alaskan pipeline: 48 inches in diameter, 810 miles long . . . made in Japan. U.S. government regulations and lack of low-cost money meant our steel mills didn't have the equipment to build the pipe.

Table 1.1.   Financial Data for a Recent Twenty-Year Period[a]

Country	Increase in Money Supply (%)	Increase in GNP (%)	Expected Inflation[b] (%)	Actual Inflation (%)
Brazil	44.7	9.1	35.6	32.1
Japan	16.8	8.4	8.4	6.1
Italy	16.5	4.3	12.2	9.1
Spain	16.2	6.3	9.9	10.5
Mexico	15.8	6.1	9.7	8.4
France	10.4	4.1	6.3	6.4
Netherlands	9.5	4.2	5.3	6.4
Sweden	9.1	3.1	6.0	6.6
Germany	8.7	3.9	4.8	4.4
United Kingdom	8.1	2.5	5.6	8.3
Canada	8.1	4.8	3.3	5.3
Switzerland	7.8	2.8	5.0	5.1
Belgium	7.1	4.2	3.9	5.2
United States	6.1	3.6	2.9	4.7
Average	13.1	4.7	8.4	8.5

[a]Basic data from Market Logic, 3471 North Federal Highway, Fort Lauderdale, FL 33306.
[b]Expected inflation is the increase in the money supply less the increase in GNP.

rate of inflation for the example period as 8.4 percent. The average inflation for the 14 countries turned out to be 8.5 percent! These data are for 280 country-years, and they are convincing. Since the money supply in our country is mostly under the control of the Federal Reserve Board, which is mostly under the control of the government, inflation is our own doing. To have inflation, two things must occur:

1. The government (that is, the president and Congress) must agree on a deficit budget.
2. If the U.S. Treasury can sell the federal bonds printed to raise the money to cover the deficit, interest rates

go up because money needed by industry is with-drawn from the lending sources. If the Treasury is unable to sell the bonds, the leftovers are delivered to the Federal Reserve, which credits the Treasury's account *as though it had deposited cash,* and the Treasury writes checks against the amount.

The second step is the one that does the big harm. That's the one that causes inflation. And *that,* in turn, does the following:

1. Raises interest rates, because few will lend money knowing that when it is paid back they will receive less buying power than they have now. (Almost nobody outside of the financial world realizes the import of this facet. The bond market is far bigger than the stock market, and it has virtually been destroyed. Many of us feel that it can *never* come back in the sense of a true bond market where capital is preserved at all times.)

2. Prevents young people from buying homes and cars, since salaries rarely rise as fast as inflation. The latter, since Social Security is *fully* indexed, is what has made serious trouble for that agency.

3. Discourages saving, which as we saw earlier is essential for business.

4. Makes accumulation for a funded pension based on early lower wages completely inadequate to provide an inflated pension at retirement.

5. Destroys the buying power of fixed pensions. Figure 1.1 shows how even a 5 percent inflation rate cuts a fixed pension in half in only 13 years, a man's life expectancy at age 65 (women have 18 years to go).

6. Requires higher taxes to pay the interest on the federal bonds printed to pay for the deficit. (The $180 billion deficit accumulated during Mr. Carter's four years as president works out to $75 a year for every man, woman, and child in the United States, *forever!*)

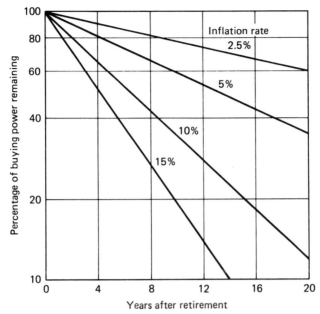

Figure 1.1.   The effect of several rates of inflation on the effective buying power of a fixed pension.

7. Prevents manufacturers from depreciating their tools so that they can buy new ones needed to stay in business.

8. Destroys the rental business because rents cannot be raised enough to pay for the units.

This list delineates the terrible consequences of continually spending more than a government takes in. However, inflation can go on for a long time while a government survives. Witness Brazil, where inflation has averaged 32.1 percent for the last 20 years. The country still functions and the growth of the GNP exceeds that for all countries with lower inflation rates. The problem that arises is that raw materials from other countries become exceedingly expensive. Foreign trade will, sooner or later, come to a halt, and with it goes the local economy. Friedman has described inflation as a "tax imposed without anybody voting for it." That's *almost* true: nobody but Congress and the president.

1.3.   *MUTUAL FUNDS*

Since inflation will be with us for many years, most people would like to have more income now, or to save (at an accumulation rate higher than inflation) for more income later.*
What should they do?

Provided they have the money, our country offers an almost endless array of investment opportunities: land, rentals, notes, stocks, bonds, options, oil rights, mineral rights, partnerships, mutual funds, and much more. One of these, mutual funds, is what this book is all about. Mutual funds have the following unique features:

1. Can be purchased with so little down that anyone can get started.
2. May be added to as frequently or infrequently as one desires, and with very small amounts of money.
3. May be partly or totally cashed in at any time.
4. Have a negligible chance of failure.
5. Make their profit with a substantial tax shelter.
6. Require no maintenance.
7. Incur no liability and require no liability insurance.
8. Have a high certainty of a good or even excellent rate of profit over a long period of time.

*How much do you need to put away? With 10 percent inflation it takes 25 percent of your yearly income to have a "good" retirement. Don't despair. Your company is putting about 10 percent away for you, and Social Security a few percent more. A serious investment program of about 10 percent *every year* will do the trick.

9. Require little effort on the part of most investors (but a fair amount if you are an "aggressive" investor).

10. Remain fluid, immediately available for borrowing against so that money needed for a special circumstance won't force you to sell out.

11. Require no taxes unless they make a profit (unlike land).

12. May be set up so that profits may be automatically reinvested, no matter how small.

13. Have many "fringe benefits" unavailable with other investments.

One group of mutual funds—the one this book is all about—is called *no-load funds*. These are sold only by mail or telephone, and having no salespeople means paying no sales commissions. By not requiring any commissions no-load funds make it practical to get out when the market is going down, and get back in when it turns up.

If you are a long-term investor not interested in spending time on your investments, no-load funds have the advantage that the usual 8.5 percent commission ends up in your pocket instead of somebody's else.

1.4. THE STOCK MARKET

Mutual funds are a group investment in the stock market, so before we go into funds we need to look at the larger picture. Basically the stock market is the financial heart of the United States. To start a company, that is where you would go to raise the money. A lot of others have done this in the past, and the stock market now consists of some 60,000 corporations, ranging all the way from tiny ones you and I never heard of to the financial giants (which were once tiny themselves). By meeting

		New York Stock Exchange	American Stock Exchange
1.	Shares publicly held	600,000	25,000
2.	Market value of publicly held shares	$10 million	$1.25 million
3.	Number of stockholders	1,500 holders of 100 shares or more	750, including 500 holders of 100 shares or more
4.	Demonstrated earning power after income taxes	$1.2 million	$150,000 last fiscal year
5.	Net tangible assets	$10 million	$1 million

certain specifications such as issuing a large number of shares,* turning over a certain amount of business a year, and having over a certain minimum number of stockholders, about 3,000 of these corporations are listed on the various exchanges. The New York Stock Exchange (NYSE) has about 1,800 and the American Stock Exchange (Amex) has about 800. The "unlisted" corporations, because they are smaller or because they just don't want to be listed, have stocks that may be purchased "over the counter," which means not through exchanges but person to person. The *Wall Street Journal* carries 2,100 of these. The relatively small size of the American Stock Exchange compared to the New York Stock Exchange wil come home when I point out that at one time you could buy all the stocks on the American Stock Exchange for less than what it would take to buy all of IBM!

*In order for a corporation to qualify for admittance to the New York Stock Exchange or the American Stock Exchange it must meet the following minimums:

Investors in the stock market and the approximate percentages they own are as follows:

Pension funds	15	percent
Not for profit companies	6	
Mutual funds	6	
Insurance companies	5	
Foreign investors	3.5	
Others	13.7	
Total	49.2	percent

Some 32 million individuals own the remaining 50.8 percent. The total value of all the corporations in the United States fluctuates like mad, and is probably about $3 trillion.

It must be admitted that with any investment there is the risk of having a loss. But equally important, in an inflationary period there is no "risk" of a loss if you keep your money in cash—it becomes a *certainty*. Your dollars will absolutely buy less as time goes on. So investments really are a necessity, and as we shall see, the risk can be divided into a number of balancing areas so that, over a period of time, a serious risk is most remote. And *that* really is what investing is all about.

When one invests in the stock market there is some good news and some bad news. The good news includes the following:

1. The stock market is in a historical long-term uptrend.
2. If you buy a stock or bond you can only lose 100 percent of that investment, but there is no limit on how much you might make.

On the bad news side:

1. If you buy a stock and it goes down 50 percent, it will have to go up 100 percent to get even.
2. There are three risks that are inherent in investing in a single stock:

   a. The market may go down and pull your stock down
       with it without regard to any bad news about the
       stock.
   b. The management may turn out to be incompetent.
   c. The product may turn out to be poor.
3. If you buy a bond, interest rates may go up. This in
   turn drops the value of your bond.

As we shall see, wide diversification, professional management, and a number of other factors to be brought out later
can keep risks low and the prospect of gains high.

So those are the advantages and the disadvantages. The way
to keep most of the advantages has been stated very simply by
Jay Schabacker (of the Switch Fund Advisory): "We are primar-
ily in business to keep you from losing money, and only secondarily in business to guide you to profits." Those of us who
have been around a long time know he is right.

1.5.   THE MUTUAL FUND INDUSTRY

The U.S. mutual fund industry is centered in the general stock
market. It is a venerable industry that began in 1924 when the
Massachusetts Investment Trust and the State Street Investment Corporation came into being. These were both commission-type funds, and they were followed by many others. The
idea of doing all the fund business by mail began in 1928 with
the Scudder Income Fund, a no-commission ("no-load") fund.
The newest type of fund, called *money market*, began in 1972
with the Reserve Fund. Thus we currently have some funds
that charge commissions to buyers (almost never to sellers),
and those that do not charge commissions. All funds may be
classed as (1) stock, (2) bond, and (3) money market funds.

All three types have prospered over the years. At first the
load funds dominated the area, but then the no-loads passed
them in total assets in mid-1979, having moved up from 7.7
percent of the fund business in 1969 to 53 percent in 1979.
In 1978, the money market funds whizzed by the stock and
bond funds to emerge by far the largest in total assets. In total

number of individual funds, the load funds are still in front. In mid-1982 the count was approximately as shown in Table 1.2. About a third of the total assets of all mutual funds are held by institutions such as trusts, pension funds, and foundations, and funds account for about a third of all the trades that take place in the various markets each day. The total assets of $238 billion mean, according to David Silver, president of the Investment Company Institute, that "Mutual funds are now the fourth largest type of financial institution in the United States. Only commercial banks, savings and loans, and insurance companies have greater assets."

1.6.   THE ADVANTAGES OF MUTUAL FUNDS

Mutual funds make money for their shareholders from four basic sources:

1. Dividends, which are fully taxable the same as income (less the first $100).
2. Short-term capital gains from profits made in less than 12 months.
3. Interest from lending surplus cash, also taxed the same as income.

Table 1.2.   The Mutual Fund Industry in Mid-1982

Fund Type	Number of Funds	Total Accounts (millions)	Total Assets (billions)	Average Account
No-load stock and bond funds	240*	3	$20	$6,000
No-load money market funds	200	12	200	16,000
Load stock and bond funds	350	3	18	6,000
Total	790	18	238	

*Run by 150 fund companies.

4. Long-term capital gains from profits in stocks held more than 12 months. These profits are taxed at 40 percent of the taxpayer's normal rate.

When you add up all this income and take out expenses you get the data in Table 1.3, which shows an average for all the aggressive growth and growth funds over the very long term as 12 percent. I certainly don't advocate buying average funds; I'll help you find the very best, and they should do quite a bit better, plus of course, you'll have the important advantage of moving out of laggards as necessary. Funds have had their bad years, such as 1973–1974 and 1981–1982, when they made a whole lot less than the average. Figure 1.2 illustrates the share price movement of a well-run middle-of-the-road growth fund (Mathers) from January 1, 1967, to the middle of 1982. In general I prefer funds that have a greater resistance to market drops, or, as I'll explain later, I get out and put my money into money market funds. Figure 1.2 does have a lot of meat in it. First of all, the growth for the entire 14 years up to early 1981 is at an average rate of 15.8 percent and increases the original $10,000 investment to $78,000, provided money was available to pay taxes on profits as they were distributed. During the bull market of the late 1970s, the growth rate was about 33 percent a year. Had a reasonably effective timing program been employed, the end result could have been over $300,000, an average growth rate of 28 percent a year. On the other side, it would have taken five years for monies invested in 1972 to return to their original value. The yield from just holding the original purchase was far greater than inflation. For reasons I'll discuss later, almost no investors in individual stocks did as well as the Mathers Fund during this period.

Making money is one thing, but these days it is important *how* you make money. Here mutual funds shine. Few people realize that funds, through a special law, *pay no taxes on their profits.* They turn the whole amount over to their shareholders. This is a far cry from ordinary corporations, which may have to pay up to 50 percent of their profits to Uncle Sam before paying any dividends to you. In addition, most of the fund profits come from long-term capital gains.

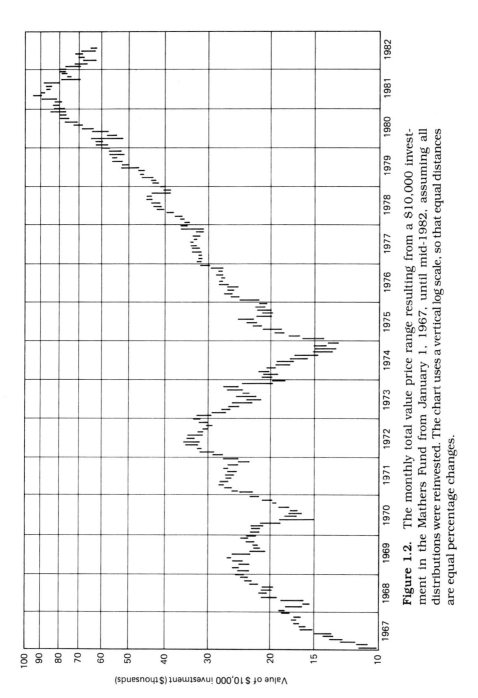

Figure 1.2. The monthly total value price range resulting from a $10,000 invest-ment in the Mathers Fund from January 1, 1967, until mid-1982, assuming all distributions were reinvested. The chart uses a vertical log scale, so that equal distances are equal percentage changes.

13

1.3.   Sources of Average Yearly Profits Made by Aggressive Growth and Growth-Stock mutual funds over the Very Long Term.

Source of Profit	Very Approximate Yearly Profits (%)
Profits on stocks owned	10.2
Dividends	3.0
Profits made on dividends reinvested	0.1
Interest on loans made	0.1
Management fees	−0.5
Housekeeping expenses	−0.9
Net to shareholder	12.0

In Section 1.3 a rather substantial list was presented covering the good things that arise investmentwise when one owns mutual funds. In this section we are more concerned about *how* they arise, and what advantages they bring.

(I am sure the following fourteen paragraphs will cause a lot of rethinking among the many individual investors in stocks, bonds, options, land, rentals, mortgages and other vehicles. The list will make anybody wonder why he or she is working so hard on investing when it costs so little to have others do it for you.)

1.   **Professional management.** Managers are hired to work full time to watch over a fund's investment portfolio and to make decisions on what to buy, sell, or hold. The managers are the ones who get the credit when a fund makes a lot of money, but, as we shall see later, their influence is not the only item that makes funds a good investment, either short or long term.

2.   **Diversification.** Stock is held in a large number of companies, usually *not* in a single field such as airlines or electronics. Diversification through numbers alone prevents the unexpected collapse of one investment from being a calamity to the whole. What is diversification

worth? Well, it's not much of a sample, but Table 1.4 shows a number of averages for a "good" and a "bad" day in the market. Funds at least keep you from losing a large fraction of your estate in *one* day. The day I started my daughter in her first mutual fund with a $500 investment, she had a share in a full portfolio of over 100 stocks. That's impressive.

3. **Freedom from onerous decisions and housekeeping.** Until you have owned stocks in your own name, you cannot imagine the time and effort they require. You may ignore everything and just accept dividends, but if you make even rare trades to try to put your money into more advantageous positions, you must study, get advice, and act. If this is not enough, add the worry that comes later on when you have accumulated a fair amount and daily market swings amount to several hundred dollars. It's mean. Then there's the mechanics of it all. If you own stocks you have to protect the certificates, decide to buy or sell warrants, sign proxies, and exercise rights. Letting a professional do all this for a small yearly fee is cheap, believe me.

4. **Cash flow.** There is a steady flow of new money. It is shown in Chapter 2 that when the cash flow is large—like 50 percent per year of the total value of the fund—the manager is greatly helped.

Table 1.4.   Comparison of Some Averages on a "Bad" Day and on a "Good" Day

	Bad Day	Good Day
Dow Jones industrials (points)	− 14.76	+ 14.30
Dow Jones industrials (%)	− 1.57	+ 1.55
Standard & Poor 500 (%)	− 1.50	+ 1.50
All funds (%)	− 1.4	+ 1.0
10 growth funds (%)	− 2.1	+ 1.6
10 best stocks (%)	+ 5.3	+ 16.6
10 worst stocks (%)	− 11.5	− 9.1

5. **Reinvestment of dividends.** When you own stocks worth a few thousand each, the dividends checks run around $20 each. It is not possible to reinvest this small an amount in stocks without paying whopping commissions. Mutual funds will reinvest *any* dividend. This turns out to make a big difference, worth about 3 to 4 percent per year.

6. **Buying tax losses.** After a fund has suffered a decline in value—usually this occurs during a market drop— the stocks that have been sold at a loss represent a potential amount that will be used to offset capital gains made in the future. When you buy a fund in this position you will *not have to pay taxes on capital gains until the tax offset is used up.* See item 7 in Section 1.7 for the opposite effect.

7. **Continuity of management.** I have never seen this mentioned before, but mutual funds registered jointly or in trust (see Chapter 8) can furnish continuous management and income in the event of death. This may seem like a morbid subject, but those who have not been through the death of a parent simply have no conception of how an estate can get tied up. My personal experience concerns almost all of my mother's estate being in a family venture—the New York and Honduras Rosario Mining Company. During the year after her death, during which the estate was tied up, a revolution broke out in Honduras, and my brothers and I faced the possibility of losing our inheritance. It wasn't a large sum, but we didn't want to lose it. I am happy to add that things did work out satisfactorily. Even in ordinary cases, it is mighty comforting to have a manager watching over the investments and *able* to make changes, whether the ownership is tied up or not.

8. **Redemption.** By regulation, all open-end mutual funds must upon demand redeem your shares at the current price (sometimes less a redemption fee of about 1

percent). Unlike closed-end funds, for which a buyer must be found, open-end funds make their own market.* Be sure you do not think you can get your money back—you get whatever the fund is worth the day you redeem it. This might be more or it might be less than you paid.

9. **Individual attention.** Another advantage, which doesn't have a percent value to it, is that the smallest investor in a fund gets exactly the same investment attention as the largest. Brokers tell me that they need 400 accounts to make a living. What with that and trying to keep up with some reasonable fraction of the 60,000 corporations in the United States, a little investor isn't going to get a lot of attention.

10. **Funds may be your only chance.** A further overwhelming factor may be that since funds can be started with very little down and built up with small additional payments, they may well be the *only* investment a lot of us can afford.

11. **Funds pay minimum commissions.** Funds buy stocks in such large quantities that they always qualify for minimum sales commissions. On an average purchase of $1,000 worth of stocks, it will cost a small investor $60 (6 percent) to buy and sell. On a $100,000 purchase the number is a fraction of 1 percent, or less. Sales larger than this are frequently negotiated without employing a stock salesman (broker) and only a transfer fee is paid. Many investors would show a profit instead of a loss if they could save 6 percent on every cycle. Another way to look at this is that you and I pay about 30 to 90¢ a share to buy a stock, but mutual funds run about a quarter of that. On the other hand,

---

*Open-end funds issue and sell new shares as long as people want to buy them, and frequently the fund grows and grows. Closed-end funds are incorporated for a fixed number of shares. After these are sold, newcomers have to buy shares from somebody else who owns them. More on this later, in Section 1.12.

many of them do a fantastic amount of trading (to get out of stocks that go down, mostly) and it's a lucky thing they can do it cheaply.

12. **There is a record of past performance.** Advisory services, stockbrokers, and you yourself as an investor have a record of past performance, but defining it is almost always a very difficult job. Funds have a completely open record, embarrassing though it may be from time to time.

13. **Funds have few secrets.** By law you get informed if the fund is sued or any other significant changes occur.

14. **Funds can be timed.** Whereas individual stocks react violently from day to day, the movement of a wide portfolio is much smoother. This makes it possible to spot trends and act on them.

The net result is that you as an individual can do a mighty fine job of investing by buying and occasionally switching mutual funds, and that's what this book will help you do.

1.7. THE DISADVANTAGES OF MUTUAL FUNDS

Aren't there any disadvantages? Well, finding disadvantages with an investment that takes very little money to start and that is likely to return more than an average of 12 percent per year over the long term is a bit difficult, but there are *arguments* against them. These go as follows:

1. Most mutual funds (but not the kind this book advocates) charge a sales commission of about 8 percent.* This is paid when you buy (for $100 you buy $92 worth of the fund), but it covers buying *and* selling. It is a charge that keeps many people away from mutual funds. We are going to beat this disadvantage by buying no-load funds. They don't charge any

*Throughout this book I use 8 or 8.5 percent as a typical commission for load funds. Actually commissions vary from zero to 8.75 percent, with three-quarters of them 8 percent or better. They are graded downward for large sales as shown in Table 5.2.

commission because no salesman is involved. But, to be honest, even an 8 percent commission is less than regular commissions on stock sales when a small amount, like reinvesting dividends, is involved.

Sometimes the 8 percent commission is referred to as "9.2 percent." The 9.2 percent arises from using the after-commission dollars, instead of the more natural before-commission dollars, as they do in stores. I was against this practice for many years, but my no-load friends have me convinced that using the after-commission base makes sense. In a nutshell what they say is that when you send a load fund $100 you end up with a $91.50 addition in your account. Had you sent it to a no-load fund you would have ended up with $100 in additional shares, and the difference—$8.50—is 9.2 percent of the $91.50. I guess it really doesn't matter how you talk about the commission. It's money that's lost as far as you are concerned.

Perhaps I will get too complicated here, but 8 percent paid when you buy, coupled with no charge when you sell, is a lot less than paying 4 percent when you buy and 4 percent when you sell at a *profit* a few years later, as the second 4 percent is figured on the sale price. Could be a big difference.

We may also bear in mind that—excluding the small mailing fees, federal transfer taxes, New York State sales tax, Securities and Exchange Commission fees, possibly an odd lot fee (for stock buying), and a local sales tax—the 8 percent commission is the *only* cost for the load funds. If, for instance, you own a house and contemplate selling it for the real estate man's 6 percent commission, think again. You may well have to pay a total of over 10 percent. I did.

2.   The second disadvantage (or argument is a better word) is that, holding large quantities of stock, a mutual fund can't sell out when the market is headed down. This is a biggy. It is essential not to ride the market down. This is more an argument against buying the wrong funds.

3.   Some argue that you lose control of your money. I don't see this. The daily newspaper will list the price of your mutual funds (if it has 1,000 shareholders), so you know how it is doing on a daily basis. You get a statement every time you make a new purchase, and every time the fund issues distributions and reinvests them for you. But it is true that you have lost the ability to say what will be bought and sold. With most of us, we're better off.

Maybe we should talk a moment about seeing the price of a share in your daily newspaper. Everybody likes to know how his or her investment is doing. (Later we'll learn that share price isn't a very good indicator for how funds do because they keep giving you more shares and it's the total value of your account, not the share price, that counts. But for now we'll talk share price.)

You can find the current price per share in the mutual fund columns of the financial page of almost every newspaper, sometimes under the heading of "Investment Companies," and as I said before, the price only has importance on a day-to-day basis. (The changes due to distributions make tracking via share price impossible over the long term.) The name of the fund will be given (possibly located under the group heading rather than its popular name), along with two prices and a difference from the day before. The first price is the bid or net asset value (NAV) per share price, which is simply what you can get if you ask the fund to redeem your shares. The second price is the asked price, or what you would have to pay to buy some more shares; in short, the real value from the first column plus the maximum commission charged if the fund is a load fund. If the two are the same, the fund is a no-load. Instead of the same price, you will usually find the letters *NL* in the second column. The price of the share is given in dollars and cents, not eighths of a dollar like stocks, and the difference from the day before's price, unfortunately, is given in cents with a plus or minus sign as appropriate. I say "unfortunately" because the difference in percent would be worth a great deal more. It throws you off to see that your $40 share has gone down 40¢, while your $11 share has gone down 11¢. The drop is the same for both, 1 percent.

Let me tell you how to read the price changes and make some sense out of them. Just look at the dollar values and move the decimal two places to the left. Thus $13.52 becomes 13. Then, if the price change is + 15¢, it went up a little over 1 percent.

Over a period of time you will note which of the funds you are watching go up (or down) more than the others. Those are the most volatile ones, and later on we will see that those are the ones that bear watching and should be sold when a decline develops. You may expect to see some funds move twice as much as others, in *percent*. Funds that have been successful and increased in share price often split the shares to get a lower price so they won't show a large drop in *cents* on a down day.

4.   Mutual funds charge a managing fee, which is usually about 0.5 percent per year. (This has always been a good deal, in my opinion.)

5.   There is also a housekeeping fee of about 1.0 percent per year.

6.   A very few funds charge a redemption fee when you sell out. This, when it is charged, runs about 1 percent.

7.   When you buy a mutual fund you may be taxed for profits you never got. This can come about in this manner. Suppose a mutual fund has bought some stock at $100 and it has risen to $120, and suppose on this particular day you come along and buy the fund for $120. If they were to sell the stock and send you a $20 capital gains distribution to reinvest if you want to, you would owe capital gains taxes on the distribution. Thus, you might pick up a small tax burden when you start in the fund. Later on, these dividends are profits on which you are glad to pay taxes, or glad to get, at least.

8.   "The market can't keep going up forever." There's no reason why it can't or shouldn't as long as the economy keeps growing.

9.   Mutual funds make you pay taxes you would avoid. This is true, but not very important to me. Each year, typically, they take profits in some of the stocks that have gone up, and by law must send the money to you. You must then pay taxes on these capital gains, and this may well be during the highest earning period of your life when your tax rate is highest, instead of later. You have to pay even if you never "see" the money, as it is reinvested in more fund shares. As I said, all this doesn't worry me a lot. It might worry a large stockholder.

10.   The value of mutual funds goes up and down. This is surely true. If the stock market has one characteristic you can count on, it is that it will go up and down. Thus you should arrange your finances so you will not have to sell out at the bottom. This protection is not hard to achieve: Don't borrow heavily on your funds, I suggest not over 30 percent, and use the market timing techniques discussed in Chapter 4.

11.   The fund may cash you out. Most funds, when an account gets below a certain minimum (usually around $100) reserve the right to cash you out after giving you due notice and a chance to add to your account. I can't say that this is a big disadvantage.

12.   "Mutual funds don't do any better than the market averages." Years ago it was a popular thing to study mutual funds and point out that they didn't do as well as the Dow Jones industrial average, or stocks selected at random* or all sorts of things, *none of which you as an investor could do—* like buying all the stocks on the Big Board. The study game has been pretty well worn out and I haven't seen one for years. Let's look at the old ones that are still widely quoted. The five best known are as follows:

a.   In 1962 the Wharton School of Business of the University of Pennsylvania showed that only 13 percent of the funds they studied (circa 1953–1958) outperformed the Standard and Poor average of 500 stocks. This conclusion produced screams from the fund aficionados who pointed out, heatedly, that funds held cash as well as stocks, and it wasn't fair to compare their performance with an average made up of stocks only. So the analysts tried again, this time disregarding the cash and bonds, and came up with the conclusion that only 46 percent of the funds did better than the S & P 500.

b.   In a study reported in 1965, two members of the Wharton team had a little more fun at the expense of mutual fund

*In 1975 a widely quoted system for buying stocks was nothing less than a dog! His owner would spread out the *Wall Street Journal* and he'd buy the stock that his dog's paw pointed at. All this proves is that a lot of stocks go up in a bull market.

managers. They selected portfolios at random (dart-board technique) and these, on the average beat the performance of "50 well-known funds." This got a lot of attention. People began to ask, "Just what do those fund managers do to earn their money?"

c. Another study was made in 1966 by the Arthur Wiesenberger Company. Their analysis went down the same track and showed that only 44 percent of the funds beat the New York Stock Exchange average over the previous 10 years (1955–1965).

d. A more recent study, again by the Wharton School of Business, showed that an investor (a very rich one, I guess) would have come out ahead of funds if he bought every stock on the New York Stock Exchange.

e. Finally, rather than compare averages, *Fortune* magazine in 1967 analyzed what the top-notch fund managers sold and what they bought with the money. By and large, the stocks *sold* did as well as the new ones *bought,* a most embarrassing state of affairs.

Your writer doesn't particularly like any of the first four studies for the simple reason that any real life fund has housekeeping and management expenses and its performance should never be compared with an average, which does not. If you will take the record for any 10-year period, and I have done this for many, subtract 2 percent per year from the Dow Jones industrial average to pay for housekeeping and management, you will find that about two-thirds of those fund managers trying for profit (some try for income or stability) beat the Dow Jones. Now maybe 2 percent is on the high side for total expenses, but the general conclusions hold up well. The average performance of all mutual funds is fairly close to that of the market, and the performance of many growth-oriented funds, though somewhat better, is still less than we would expect. We may draw two conclusions from all this:

a. Since hundreds of full-time fund managers working very hard to make a profit in the market can't do much better than the averages, it must be very hard to make it big in stocks.

b. If it is so hard for many full-time managers to beat the averages, there is no reason to believe a part-time amateur can do better.

It wouldn't hurt to read these conclusions again. Those of us who have had good years in the market, and really feel that we won't make any of those "stupid mistakes" again, need to revise our opinions. Full-time managers with advisers and computers at their disposal, trying hard for good profits, year in and year out average about 12 percent per year.

All this must be very disconcerting to the fund salesmen who carefully examine the record of literally hundreds of funds and with the greatest care try to select the best for their clients. Something always seems to happen to last year's genius. He and his supporters claim that "it's not his kind of market," implying that when his kind of market comes around he will again lead the pack. It rarely happens. Chapter 2 has a lot to say on this. And how well do individuals do in the market? As H. H. Burbank, associate professor at the Harvard School of Business, has said, "97 percent lose money, 2 percent break even, and 1 percent make money." For an individual, just equaling the market averages would be mighty fine.*

Let me now add a few words about the market averages referred to earlier. The Dow Jones industrial average† consists

---

*See *Wiped Out,* by Anonymous (New York: Simon and Schuster, 1966). This is the story of a man who with the help of sincere brokers ran a $60,000 inheritance into $297.78 in two years during a bull market. Not easy to do, but he did it.

†Presently the 30 stocks in the industrial average are the following:

Allied Corp.	General Foods	Owens-Illinois
Aluminum Co.	General Motors	Proctor & Gamble
American Brands	Goodyear	Sears, Roebuck
American Can	IBM	Standard Oil of
American Telephone	Inco	California
& Telegraph	International Paper	Texaco, Inc.
Bethlehem Steel	International Harvester	Union Carbide
DuPont	Johns-Manville	United Technologies
Eastman Kodak	Merck	U.S. Steel
Exxon	Minnesota Mining	Westinghouse
General Electric	& Manufacturing	Woolworth

of the adjusted price of 30 of the largest and most successful corporations in the country. It is often used as a sample of what the "market is doing" but actually only tells what the blue chips are doing. *You could buy* the stocks in the Dow Jones if you had the money, and they would make a very high quality group.

The Standard & Poor's 500, the Value Line 1100 Stocks, and the Indicator Digest Average (IDA) are three other well-known indices. These would take an *awful lot of money* to buy without having to pay unreasonable commissions.

I hope this covers the "disadvantages" of mutual funds. Now let me show you how to make them look worse:

1. Hunt through data until you find a year when a specific mutual fund (or several) went up less than the Dow Jones industrial average and complain that they don't equal the averages—why buy them? We have already discussed that you can't buy the averages, and I guess that's enough on that.

2. Compare a bond fund managed for stability with an average not constructed for stability, particularly during a rising market. (But never during a falling market, because the stability fund would then show up better.

3. Attack fund officers and fund managers as though they were out to "get you," pointing out how much money they get. But never point out that both groups are almost invariably fund owners too and just as anxious as you for the value of the shares to advance.

4. Attack the principle of funds because "they could dump large amounts of stock during a market drop and cause a landslide." They could, but they don't.

5. Compare a fund's performance, not counting reinvesting dividends, with some average like the S&P 500, also not investing dividends. As a shareholder you can reinvest dividends, but the averages cannot.

These corporations account for one-third of the total value of the stocks on the New York Stock Exchange. They're the big ones.

I guess you can count on this sort of thing against funds, insurance, doctors, or most anything else. We are going to get around the biggest objection—the 8.5 percent commission—by only buying funds that don't have it.

1.8. NO-LOAD FUNDS

The reluctance of many investors to pay an 8.5 percent commission on each dollar invested in the commission-type mutual funds led to the creation of mutual funds sold only by mail, without any commission, which came to be called *no-loads*. They are open-ended funds just like those we have been discussing that issue new shares any time some new money comes in, and redeem shares whenever they are so requested. The no-loads bear the same resemblance to the load funds as does the mail-order branch of Montgomery Ward to its retail stores. You save the commission. Doesn't the absence of a sales organization hurt the performance of a fund? No. Many studies have shown that the performance of the two types is identical.

The Securities and Exchange Commission (SEC) in its *Institutional Investors' Study,* summary volume 1971, page 31, said: "There is no appreciable difference between the performance of funds that charge sales loads and those that do not." They were referring to profit *after* the shares had been bought.

There is a difference, and it is important, between having 100 percent of your money invested in no-loads and having 8.5 percent siphoned off for the sales organization of the load funds. That's the basic dollar difference, and it can get pretty big. For instance, suppose you buy $6,000 worth of a load fund and incur a $500 commission. Had you kept the $500 by buying a no-load fund, and had it grown at a quite reasonable 12 percent per year, in 10 years it would become $1,550, and in 20 years, $4,800. That's a lot of commission. But even more important, as a shareholder in a no-load fund you are free to switch in and out of the market without paying a commission on each move.

You would think that it would be easy to say whether a mutual fund charges a commission or not, and in general it is. The commission-type funds usually charge 8 to 8.5 percent to buy and nothing to sell. The no-load funds make no charge to buy or to sell. Unfortunately, there are a few funds that charge commissions like 0.5 percent or maybe as much as 2 percent to buy and nothing to sell, and a few that charge a special fee, usually 1 or 2 percent, if you sell within, say, 60 to 90 days after buying. Why do funds make these peculiar small charges? In general the charges are aimed at reducing excessive trading by their shareholders, which bothers the portfolio managers because they have to hold extra cash on hand, and of course, extra trading means extra paperwork.

I don't get excited about ½ or 1 percent charges, but 2 percent begins to get my dander up, and 8.5 percent on sales (and on all dividends paid in the future) absolutely turns me off. Indeed, if you will look at the average earnings of mutual funds and subtract 8.5 percent for any money you put into a commission fund that year, it will impress you.

Aside from not having a sales charge, is there anything basically different between load and no-load funds? The answer is *yes*, but the difference is both inexplicable as to origin and unmeasurable as to effect. Even so, here it is: according to the Investment Company Act of 1940, a no-load fund need only have one person on its board of directors who is *not* affiliated with the fund management group. (See Section 5.5.) It may of course have more. On the other hand, if a sales charge is levied, 40 percent of the board of directors must have no affiliation with the fund management group. One could hence argue that it could be—but not necessarily is—harder for a no-load fund to fire its management group and get another than it might be for a load fund. As noted previously, nobody has ever evaluated this difference as good or bad.

Two trivial arguments against no-load funds that we might as well dispose of now are that they are small and hence their expenses are proportionately larger than for load funds, and that there are not enough of them to give a buyer a wide choice. The first point is true, but there are small load funds, too. Still further, unless expenses are wildly out of line, they are entirely secondary to performance and to the 8.5 percent commission for a load fund. As for numbers, there are plenty of no-load funds. Of the total of about 790, 240 are no-loads. Of the 540 listed in the *Wall Street Journal* each day, 200 are no-loads. (The not-listed funds do not yet have the 1,000 shareholders needed to qualify for being listed.)

Now while I like no-load funds more than load funds, I admit to three deficiencies with the no-loads:

1. When a person is just starting out in mutual funds he or she may have many, many questions that I could not anticipate for this book. It would be entirely reasonable for the first fund purchases to be of the load type in order to get the benefit of talking with a broker—and by the way pick one who either specializes in funds or doesn't sell anything else at all.

2. There are times when it is nice to have a broker go to bat for you when a fund won't answer a question or an acount is mixed up or you want to change registration or swap funds.

3. It is more convenient to call your broker and make a trade than to write a letter or send in a form and then wait a week or so to find out what happened. (The trade date isn't delayed more than mail time, as we shall see later—and often you can just phone the fund directly.)

What do brokers say about no-load funds? Well, let's go a little further back and ask what they say about funds. Most of the time, very little. They would much rather have the commissions from a bunch of sales than a single commission from a fund sale. If you ask them directly almost all will agree that funds are a good vehicle and everybody should own some. Should you ask about no-loads, you may get a disparaging remark since there is no commission in no-loads for brokers. Often you get a motherhood statement such as "You get what you pay for" or "I wouldn't buy that trash." A few brokers will say, "Of course we don't sell no-loads, but if you have one you want we will be glad to buy it for you." They also hope that by selling some no-loads the fund managers will send some stock business their way.

So really the question as to why people buy load funds when they can buy funds without commissions boils down to the fact that a lot of people never heard of them, or they do not want to do a little work to save a lot of money. It is hoped that this book will make it easier for those who want to invest in them.

1.9.   HOW DO THE ADVANTAGES AND DISADVANTAGES BALANCE OUT?

I believe the data presented in Sections 1.6 and 1.7 and the rest of this book justify the conclusion that any investors buying and switching a small group of funds for aggressive growth or buying and holding a small group of growth funds for a long-term purpose will achieve their goals. It does not appear that one could seek more from an investment. In addition, the small down payment needed to start, plus the small additions acceptable to most funds, may well make mutual funds the *only* investment feasible for many.

The real arguments for owning no-load mutual funds are as follows:

1. You get professional management, which at the worst should be better than an amateur's part-time effort.
2. You get diversification so that no single calamity will be a calamity to you, and your ratio of risk to profit is minimized.
3. You get freedom from housekeeping and decision making.
4. You may have dividends reinvested no matter how small they are.
5. You may select funds that have a large percentage cash flow, but some switching usually becomes necessary (see Chapters 2 and 4).

6. You get a number of fringe benefits.
7. You're able to switch without incurring commissions.

1.10.   DO FUNDS BEAT INDIVIDUAL INVESTORS?

This really big question is whether you should be in funds, or out on your own in the market. I wouldn't argue that some people probably have made a lot of money in the market, but I would have to add I never met one. I used to be a consultant for a large brokerage house, and hence got to go to many of their parties. Being an appreciator of beautiful women, I'd occasionally ease a broker's wife over to a corner for a private chat. And what did I learn? Well, never mind about *that,* but I did learn that their husbands couldn't make any money in the market. "Charlie's clients do fine," they would say, "but what we buy always go down." What they really meant was that Charlie *talked* about those who did fine.

Elsewhere we mentioned the enormous percentage of those who lose money in the market. Couldn't they take an advisory service to learn what to buy? Well, it turns out that buying a stock advisory service and doing as well as their "special portfolio" are two different things. But let me make the attempt.

There are over 200 stock advisory services. In general they disagree on what stocks to buy and when to buy them. No accurate audit exists as to which services are best. Most of them are dishonest—not in the sense of trying to cheat people by recommending stocks they know to be worthless, but in the sense of presenting a record that cannot be duplicated by those who pay for the service. This comes from seven sources.

1. Nearly all stock advisory services state portfolio changes after the fact. "Since the outlook for United Beans has deteriorated we have swapped it for Undertakers' Life Insurance." How long ago the event took place depends on the service. For those reports issued monthly, it could have been 29 days ago . . . and with the benefit of considerable hindsight. One of the most esteemed services (from a performance standpoint)

corrected its market timing plot by saying, "It is now evident that our indicators showed that *last May* was a 'buy' area," and darned if they didn't retroactively add an arrow to their chart with a "buy" label—the following August! Another service I once took (at $500 a year) in their market letter dated one Friday said "Kaufman and Broad was added to our model account last Monday at a price of 25½. On Tuesday the issue was quite strong and closed at 26½." The model account had a profit before the subscribers heard of the recommendation! I have only seen one service that said "If we can buy General Motors at less than $45 next Monday, we'll do it." I could equal the performance of *that* service if I had the money to buy all their recommendations. But almost all cheat their customers by claiming that they bought last week or whatever. A few services offer to wire their special customers (who pay extra) so they can beat the regular subscribers. I tried this "hot tip" extra service. It only cost me $600 before I wised up.

2.   Another practice of a number of large services is to let the boys in the office buy before the recommendation is sent to the paying subscribers. I once went back and plotted a number of special situations the week *before* they were released. Sure enough, *they went up the week before*, and fell after the subscribers got them. Indeed, after I worked my way into the inside, I had people call me and say "Hey, our special situation next week will be . . ." In short, you as a subscriber can rarely buy at the recommended price, nor can you sell at the "sell" price. There's one born every minute. This doesn't happen with mutual funds. If 200 people want to buy mutual fund X on Monday morning it doesn't change its price one iota; it just gives the fund some cash flow.

3.   Many services recommend so many stocks that almost nobody could take their advice. One large service kept a running list of how you as subscriber should buy and sell, and at the end of 10 years quietly abandoned the feature because it did terribly, in spite of the help given by the subscribers who bought late. This is still another argument to the effect that it is very very hard to make money in the market, particularly without a large percentage cash flow.

4.   Many services conveniently forget commissions. One book by a well-known and respected stock analyst has a list of short-term trades made according to his timing method. The profits are all small—like a half-point or maybe a point and a half.* In the aggregate the particular paragraphs show a profit of 16 points. When round-lot commissions were added in, the profit was halved.

5.   The best funds each year beat the best advisory services. Why? See Chapter 2.

6.   It isn't fair to add in the human failures of subscribers who may be out of town when a particular action is recommended, but such a situation nevertheless can affect one's ability to follow the service's advice. Another failure might be not having enough money to make all the buys recommended.

7.   It also sounds like mumbo jumbo, but there is a difference between hypothetical investment "play money" and real money. For an illustration, one service I know of showed a paper profit one year of 41.0 percent. The same man ran a real live mutual fund. And how did he do that year? He lost 2.2 percent.

So take the published record of an advisory service with a great big grain of salt. I have never met anyone who could equal the published performance, including me. And I surely tried for 25 years.

Is there any way to really show that there is a reason for funds to beat individuals? There surely is. In the *Financial Analysts Journal* of March/April 1972, Haim Levy and Marshall Sarnat presented something I had been looking for a long, long time. Here is the story. Basically, every investment has two balancing parameters—*profit* and *risk*. One would like a big profit with a little risk. This is hard to find. Indeed, with many investments you never really know the risk. In the case of stocks the risk is really the variability, as you may buy at a peak and be forced to sell at a valley. Taking a 10-year period, one may

*In the stock market "points" are dollars. Prices are quoted in eighths of a dollar. No, I don't kow why.

easily compute the average profit, and from the price oscillations, the variability or risk. For the period studied by the authors, the S&P average was a profit of 10.6 percent per year, and the variability was 11.7 percent per year. A plot was made of average yearly profit against average risk (Figure 1.3) and a point made for the S&P data. Next, horizontal and vertical lines were drawn through the point.

Now consider either a fund or a stock. If the profit is more than that of the S&P average, the fund will plot *above* the horizontal line *AB*. If it is less, it will plot somewhere *below* the line *AB*. If the risk (variability) is more than the S&P, it will plot *to the right* of the vertical line *CD*. If it is less, it will plot *to the left* of *CD*.

The two lines *AB* and *CD* divide the chart into four quadrants, labeled I, II, III, IV. Any fund or stock that plots in zone I has more profit and less risk than the S&P. In zone II it has more profit but more risk. In zone III, the profit is less and the risk is more—clearly undesirable—and in zone IV the profit is less and the risk is less. If a selected fund or stock plotted in zone I, it would obviously be a better investment than the S&P, having more profit and less risk. Unfortunately, most funds plot in zones II and IV, so we have to refine the approach. This we do (Figure 1.4) by adding a zero risk bond that pays 6.5

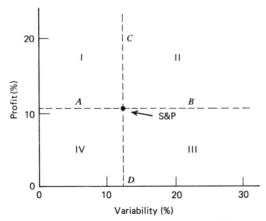

Figure 1.3. Profit versus variability, stocks only.

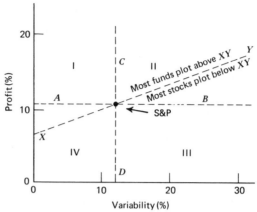

Figure 1.4.   Profit versus variability, bond and stocks combinations included.

percent at point X. Connecting X and S&P, we have a line along which will plot all portfolios of the bonds and the S&P, all the way from owning no stocks at point X to owning no bonds at point S&P. The line extending X–S&P to Y exists when the account is leveraged by borrowing on the portfolio to buy more stocks.

Now we are in shape to make our comparisons. Any funds that are *better* than any combination of bonds and the S&P will plot above the line X–S&P because they have more profit and less risk. Any fund or stock that is worse will plot below.

The study then took various stocks and combinations of several stocks and found that, when the risk was considered, they plotted below the line X–S&P, but *funds plotted above.* This is the essence of our proof. *Basically it is better to hold a large number of stocks than only a few and that is what funds do.* Two more factors strengthen this conclusion: Funds permit reinvesting dividends, no matter how small; and a few funds help their own performance for a limited time while a large percentage cash flow is coming in, by repeated buys in a few stocks, which drives their price and the per share value of the fund up.

I'll admit that individuals get more fun out of running their own portfolios. I believe it costs them a lot of money.

1.11. THE CATEGORIES OF MUTUAL FUNDS

Basically, mutual funds may be categorized three ways:

1. Whether or not a commission is charged to buy or sell.
2. Whether they are closed-end or open-end funds.
3. Whether they are stock or bond funds, or money market funds.

Commission and no-load funds are discussed in Section 1.8; closed-end funds in Section 1.12. The many types of no-load, open-end funds are discussed in Section 1.13.

1.12. CLOSED-END STOCK AND BOND FUNDS

I briefly mentioned closed-end funds earlier. Here comes a little more depth.

If you and I and several others pool our money, form a corporation, and hire a manager to invest our money and pay us the profits, that's *not* a mutual fund. That's a simple corporation-for-profit and before it can distribute profits, it must pay taxes on them, and you, I, and the other investors will get less than all the before-tax profits.

If we do the same thing, raise some money, sell some shares, agree to distribute *all* the profits, and get approval from the SEC,* that's a closed-end fund: The total number of shares is closed. Whatever the fund started out with, that's it. Closed-end funds don't have to pay taxes on profits—all profits go to the shareholders after legitimate expenses for operations. Closed-end fund shares are listed on the various exchanges and the usual commissions are charged to buy and sell.

Unlike open-end funds, where the shares are sold and bought back *by the funds*, the shares of closed-end funds are bought and sold *by the public.* You will find quotes for them in the

---

*The two main requirements as far as investments go are (1) the fund must derive at least 90 percent of its gross income from dividends, interest, and the sale of stocks or bonds; and (2) the fund must derive less than 30 percent of its gross income from securities held less than three months.

Tuesday *Wall Street Journal* under "Publicly Traded Funds." The price of a share of a closed-end fund is determined in the same manner as that of a stock—it's what the public will pay for it, and, strange to say, the public usually prices closed-end stock funds at a substantial discount from the true worth of the stocks in their portfolios. This is for a couple of reasons:

1. The distributions are normally not reinvested automatically, hence the funds' performance when plotted shows up (erroneously) at substantially below the performance of funds when distributions are included. (See Section 4.3.)
2. The pay for the managers is independent of the performance or the size of the closed-end funds, hence nobody is pushing them.

An argument (I can't call it a "reason") has been advanced that the discount is the market's way of balancing the commission costs as compared to no-load funds. This could be, but it doesn't explain why closed-end funds were discounted long before no-load funds became a substantial industry. At any rate, despite the fact that buyers of shares in closed-end funds get diversification, professional management, good performance, and lower housekeeping costs, such shares normally sell at a discount of from 10 to 20 percent of their net asset value per share,* and shareholders do get 10 to 20 percent more money working for them than from an open-end fund. They may also buy shares on margin, as arranged by a broker at the time of purchase. The percentage you have to put up to buy on margin varies from time to time as the Federal Reserve Board endeavors to encourage or discourage investing. Typically it ranges from 50 to 70 percent; that is, you put up the 50 to 70 percent and the broker arranges to lend you the remaining amount, charging interest at current rates, of course.

The previously mentioned discount from true market value means that many closed-end funds are clear candidates for

---

*In short, if you start a closed-end fund you are almost certain to lose money in that the market will discount your portfolio.

takeover either by a rich combine or by their shareholders, as an immediate profit of from 10 to 20 percent is available either through sale or by becoming open-ended.

There are about 11 closed-end stock funds with assets of about $3.5 billion, 12 specialized closed-end funds with assets of about $1.8 billion, and 23 closed-end bond funds with assets of about $1.7 billion, for a total of around $7.0 billion. Although this is a substantial amount of money, it is far smaller than the assets of the no-load fund industry. The organization that represents the closed-end funds is the Association of Publicly Traded Investment Funds (201 North Charles Street, Baltimore, MD 21201).

Although closed-end funds are, in my opinion, a better way to invest for small investors than buying individual stocks, they are not for us, for these reasons:

1. They sell at customary stock exchange commissions and taxes (say, 3 percent to buy and 3 percent to sell), so that a running account to add, say, $50 a month would result in very high expenses.

2. Automatic reinvestment of dividends and capital gains distributions, when available, is expensive for small investors.

3. There is no continuous stream of money coming in to help.

4. They have no withdrawal plans, nor redeeming arrangements for small amounts.

5. There aren't any no-load closed-end mutual funds.

6. Although the death of a large stockholder or any type of forced liquidation could cause an *open-end* fund to redeem a lot of shares and maybe sell some stocks, a large sale of a *closed-end* fund can cause the same market reaction as any single stock being dumped.

Closed-end bond funds are organized and run in a manner paralleling the closed-end stock funds. Again, the same list of objectives given for the closed-end stock funds applies, with one minor change of effect: The discount at which the bond funds usually sell—it averages about 3 or 4 percent—becomes an advantage in that those seeking income receive 3 or 4 percent more than they would had they purchased the bonds directly. This works toward overcoming an objection I have to open-end bond funds (see Section 1.13, item 15) in that management fees and housekeeping expenses seriously reduce the shareholder's yield. In rare cases the discount of the closed-end bond funds is substantial, and yields exceeding other investment vehicles are possible, even when commissions are included.

The daily price of each closed-end bond fund may be found in a separate box in the *Wall Street Journal* each Wednesday, along with the net asset value per share. I am not aware of any service devoted to closed-end bond funds, possibly because there are only 23 of them. As I point out later, if you can afford to collect about 20 bonds directly, you will probably come out ahead of a closed-end bond fund.

In a sort of parallel to the closed-end funds, some corporations have such a diversity of products that brokers sometimes refer to them as "the same thing as a mutual fund." To me they are subject to the same arguments as the closed-end funds, as outlined earlier, and these arguments keep me out of both closed-end funds and diversified corporations, in favor of open-end mutual funds.

1.13. THE VARIOUS TYPES OF NO-LOAD, OPEN-END MUTUAL FUNDS

First of all, since this is a book on no-load, open-end funds, starting now I'll just call them *funds* or *mutual funds*, with the no-load and open-end features implied. When it becomes necessary to mention either closed-end or commission-type funds, they will be so designated. Of the no-load, open-end stock and bond funds (as distinct from no-load, open-end money market funds), almost everybody would be satisfied if they were described by their purpose in life, such as:

1. Aggressive growth (small companies, high risk).
2. Growth (larger companies, less risk).
3. Growth and income (growing companies with dividend records).
4. Income (utilities and other good payout companies).
5. Fixed income (bonds and preferred stocks).
6. Balanced (stocks and bonds).
7. Specialty (selected investment areas).

However, things aren't that easy. We find all sorts of classifications that describe each fund's aims. It is when you add in their policies—*how* they plan to achieve those aims—that simple classifications blow up, and we find ourselves with some 20 different types of funds. Next, when you add in how well they achieve their aims, there is a whale of a lot of disagreement as to what kind of fund each is, and each advisory service and investor has to use his or her own judgment. I shall list the many types in the next few pages, and I think you will be amazed at how many different methods people find to endeavor to make profits or income with mutual funds. When the chips are down and we get to actually selecting funds to buy, in Chapter 4, the grouping is simply what I think you would prefer: *aggressive growth* for those who want to make the most profits and don't mind doing some work to get them; *growth* for those who will settle for good profits and very little work; *income* for those seeking income now or later; and *preservists.* A few closed-end and commission-type funds are included because they represent possible types for future no-load, open-end funds.

After you decide on what types of funds you would like to buy, how do you find out how they compare and where do you get their addresses, since no-load funds are essentially a mail-order business? Comparisons of how the various funds are doing (and have done) are presented in the advisory services listed in Section 4.2. You may write for a sample copy or take a trial subscription.

There are several ways to obtain fund addresses:

1.   The main fund groups are listed in Section 4.4. Other funds are listed in Appendix C.

2.   Write to the Investment Company Institute, 1775 K Street, Washington, DC 20006, or the No-Load Fund Association, Valley Forge, PA 19581, and either will send you a list.

3.   Write to the No-Load Fund Investors, P.O. Box 283, Hastings-on-Hudson, NY 10706, and order a copy of the *Handbook for No-Load Fund Investors*. It has by far the best and most complete list of no-load funds ever assembled. The data provided include:

Name of fund	Minimum starting
Address	amount
Telephone number	Minimum subsequent
Accepts collect telephone	amount
calls?	Telephone orders
Adviser's name	accepted?
Fund objective and	States where qualified
policy	Telephone switch
Year organized	available?
	Date of distributions
	Shareholders' services
	Redemption fee?

Following are brief descriptions of the various types of mutual funds, along with examples of each where applicable. The examples are simply well-known funds; they haven't been selected on the basis of being recommended or not recommended for purchase at this time.

1.   **Aggressive growth funds.**   The funds trying for maximum profits are called *aggressive growth* or *performance* funds. Besides being identified by their prospectuses as being able to

buy on margin or "go short,"* they are identified by their port-folios often being in American Stock Exchange or over-the-counter stocks, and by their volatility. You can identify volatil-ity by noting how much they move each day on Wall Street (see Section 1.7). Plots of their performance also show their volatil-ity (see Figure 4.10). Examples of aggressive growth funds include Constellation Growth Fund, Dreyfus Number Nine, Vanguard Explorer Fund, 44 Wall Street Fund, Hartwell Lever-age Fund, Pennsylvania Mutual Fund, Scudder Development Fund, 20th Century Investors, and 20th Century Ultra Investors.

2. Growth funds. Growth funds invest in growing companies but of a safer grade than those selected by the aggressive growth funds. They also avoid speculative tech-niques. They are diversified, which means they own stocks of 20 or more companies. A few growth stocks have shown remarkable resistance to market drops. I'll draw attention to them in later discussions. Examples of growth funds include Acorn Fund, Afuture Fund, American Investors Fund, Colum-bia Growth Fund, Dodge and Cox Stock Fund, Evergreen Fund, Fidelity Asset Investment Trust, Mathers Fund, Nicholas Fund, Rowe Price New Horizons Fund, and Weingarten Equity Fund.

3. Balanced funds. Balanced funds usually have high-quality stocks, some preferred stocks, and some bonds. Exam-ples of balanced funds include Dodge and Cox Balanced Fund, Good and Bad Times Fund, and Stein Roe and Farnham Balanced Fund.

4. Income funds. Income funds quite naturally invest in stocks that have a good record of paying dividends. Many of

*Going short is a technique used by sophisticated investors to make money in a declining market. It works like this: When an investor feels strongly that a certain stock is going down in price, he borrows a certificate for, say, 100 shares and promises to replace it when asked. He then sells the stock and pockets the money. If the stock goes down he rebuys the 100 shares for less money and replaces the certificate. During the time the certificate is "miss-ing," the "shorter" has to pay any dividends that may be declared. Still further, an investor who buys a stock (goes "long") can only lose 100 percent of what he paid for the stock. A shorter, on the other hand, might have to pay three times what he got for the stock sold when the time comes to replace it. Not a game for amateurs.

these are blue chips, preferred stocks, and utilities. They would also avoid risk techniques. Examples of income funds include American Investors Income Fund, Dreyfus Special Income Fund, Fidelity Equity Income Fund, Financial Industrial Income Fund, and Vanguard Wellington Fund.

   5. Stability funds.   In years past there were stability funds whose portfolios consisted largely of preferred stocks and bonds, selected to have a minimum of price fluctuations. The collapse of the bond market has made the term *stability* hard to justify, and I am unaware of any fund using it. In today's world, stability can best be obtained in bond funds or money market funds that invest only in government securities.

   6. Specialty funds. Specialty funds arbitrarily limit themselves to investing in only one area of industry (electronics, aviation, and such), or precious metals (gold stocks); they may even use a social conscience limitation (no tobacco or arms production stocks). These funds give investors a little control over where their money will be used. Gold share funds could actually be a separate category, but they are a type of specialty fund. Some categories of specialty funds and examples are as follows:

Aviation	National Aviation and Technology Fund
Energy	Able Associates Fund, Energy Fund, and Northeast Investment Trust
Foreign investments	GSC Performance Fund, GT Pacific Fund, Rowe Price International Fund, Transatlantic Fund, and Scudder International Fund
Gaming	Gaming, Sports, and Growth Fund
Gold shares	Golconda Investors, Lexington Goldfund, and United Services Gold Shares Fund
Medicine	Medical Technology Fund
National resources	Able Fund, Omega Fund, Rowe Price New Era Fund
Oceanography	Steadman Oceanographic, Technology, and Growth Fund
Public utilities	Energy and Utility Shares

Regional	North Star Regional Fund and USAA Mutual Fund, Sunbelt Era
Social conscience	Dreyfus Third Century Fund, Foursquare, and Pax World Fund

7. Option funds. Option funds, rather than being concerned with stocks or bonds, write puts and calls. Such funds could be incredibly volatile. Examples of option funds include Analytic Optioned Equity Fund, Directors Capital, and Gateway Option Income Fund.

8. Multi funds. Multi funds were a sort of "fund of funds," and were intended to do the selecting and switching for you. They were not successful and have dropped out of the picture.

9. Exchange funds. Years ago there were exchange funds that would take over your portfolio at its present value and meld it into a wide number of investments to increase your diversification, without incurring any taxes that ordinarily would be due should an appreciated stock be sold. There are few if any of these now, but many funds will accept your stock shares as payment if they already own the same stock. You save commissions.

10. Dual funds. Dual funds give all their *dividends* to a select half of their shareholders, and all the *profits* to the other half. Oversimplified, an equal amount of income and capital gains shares are sold and the total proceeds invested. The income shareholders (50 percent) get *all* the income; that is, all the dividends and interest minus all the operating expenses of the fund; the capital gains investors (who put up 50 percent of the capital) get *all* the capital gains. Thus each class of stock ends up utilizing twice as much money as it has invested. In theory the income investors would get say 2 × 3.5 percent dividends and the capital gains buyers might get 2 × 20 or 30 or more percent capital gains. There aren't any no-load dual funds, nor has the concept caught on.

11. Tax-deferred annuity funds. In 1980 a ruling by the SEC (which is still subject to cancelation) apparently allowed mutual funds to be combined with annuities so that interest earned by the fund would remain tax free and would not have to be reported until, at some later date, the fund was converted into an annuity. At that time it would come under the usual rules for annuity taxes. This ruling was ideal for a money market/ annuity fund, since money market funds are earning very high interest rates, which under normal circumstances would be fully taxed. Dreyfus, Fidelity, Bankers Security, and several other fund companies currently offer these tax-deferred annuity funds.

12.   Tax-managed funds.   You really don't need to know about tax-managed funds except for general interest. The Tax Relief Act of 1981 reduced taxes so that this special group of funds has little allure. There is a section in the general tax laws that is called the "dividends received deduction." In essence, *corporations* may deduct 85 percent of dividends they receive and pay taxes on only the 15 percent remaining. (The basis of this was that the originating corporation had already paid taxes on the earnings, and the final shareholder would pay again, and it seemed that three times was getting a little too much.) Thus if a mutual fund paid taxes on only 15 percent of its dividends and reinvested the 85 percent for more capital gains, then the fund shareholder (assumed wealthy) would receive no distributions from dividends. When the shareholder sold or when a distribution was made it would be *all* capital gains. About a half-dozen funds use this arrangement, and so far, especially with the current reductions on taxes, they have not shown the loophole to be worthwhile. Examples of tax-managed funds include Qualified Dividend Portfolios and Fidelity Qualified Dividend Fund.

13.   Series funds.   In the preceding sections I have discussed many types of funds. In general they are separate entities, having their own management corporations, managers (who might serve several funds), and shareholders. In a number of cases there are telephone switch agreements between funds. In 1980 a new arrangement appeared wherein *one* fund managed by *one* management group had a number (or series) of portfolios—say, stock, bond, and money market—and the shareholder was free to switch from one to another. The shareholder received the treatment and distributions according to whatever portfolio he or she was in.

Offhand, it would seem that there is little difference to the shareholder whether he owns three portfolios or three funds, and indeed, such is the case. But there are substantial management and housekeeping expenses that are reduced. To start with, there is only one management corporation with its one board of directors instead of three, and only one fund board. Only one prospectus need be mailed out, and only one set of quarterly notices. Only one set of reports need be sent to the SEC. Matters of concern to only one portfolio would be voted on by those shareholders, and matters of concern to the fund would be voted on by all; one share, one vote. That last point could cause some concern, since money market funds hold at a dollar a share, whereas stock or bond funds may be many times that, and the money market shareholder would then have many times the vote. In practice this has not caused a problem, but it could.

The cost savings of the series funds are such that we may expect to see more of them. At present they do not appear to offer any disadvantages to shareholders. I would neither specially invest in a series fund nor get out if one changed to series. You only need to know they would save you a little money, a secondary consideration to how much they make for you. Back of the series fund idea is the dream that someday the IRS might rule that moving from one portfolio to another within the same fund does not constitute a buy and sell, since the money never moves into the control of the investor. It would then generate no tax considerations. So far this hasn't happened. An example of a series fund is Fidelity Select Portfolios Fund: Energy, Brokers, Medical, Minerals, Technology, and Utilities.

14.   IRA managed funds.   Fund managers are limited by not wanting to burden their shareholders with short-term capital gains, and this in turn deters them from being as mobile as they might want to be. In IRA accounts, no taxes are incurred until the money is withdrawn and short-term or long-term gains are not different to the shareholders. A few funds are being set up to take advantage of being free from tax considerations. The same has been true of offshore funds and some foreign funds. It remains to be seen how the new IRA funds perform before any definite recommendation can be made. This freedom from concern about short- or long-term gains is also of enormous importance to those practicing telephone switching with their IRA accounts. Examples of IRA managed funds include Gintel ERISA Fund, Mutual Qualified Income Fund, and Partners Fund.

15.   Bond funds.   The advantages of mutual funds that generate income by buying corporate, federal, or municipal *bonds* are not nearly as compelling as they are for funds that generate capital gains through buying common stocks. Top-notch *stock* funds often average long-term earnings of 15 to 20 percent, possibly 10 percent more with some timing efforts. The 1.5 percent cost of managers and housekeeping taken from dividends (which probably would be taxed as income) is not onerous. Corporate and federal *bond* funds produce a fully taxable yield of possibly 7 to 13 percent, depending on current interest rates, and the loss of 1.5 percent becomes 10 percent or more of the taxable income. The municipal bond funds produce a lower income yet, and the housekeeping and management fees total a higher fraction of the income remaining.

The bond funds have the advantages of leaving management to the managers, taking care of the housekeeping chores, diversification, permitting small additional investments, and having distributions reinvested, but there is little or no advantage to having a good cash flow. (See Chapter 2.) If new money comes in while interest rates are rising, new bonds will be bought with better "coupon rates," (interest rates) and the average yield of the portfolio will increase. Should the new money come in when interest rates are falling, the opposite is true and bond fund buyers lose a little of their ability to lock in a high yield.

The advantages of buying a portfolio of individual bonds directly without participating in a bond fund are many:

a.   Investors are spared a loss of, say, 10 percent of their income.

b.   They may, during periods of high interest, lock in those rates for the life of their bonds.

c. If they buy bonds with a not-too-far-away maturity, they may wait out a market drop in bond prices and receive the bonds' face value.

In the next few pages I am going to discuss buying bonds quite thoroughly. You should become competent to make a decision between buying bonds yourself or buying a bond fund.

When corporations need to raise money, they have the choice of short-term borrowing, issuing bonds, or issuing new stock. If the problem really is short term, they go to banks or money market funds and pay (in 1983) 12 to 16 percent. If they issue bonds they might pay only 10 to 14 percent, but they are locked into paying this for a long time, and paying back the principal some day. (Some bonds are "callable," which means that the company issuing them can pay them off early, usually at a small profit to the original bondholder.) Bond interest (like short-term interest) is an expense like a gas bill. It gets paid with before-tax income. New *stock* dilutes the value of the current shares, which usually respond by going down in price. (Theoretically, and often practically, the price goes back up when the new money starts earning.) However, the corporation will only pay dividends on its stock if it earns money and does not need it for something else, and it *never* pays back the purchase price of the stock.

All bonds are issued in $1,000 units. Although a company might have several bond issues, it has only one common stock.

Investors identify bonds by the interest rate printed on the bond (also called the *coupon rate*) and the date the bond will be paid off. For example, EAL 5s 92 (read "Eastern Air Lines fives of ninety-two") are bonds that Eastern sold many years ago. At that time they could borrow money at 5 percent (hence the number 5) and they agreed to pay back the $1,000 in 1992 (hence the 92). More recently, when Eastern wanted to raise some money they had to pay 17.5 percent, due to both the company's outlook and current interest rates, so they brought out the EAL 17½s 98, meaning they would pay $175 a year interest, normally in two payments, and pay back the principal in 1998. (Any broker can tell you the exact dates on which they make payments.) By now you are wondering why any investors would at this time buy a bond paying 5 percent when they could get one from the same company that pays 17.5 percent, and that explains why the EAL 5s 92 are selling at $380. This makes their current yield about 13.1 percent, but if you hold them to maturity you will add in a profit of $620. Your "average yield to maturity" is hence about 15.3 percent. You could make a little more by buying the newer bonds, but you would be locked in longer and get your money as fully taxed interest, instead of part being capital gains.

Confusingly, bonds are quoted in the daily paper as a *percentage* of their $1,000 maturity value. Thus the Eastern bond mentioned as selling at $380 would show in the bond column as 38. It will take you a few moments to figure out what you would have to pay for a bond listed at 50¼ ($502.50). The system is stupid, but that's the way it is.

Bond people rate the quality of bonds with a simple code: AAA for the best, AA for slightly lower, on down to C, for bonds that are least secure. Bonds having rating of BBB or higher are called *pension grade* and are by law suitable for pension funds. The higher the rating and the closer the date of maturity, the less risk a bond will have. But in truth a bond entails little risk, in fact none at all unless the company goes bankrupt. Even if the company is sold, the new owner cannot shirk paying the bonds. You will get interest payments when due, but the price you can get for the bond should you want to sell it does fluctuate with current interest rates.

Table 1.5 has been prepared to show the wide variation of yields available in so-called fixed-value vehicles, at least in late 1982. The table is for medium-time-to-maturity bonds unless otherwise noted. In a normal world long-term bonds would pay less than short-term ones, but with inflation the reverse has been true. We see that the basic principle of more pay for more risk usually applies. When the prices get out of "proper" position buy opportunities are presented, as they are with common stocks. The risk of different bonds is not clearly defined. If the United States, the corporation, or the municipality issuing the

Table 1.5.   The Wide Spread in Yields Available in Late 1982

Investment	Yield (%)	Investment	Yield (%)
Bonds rated CCC	16.0	20-year Treasury bonds	12.2
Bonds rated B	15.0	10-year Treasury bonds	12.1
Bonds rated BBB	14.0	Average of all	11.3
Bonds rated A	13.8	Money market funds	11.0
Bonds rated AA	13.5	Municipal bonds rated A	10.0[b]
Bonds rated AAA	13.0	1-year all savers	9.8[b]
90-day bank certificates of deposit	13.0	U.S. savings bonds	8.0
30-month Small Savers certificates at savings and loans	13.0	Dow Jones industrial average, dividends	6.7
13-week Treasury bills	12.5	Savings and loan passbooks	5.5
		Bank savings accounts	5.25

[a]The order is expected to remain similar even though the yield levels change.
[b]Tax exempt.

bond survives, the interest will be paid as due and the face value paid at maturity. Between then and now, the price may be below or above what you paid.

Returning to Table 1.5, we see that at the time the table was constructed, very low quality corporate bonds paid about 16 percent per year, and higher grades paid less; then money market funds (which hold mostly high-grade certificates of deposit and federal securities) list with yields around 13.3 percent; tax-exempts come in around 12.8 percent; and the table continues down to savings and loan (S&L) savings accounts at 5.5 percent. The spread is truly profound.

There are four different types of bonds:

a. **Government bonds.** The U.S. Treasury issues bills, notes, and bonds, and other agencies issue government-backed bonds. All carry AAA or AA ratings and are the safest investment of all. During their lifetime they may sell below their original cost when interest rates are high, but there is insignificant risk of not being paid off at maturity.

b. **Corporate bonds.** Corporate bonds are found at all levels of quality, from AAA on down to C. As I said previously, if the company survives, the bonds will too. High-grade corporate bonds of the type that cannot be called before maturity offer a chance to lock in very high yields.

c. **Convertible bonds.** Convertibles are bonds that may, at the owner's option, be converted into a specific number of shares of the corporation's stock. Thus convertibles offer the security of bonds with the possibility of making a profit. For this added feature they usually sell to give a lower yield than regular bonds.

d. **Municipal bonds.** Municipal bonds (called *munis*) originally had two reasons to exist: a tax-free yield and a wide-open estate loophole. The tax-free yield was set up in order to help municipalities raise money for improvement at a low cost. In all cases federal taxes on the interest are forgone, and usually state taxes that would be due in the state in which they are issued are too. Sometimes other states honor this feature as well (see Table 1.6). The second reason for their existence is that they are almost always issued as "bearer bonds," which means that they are not registered in anybody's name.* You pay for them and get bonds with coupons that become due every six months. If you clip the coupon and take it to your bank they will collect the interest due you, usually for a fee of a few dollars. You could mail the coupon to the bank that makes the payments for the municipality and get the full amount, less the cost of registered mail. Since no owner's name appears anywhere on the bond, whoever has possession of it may claim the coupons and, upon maturity, get the face value of the bond. If you lose the bond you lose the interest and the value of the bond—just like losing cash.

Although the first purpose, that of saving cities, counties, and states part of the cost of raising money, is quite laudable, the use of the nonregistered form is frankly a wide-open loop-

*A tax law change will end this in 1983.

Table 1.6.   Does Your State Respect the Tax-Free Provisions of Municipal Bonds?

State	State's Own Bonds	Other States' Bonds	State	State's Own Bonds	Other States' Bonds
Alabama	No	Yes	Montana	No	Yes
Alaska	No	No	Nebraska	No	No
Arizona	No	Yes	Nevada	No	No
Arkansas	No	Yes	New Hampshire	No	Yes
California	No	Yes	New Jersey	No	Yes
Colorado	Yes	Yes	New Mexico	No	No
Connecticut	No	No	New York	No	Yes
Delaware	No	Yes	North Carolina	No	Yes
Florida	No	No	North Dakota	No	Yes
Georgia	No	Yes	Ohio	No	Yes
Hawaii	No	Yes	Oklahoma	Yes	Yes
Idaho	No	Yes	Oregon	No	Yes
Illinois	Yes	Yes	Pennsylvania	No	Yes
Indiana	No	No	Rhode Island	No	Yes
Iowa	Yes	Yes	South Carolina	No	Yes
Kansas	Yes	Yes	South Dakota	No	No
Kentucky	No	Yes	Tennessee	No	Yes
Louisiana	No	No	Texas	No	No
Maine	No	Yes	Utah	No	No
Maryland	No	Yes	Vermont	No	No
Massachusetts	No	Yes	Virginia	No	Yes
Michigan	No	Yes	Washington	No	No
Minnesota	No	Yes	West Virginia	No	Yes
Mississippi	No	Yes	Wisconsin	Yes	Yes
Missouri	No	Yes	Wyoming	No	No

hole by which bond owners may give them to their children in amounts above the limits at which gifts are taxed, or slide them by estate taxes by simply passing them to the heirs without records or comments. With gifts up to $10,000 a year being tax free, the estates shortly to be tax free up to $600,000, the unregistered feature loses a lot of its allure. Buying a bond fund deprives the purchaser of the loophole feature, which as we noted will be rarely needed, but the usual advantages of professional management, diversification, and not fooling with those "darn little coupons" remain. The last reason can be overcome by letting your broker keep the bonds and collect the money, one of the last free services remaining in this cost-conscious world.

How to make the choice of buying municipal bonds for higher after-tax income than from corporate bonds is quite simple: Divide the yield from a muni of quality equal to that of a corporate bond by the value (1.00 − your end tax rate), and if you come out ahead in after-tax yield, buy the muni. Thus the tax rate for a muni shown in Table 1.4 of 10.0 percent becomes 14.3 percent for a 30 percent bracket, and 16.7 percent for a 40 percent bracket. (See Table 1.7 for other rates.) Even with interest rates expected to come down, munis remain attractive. The unexpectedly high yields are probably traceable to a slightly lower liquidity should you want to sell, the soluble coupon problem, and the hazard of losing the bond.

Table 1.7. Required Equivalent Yields for Taxable Investments Compared to Tax-Free Bonds Paying 6 to 15 Percent per Year

Tax-Exempt Yields (%)	Tax Bracket (%)				
	30	35	40	45	50
6.0	8.6	9.2	10.0	10.9	12.0
7.0	10.0	10.8	11.7	12.7	14.0
8.0	11.4	12.3	13.3	14.5	16.0
9.0	12.9	13.8	15.0	16.4	18.0
10.0	14.3	15.4	16.7	18.2	20.0
11.0	15.7	16.9	18.3	20.0	22.0
12.0	17.1	18.5	20.0	21.8	24.0
13.0	18.6	20.0	21.7	23.6	26.0
14.0	20.0	21.5	23.3	25.5	28.0
15.0	21.4	23.1	25.0	27.3	30.0

Here are several additional pionts you need to know in order to judge whether you want to run your own bond portfolio instead of having fund managers do it:

a.   Commissions to buy (or sell) bonds are much smaller than to buy an equal dollar's worth of stock; say $25 for the first $1,000 face value, and $10 for each additional $1,000. Thus, in order to get diversification *don't* buy nine different $1,000 bonds and pay $225 in commissions when you could buy three bonds for $3,000 each and pay commissions of $135 total. (A friend of mine always buys four bonds because he has four kids and this will make the division easier. Since new bonds come out in $5,000 units with *no* commissions at all, I suggested he have one more kid. He didn't think I was funny.) One problem: There is a pretty wide spread between the bid and asked price of bonds, and it wouldn't hurt to call several brokers to get the best actual price.

b.   If you sell a stock the day before a dividend goes "X" (i.e., the dividend is declared), you lose the dividend; the new owner gets it all. If you sell a bond at, say, six months less one day, the buyer gets to pay you roughly 179 days interest, a fair arrangement. Similarly, when you buy, usually a fair amount of money goes to pay the interest due the previous owner. The statement you get from our broker has a little box that says "Interest paid, $250." When you get your interest check for $300 a month later, don't pay taxes on the whole $300; just pay on the $50. This only applies during the first pay period, because after that you will be the owner for the entire six months.

c.   Interest rates fluctuate; indeed, the roller coaster bond market has all but destroyed rational bond investing. The rise in interest rates caused the fall in price of the $1,000 Eastern bond discussed earlier from $1,000 to $380. Although the bond will go up substantially should interest rates come down to "normal," if you buy a high-interest-paying bond at par, don't look for a substantial rise in price well above $1,000, for a drop in interest rates. People don't like to buy a sure loser at maturity, even when that is 20 years away.

d.   Bonds close to maturity will not drop a whole lot as interest rates go up because they will soon be worth $1,000. This hurts bond funds as far as stability of price is concerned, as they have bonds of all maturities, and they replace those that mature with new ones.

If you want to get some income, and lock it in for many, many years, and have that income as big as possible for the bond quality you like, you will come out ahead if you collect a diversified stable of bonds rather than have a fund do this for you. The advantages that mutual funds have over you for a stock portfolio do not exist as large enough to justify the substantial loss of income.

The arguments I have given *against* buying bond funds do not apply if you are buying to try for a profit when interest rates go down. In that case the funds are far superior to buying individual bonds. They are instantly liquid, and the price is available on a daily basis in your newspaper.

Examples of bond funds include:

Corporate bonds	Boston Company Income Fund, Dreyfus A Bonds Plus, Fidelity Corporate Bond Fund, Fidelity Hi-Income Fund, and Value Line Bond Fund
Federal bonds	Babson Income Trust, Fidelity Government Securities Fund, and Vanguard Fixed Income Securities Fund
Tax-free bonds	Dreyfus Tax-Exempt Fund, Fidelity High-Yield Municipals, Nuveen Municipal Bond Fund, Oppenheimer Tax-Free Bond Fund, and Rowe Price Tax-Free Bond Fund

16. Money market funds. Money market funds are an entirely different type of investment than stock or bond funds. When large corporations, banks, and sometimes the federal government need short-term cash, they borrow in what is called the *money market*. The sums involved are huge, and since collateral is normally not required, borrowers pay a high rate of interest. By pooling the money from a large number of investors, money market funds provide the big money required for this type of investment, and in turn pass the high interest rates along (less expenses of course) to those who provided the money in the first place.

As far as how you as an investor should consider money market funds, think of them as a high-interest-paying mail-order bank, without any government insurance for your account. Like a bank, they accept your money, give you some checks that you may use to pay for whatever you want, and offer complete liquidity in that you can cash out anytime, unlike certificates of deposit and other fixed-period vehicles.

Money market funds, although serving in many ways like banks, have a lot of cost-saving advantages over banks: no need for sumptuous buildings, working under banking regulations that require certain reserves, or handling the paperwork for tiny accounts. To ensure minimum expenses, they also have a few regulations of their own:

a. Initial deposit must be—as spelled out in the fund prospectus—from $5,000 on down to as little as $1,000. Additional deposits may be required to be over $100 or even $250. Although there is a starting minimum, they do not customarily close your account should you go below it. Many investors use money market funds for switching to stock funds and vice versa, and it would be senseless to require opening a new account each time.

b. Each check you write must be for $500 or more; some funds permit as little as $250. It must be apparent to any investor that the minimum value for each check written poses no problem should a smaller amount be required. The $500 check may be written and deposited in a bank; the needed amount used, and the remainder redeposited in the money market fund.

c. Many funds request that you do not write against any checks you deposit until 15 days have passed. This is to give your check time to clear, but it does not affect your earning interest from the day they receive the check.

d. Some money market funds now charge a few dollars a month for housekeeping expenses. You should check with a fund before you invest it and avoid fees if possible. They can represent a large percentage of your monthly profits.

The foregoing advantages have worked out so well that the growth both in numbers and assets of the money markets has surpassed any and all predictions. Starting with the Reserve Fund in 1972, there are now about 155 public money market funds and possibly four dozen more run by brokers for their clientele. Of the total, about 8 are tax-free funds and 24 invest only in government securities. Of the latter, the AARP U.S. Government Money Market Trust achieved the unbelievable growth of total assets of from nothing to $4 billion in *two* years! The total value of the 12 million money market accounts was about $200 billion in mid-1982. Compare this with around 3 million accounts in "regular" no-load funds totaling "only" $18 billion. Burt Berry (of No-Load Fund X) describes this success: "In the history of finance, money market funds might be equivalent to the invention of the internal-combustion engine, the wireless, or the silicon chip." Truly, money markets have changed the investing habits of the entire financial world.

Currently banks would like to have the government regulate money market funds in much the same way it oversees commercial banks and savings and loans. They openly admit that they hope such regulation would increase the costs of running the money market funds and bring them more into line with the banks. As an amusing sidelight, banks currently get a substantial fraction of *their* lending money *from* money market funds, and, of course, turn around and lend it to the commercial world.

Money market funds do not invest in stocks and bonds, except for the few that use municipal bonds that are close to maturity to furnish tax-free yields. They are mostly in very short term vehicles, the average date to maturity being 35 *days*. These include the following:

a. U.S. government securities. These include Treasury bills which mature in less than a year, are highly liquid, and considered free of the possibility of default. Other government securities include those of various government agencies (Federal Land Bank, etc.,), which have some form of federal guarantee and are also considered to be free of risk.

b.   Certificates of deposit (CDs).   These are certificates issued by banks and savings and loans usually in $1 million units for the money market funds. They are short term, and highly liquid.

c.   Bankers' acceptances (BAs).   These are short-term discount notes arising out of foreign trade transactions. They are sold at a discount to give an effective rate or interest. They are backed by specific goods and guaranteed by both the bank and the buyer of the goods.

d.   Repurchases (repos).   Repos are very short term loans usually involving dealers who sell Treasury bills and guarantee to repurchase them in a few days at a slightly higher price. Repos are not guaranteed or insured by any government agencies.

e.   Commercial paper (CPs).   These are short-term debts issued by corporations. They are unsecured by any specific item or piece of goods. Since commercial papers are riskier than the other investments mentioned, their yield is higher.

f.   Municipal bonds.   Municipal bonds were discussed earlier in this section (item 15). A money market fund investing in munis would be attractive to those in very high tax brackets.

To get a perspective on how the portfolio affects the yields, note the following: At a time when funds invested in commercial paper are paying about 12 to 14 percent, those invested in governments pay about 9 to 11 percent, and those invested in munis pay about 7 to 9 percent, the last being tax free, of course.

Besides the previously mentioned differences between stock or bond and money market funds, there is one more uniqueness, and it is profound: the money markets take their daily return, and divided by the number of shares, subtract the expenses and then adjust the answer so that the share price stays at $1. The leftover is the current interest rate. There is a couple of percent spread between the various taxable money market funds, and don't let anybody tell you it isn't important. (That just says *they* don't have much money invested.) If you can pick up 2 percent on $50,000, for example, there's an extra $1,000 income—or as the old prospector said, "There's a 2-day liquor supply right there." The higher yield means a very, very, little more risk. Where do you find the yields for the various money market funds? In many daily papers and in the *Wall Street Journal,* each Monday.

For a fun item on money market funds, since most or at least a large fraction of the money is invested in federal securities and since their interest is not taxable by the states, shouldn't part of the interest that shareholders receive also be free of state taxes? Maybe they should, but only in Nebraska is the write-off possible. Nope, I don't know why.

Management costs are a little lower than for the stock funds, typically as shown in Table 1.8. The total expense nets out at about 1.5 percent below the gross yield of their investments.

The safety of the money market funds has really been superb. This is due to the combination of diversification and being in paper with very short maturities. In a few cases the portfolio managers outsmarted themselves by figuring that interest rates were coming down and locked in some long-term high rates. Interest rates proceeded to go up and the $1 share prices could not be maintained. Troubles like this can be easily avoided by sticking to funds with maturities of less than 30 days. Many

Table 1.8.   Typical Management Fees for
            Money Market Funds

Total Assets (millions)	Management Fee (%)
Less than $100	0.5
$100 to $400	0.45
$400 to $700	0.4
Greater than $700	0.35

funds help you with this; the Capital Preservation Fund, for example, limits itself to 7 days or less. Formal safety ratings are based on the criteria shown in Table 1.9.

Safety ratings for the various money market funds are published monthly in *Money Market Fund Safety Ratings* (3471 North Federal Highway, Fort Lauderdale, FL 33306) and in Donaghue's *Money Fund Safety Ratings* (Box 540, Holliston, ME 01746). No matter what the safety rating, investments in money market funds are not insured.

Although about 10 percent of the investors in stock mutual funds actually ask for certificates, almost nobody ever asks for certificates from their money market funds. I suspect that this occurs because the money markets are considered a holding investment rather than a long-term one.

The money market funds that invest in municipal bonds and furnish a tax-free interest several percent below that of the other money markets must by regulation have assets that do not have an average life to maturity of more than 120 days, with no one investment having a time to maturity of over a year. The tax exempts tell their shareholders how much of the interest comes from which states, so that state taxes may be properly paid. Examples of diversified money market funds include Dreyfus Liquid Assets, Fidelity Cash Reserves, Fidelity

Table 1.9.   Criteria for Rating Money Market Funds

Type of Security	Rating
Government securities only	AAA
Bank acceptances and certificates of deposits of large banks	AA
Commercial paper of top-rated corporations and branches of foreign banks in the United States	A
Deposits in foreign banks and commercial banks	BBB
Deposits in large foreign banks and medium-sized corporations' commercial paper	BB
Deposits in foreign banks and commercial paper of smaller corporations	B

Daily Income Trust, Kemper Money Market Fund, Rowe Price Prime Reserves, and The Reserve Fund. Examples of federal money market funds include Capital Preservation Fund; Dreyfus Money Market Instruments, Government Securities; and Vanguard Money Market Trust, Federal Portfolio. Examples of tax-free market funds include Dreyfus Tax-Exempt Money Market Fund and Fidelity Tax Exempt Money Market Trust.

17. Money market sweep accounts. A new type of combined money market fund account and checking account is being tried at several banks. In essence the computer sweeps your checking account every night and puts any money above a specified minimum ($1,000 to $5,000, depending on the bank) into a money market fund. No interest is paid on monies below the minimum. A big advantage is that checks of any amount (up to the total of the sweep account and the money market account) can be written, bypassing the usual money market ruling that all checks must be above $500 (sometimes $250). In turn, if you write a check for more than what is in the checking account, funds from the money market account are automatically withdrawn from the money market account. The advantage of automatically having a part or most of your idle money in a higher-yielding money market fund is substantial, and sweep accounts may indeed become standard across the nation.

18. Mutual funds in foreign countries.   Mutual funds exist in most industrial foreign countries and in general do not differ a lot from those in the United States except that commissions are usually 1 or 2 percent rather than 8.5 percent. I have avoided investing in them because the volatility of foreign exchanges and the language barriers in correspondence and literature seem like more trouble than it is worth. The International Investment and Business Exchange (725 College Avenue, Santa Rosa, CA 95404) has an office devoted to guiding investors through the intricacies of foreign investments and it would be my suggestion to talk with them or similar agencies before wandering into foreign mutual funds. A local source of help would be the World Trade office of your local chamber of commerce.

A point of advantage that the foreign funds seem to have is that down periods in our country do not necessarily match up with down periods in other countries.

19. Offshore funds. Want less taxes and maybe bigger profits? A group of mutual funds run by established managers (Dreyfus, Drexel Burnham Lambert, Lazard Brothers, and others), and situated in offshore locations (Bermuda, Cayman Islands, Luxembourg, Netherland Antilles, Panama, and the Channel Islands) operate by far different rules than do the onshore American funds, which are under the aegis of the SEC. Some do very well, but essentially all don't say how they do it and shareholders are pretty much at the mercy of the fund managers.

The point is that the offshores are located where there are no capital gains taxes to eat up profits, and dividend and interest tax rates are very low. They are not subject to U.S. laws as long as less than half of their assets are owned by Americans. They can't advertise in the United States because they aren't registered with the SEC. Identity of investors is not divulged, nor are investment strategies. Protection under our laws is largely missing: one of the great mutual fund collapses—that of Bernard Cornfield's IOS Limited, which nicked investors for some $200 million, was an offshore event. I also remember seeing the closed doors of a fund in Curacao, which seemingly did beautifully until some rude person divulged that the fund hadn't bought any of the stocks it claimed had done so well, nor could the manager be found.

The IRS seems to classify all this as "tax avoidance," which is legal, and hasn't pursued people who deal through Swiss bank accounts, or cash their distribution or capital gains checks offshore and bring the cash into this country.

It is encouraging to us here at home that most of the offshore money is invested in the United States, as this is direct evidence that this is the best place to make money.

The structure of the offshore funds as far as officers, managers, custodian banks, distributors, and dealers is much the same as that of typical U.S. load funds, and their commissions, a maximum of 8.5 percent and no redemption fees,

match our schedules. The big differences are in the distributors' total pay, the managers' fees, and the complete freedom
of portfolio maneuvering the managers enjoy.

Depending on the fund, the managers may receive just about
anything from 1 percent per year of the total assets (double the
usual rate in the United States) up to 10 percent of the yearly
profit, if any. During the 1960s this paid off for a while, indicating that being freed of long- and short-term profit considerations, diversification requirements, and other SEC regulation was a benefit. Recent records are hard to come by, indicating
that things may not be as rosy as before.

Few of us would agree with the sales gimmicks that arise
when complete freedom is allowed. Some funds offer automatic
leverage in that shareholders may at purchase time put their
shares in escrow and borrow 100 percent of their value to buy
more shares. They may also purchase an insurance policy that
guarantees them against loss; in fact some policies guarantee
a profit of up to 20 percent a year! For the elderly shareholder,
a beneficiary must be designated to whom the shares will be
transferred upon the owner's death without fuss, bother,
inheritance taxes, or probate costs.

1.14.   FUND PERFORMANCE

Well, how does the performance of each group compare? Since
you would buy the different groups for different reasons (growth,
income, taxes, etc.), it doesn't make sense to compare every
type. But for those intended to make money, an 11-year record
is shown in Table 1.10 for aggressive growth, growth, and
balanced funds. As you will note, the aggressive growth funds
go up the most in good markets and down the most in bad
ones, and depending on which year or group of years you pick,
you can "prove" just about anything you wish.

Referring to Table 1.10, you do not add percentages to get
the final total for, say, five years. You have to change them to
decimals, add 1.0 and multiply. Thus 10 percent a year for 2

Table 1.10.   Yearly Profit Average of a Selection of Funds[a]

Year	Aggressive Growth	Growth	Balanced
1970	− 18.2	− 9.1	+ 1.9
1971	+ 59.7	+ 34.0	+ 18.7
1972	+ 18.8	+ 14.0	+ 13.8
1973	− 37.3	− 29.5	− 13.5
1974	− 34.0	− 25.1	− 22.0
1975	+ 70.0	+ 40.5	+ 26.4
1976	+ 39.4	+ 36.0	+ 26.0
1977	+ 18.0	+ 9.7	− 2.3
1978	+ 25.0	+ 16.7	+ 8.3
1979	+ 49.1	+ 39.8	+ 32.4
1980	+ 55.6	+ 42.6	+ 35.8
1981	− 3.7	+ 4.5	− 3.1
Average	+ 14.5	+ 13.6	+ 9.6

years isn't +20 percent; it's $1.10 \times 1.10 = 1.21$ or +21 percent. The "drops" are handled the same way: −20.7 and −21.1 become a total loss of $0.793 \times 0.789 = 0.626$ or −37.4 percent.

As we see from the averages in Table 1.10 for the particular 11-year period the aggressive growth funds averaged about 14.5 percent a year; the growth funds, 13.6 percent; and the balanced funds, 9.6 percent. Essentially the same group of funds is shown plotted in Figure 1.5. It is interesting that the three types of funds performed almost identically for the first seven years (the larger losses were balanced by larger gains), and then the aggressive growth and growth funds moved well above the balanced funds, which just about equaled the inflation rate. Don't be misled by a small change in percentages; they mount up over a period of years.

And how much will you make in no-load funds? Well, your broker may not tell you and stay within his guidelines. The

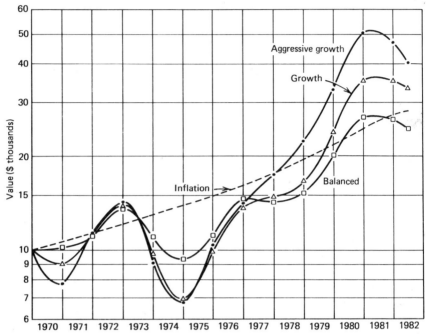

Figure 1.5. Cumulative results of investing a starting amount of $10,000 in a varying selection of aggressive growth, growth, and balanced funds, and (dashed line) the cumulative inflation rate.

SEC and the NASD (National Association of Securities Dealers—see Section 1.17) will not permit him to tell you that a particular fund "averaged 12 percent for the last 8 years." But he may tell you that had you invested $10,000 10 years ago it would now be worth $19,920 had you reinvested the profits, and there would be in addition $4,840 in dividends. Your broker may not add the two numbers together (to get $24,760) because the SEC/NASD says part of the money is profits and part income and the two mustn't be added together. You are not supposed to be able to add the two numbers together yourself and look in a set of compound growth tables and learn that the total is the same as an *average* rate of 12 percent for 8 years. One more: Your broker may not say what a $10,000 investment grew to in 8 years; only the 5-, 10-, 15-, and 20-year periods are permissible, and he can't talk about the 10 years from 1930 to 1940; he must only discuss the latest period, even though you might be very interested in how the fund fared during some special time period.

But I'm not a broker and I think you'll do better than the aforementioned averages of selected no-load funds, because I think we have a big bull market ahead of us. And if you apply yourself to the timing methods in Section 4.5, you'll do a whole lot better than the averages in Table 1.10.

1.15.   WHAT MAY A MUTUAL FUND DO WITH YOUR MONEY?

Three agencies determine what fund managers may legally do with your money—Uncle Sam, the state you live in, and the fund officers acting under the fund charter. Four agencies (add in the sales organization if there is one) who do not want you on their backs if the managers misbehave, make sure that they do. Let us start with Uncle Sam. Through his agent, the SEC, Uncle says each diversified fund must:

1. Register with the SEC if it has 100 or more shareholders.
2. Have a minimum starting capital of $100,000 before offering shares.
3. Furnish a prospectus and full accurate information about all fund business to its shareholders at least twice a year. (Most companies issue reports quarterly.)
4. Register its dealers and brokers.
5. Operate with the best interests of its shareholders at heart, not the best interest of the officers, managers, or sales organization.
6. Not make changes in organization, business methods, or investment policies without the consent of the shareholders.

7.   Keep adequate reserves for the conduct of business.

8.   Employ sound accounting methods.

9.   Earn at least 90 percent of its gross income (*gross* means before expenses) from dividends, interest, and capital gains from securities—not from other investments (such as land) that are not under the aegis of the SEC.

10. Have as a majority of the board of directors people who are not connected with investment bankers or the company's brokers. (Oddly enough, this applies to load-type funds only. No-load funds need have only one outsider on the board.)

11. If open-ended, not issue bonds or preferred stocks.

12. Make no more than 30 percent of its gross income from securities held less than 90 days.

13. Distribute at least 90 percent of its total income, or pay taxes on any undistributed capital gains at the maximum rate.

14. Put not more than 5 percent of its capital in assets in any one stock (i.e., own 20 stocks or more). (If a fund owns more than 5 percent of a corporation's shares, the corporation becomes an "affiliated person" of the fund, and transactions between the two require SEC approval.) Semidiversified funds need own only five stocks.

15. Put not more than 10 percent of its assets in "letter stock" (see Section 5.3).

16. Not enter into joint transactions with brokers or underwriters.

17. Not own more than 10 percent of the voting stock of any one company.

18. Redeem your shares in seven days or less. Funds may, however, refuse to redeem your shares:

     a. When the stock exchange is closed, or trading is restricted.

    b. When an emergency exists so that disposal of securities is not practical, or the fund cannot practically determine the value of its shares.

    c. When permitted by the SEC to suspend redemption "for the protection of shareholders."

19. Not have more than 25 percent of its assets in the stock of any one company.

20. Have the management group approved annually.

The 20 items listed need a little further discussion. Admittedly, the rules are specific, but like most rules, there are loopholes. For instance, though a fund may not buy more than 10 percent of the voting stock of a company, 10 percent is a fair portion and the corporate officers will really listen to anybody owning that much. Still further, if several funds each own 10 percent of one company, they just about have control—even though the regulations were written to avoid that very thing. Having too large a percentage of a fund's total assets in a single stock is a trap one no-load fund fell into in 1968, with the result that the mutual fund industry received possibly its worse black eye in history.

To bring the meaning of this goldfish bowl atmosphere closer to home, I would like to quote a paragraph from *How to Build Capital and Income in Mutual Funds* by David Jenkins.* In describing the effects of the regulation, he says:

> To show how this works, let us imagine that automobile manufacturers had to operate under such close supervision. First of all, you would not be able to buy a car without first being given a copy of a prospectus, which would include a complete technical description of the car and the manufacturer. Furthermore, no advertisement for the car could say that it is a good car, or that its designers know what they are doing. The manufacturer would have to point out to you how much money you will lose if you have to sell the car, and also that you might get killed by

*David Jenkins, *How to Build Capital and Income in Mutual Funds*, Larchmont, NY: American Research Council, page 20. Used by permission.

driving it. He would have to tell you how much it cost him to make the car, and how much profit he and the dealer are making. He would not be able to use any flamboyant advertising, would have to restrict sales literature to straight factual statements and would not be able to say that the car will necessarily help you solve your transportation problems or that, in fact, it will do you any good at all.

One can imagine the squealing that would occur should a "Securities Act" be passed for autos.

On top of the federal regulations, nearly all states have added those of their own. Accordingly, you might not be able to buy a particular mutual fund if its managers have not qualified for your state. (Some funds claim they don't have to, and sell anywhere. All you can do is try, or use your property in an acceptable state for an address.) This is of no great import, as there are lots of good mutual funds. It may be that the state has a limit on the maximum manager's fee such that a change would have an overall deleterious effect on their income; or they may feel the licensing fee is unreasonable; or there may be other reasons. Oddly enough, managers who handle several funds may have some of them qualified in your state, but not all.

Next comes the charter under which the fund is organized. It may very well contain many of the regulations mentioned, especially those the fund officers decide would look good to prospective investors. Thus the charter for a fund (as described in the fund's prospectus) might include the following self-imposed restrictions, many of which are restatements of the federal regulations:

1. The fund shall not purchase securities on margin or make short sales.
2. No more than 5 percent of the fund's securities shall be in any one company excepting securities of the United States. (Somebody else besides me believes in diversification.)
3. The fund shall not hold more than 10 percent of the stock of any one company.

4. The fund shall not buy the securities of any company that is less than 3 years old.

5. The fund shall not buy the securities of any company with which it has an advisory contract. (Fund managers often advise corporations as to the investing of their excess funds.)

6. The fund shall not invest in real estate or commodities.

7. The fund shall not borrow money except for temporary or emergency reasons, and then not over 10 percent of the value of the fund.

8. The fund shall not invest in the securities of a company for the purpose of exercising management or control, although it retains the right to vote as a stockholder.

9. The fund shall not make any investment that would cause more than 25 percent of its assets to be invested in any one industry.

10. The fund shall not make loans to any of its officers, or to any firms, corporations, or syndicates in which its officers or managers have a substantial interest.

11. The fund shall not purchase securities of corporations in which its officers or managers have a substantial interest.

12. Other limitations might exist according to the type of funds, such as percentage limitations on the ownership of stocks, bonds, or other securities, or nonliquid stocks.

These federal, state, and charter limits have resulted in an operation that can only be described by the word *admirable.* As far back as records go, no fund has ever gone bankrupt, although a few have gotten closed for a while. In a down market this is bad because one cannot sell out and go elsewhere. This is why I urge that even the smallest investor own more than one fund. This is a suing world we live in, and even the best of funds get sued—usually because shareholders feel the management group is making too much money. By the way, fund officers are frequently not paid, and they are absolved from losses in suits. Who gets to pay? Usually it's the management corporation.

Another limitation for the chance of misconduct lies in the fact that the managers of a mutual fund or its officers do not have physical access to the stock certificates owned by the fund; they are held by banks, as you will notice by the address when you send in your payments. Upon direction from the managers the bank pays or receives money.

Well, if a mutual fund can't go broke, do people ever lose money in them aside from errors as above? Sure. In a rising market mutuals rise more slowly than some of the glamour stocks, and people tire of the slow but sure and sell their mutuals to try for a fast buck. In falling markets some shareholders become concerned and sell out to rebuy (perhaps) at still lower prices. A section of this book is devoted to doing this right: selling near the top and buying near the bottom.

Most of what I have said concerns what a fund may *not* do with your money. Perhaps it would be useful to summarize what a typical fund *can* do with your money. The prospectus of a fund gives precise data—you get one by writing to the fund and asking for it.

The typical fund may:

1. Accept a certain starting amount of dollars, charging a commission (if it is a load fund) as stated in the prospectus, for which it of course issues shares in your name. (Somebody is always looking for loopholes. What will a fund do if it has a $1,000 first payment, and you make it and shortly thereafter withdraw $800, leaving only $200 in the account? Probably nothing.)

2. According to your instructions, send you a check or buy more mutual fund shares from your portion of any dividends received from the stocks owned by the fund, charging commissions as stated in the prospectus.

3. According to your instructions, send you a check or buy more mutual fund shares from your portion of any profits made by selling stocks owned by the fund. Commissions are not charged on reinvestment of these "capital gains." Do funds ever distribute *losses*? No. If capital losses exceed capital gains (profits), it is simply reflected by the price per share going down. (In the past decade most mutual funds have gone down in about one year out of three.)

4. According to your instructions, sell any or all of your shares and send you a check within a few days (the right to send you stock instead exists).

5. Accept any amount of money above a specified minimum as stated in the prospectus, with whatever frequency you select, to buy more shares in your name.

6. Accept money for retirement under the Self-Employed Individuals Tax Retirement Act of 1962 (the Keogh plan), the Independent Retirement Account Act of 1974 and 1981, and as a direct accumulator for a company's retirement plan.

7. At the fund's discretion distribute the dividends mentioned in (2) and (3) whenever it sees fit. Both returns from dividends and capital gains must be distributed in order to avoid the fund having to pay corporate taxes.

8. Sell shares to its employees or managers without having them pay commissions, if there are any.

9. Upon payment of a nominal fee (say $5), let you exchange your shares for shares in other funds (if any) that are managed by the same company, providing such a policy exists.

10. Arrange to send you a monthly check, providing your accumulation exceeds a minimum (usually $5,000 to $10,000) as stated in the prospectus (see Chapter 4).

11. If you have signed a contractual plan, require you to invest at the rate you signed for, or pay very high commissions on the money you have already put in. This is covered in Section 3.3.

12. Charge a yearly management fee ranging from as little as three-tenths of 1 percent to probably not over 1 percent of the current value of your shares.

13. Upon agreement of a majority of the shareholders, split the shares, perhaps giving each shareholder 100 percent more shares but reducing the value of all shares by 50 percent so that there is no change in value to the shareholder. (Funds believe the minor costs of printing and bookkeeping are worth it to increase the salability of the shares.)

14. Change managers upon agreement of a majority of the shareholders.

15. Suspend the sale of shares during the time a new prospectus is being studied by the SEC for possible approval.

16. Compute the value of a share at the close of the NYSE each day, and each successive new price shall hold until a newer price is computed.

17. With the approval of the SEC, suspend further sale of its shares if in the opinion of its directors the fund is getting too large, or it is a poor time to invest new money.

1.16.   WHAT "MANEUVERS" CAN A MUTUAL FUND MAKE?

After you have bought a mutual fund, what "deals" can the officials or managers make that might greatly change your feelings about owning that particular fund, and what can you do about it? The last question is easy to answer. If officials or managers muster enough votes to make a change you don't like, you have little chance to do anything except sell your shares.

At least the share price won't change catastrophically like those of a stock when bad news is announced, but you might have to pay some taxes if you have a profit, and a new commission to reinvest if you buy that kind of a fund.

Normally, the changes would be for your good. A typical change is a change in scope, and many funds have done this to their shareholders' benefit. Often these are specialty funds that see the errors of their ways in being limited in the areas in which they might invest, and who cast off the shackles. Examples of this might be the Texas Fund, which for the first 17 years of its life was restricted to investments in the southwest part of the United States. Another might be the Keystone S-4 Fund, which for the first 35 years of its life invested in low-priced common stocks. Both funds realized the general funds could invest in *their* areas, but *they* couldn't benefit by a wider choice. This is always bad, and worse when the funds grow large. In these two examples the funds went wide open and benefited thereby.

Another maneuver a fund might pull is to join another fund or a group of funds. Examples might be the Ivest Fund joining the Wellington group or the Gryphon Fund joining the Founders Fund. Since both fund officials and fund managers are typically shareowners in the fund in question, it would be hard to believe that a move they might make would be intended to hurt the fund. Yet the move might work out poorly. One William Street went from a load fund to a no-load fund, with poor results for the shareholders, but surely not intentionally that way. Fairfield went from a no-load fund to a load fund, with good results for the shareholders.

Another type of maneuver might be a change in policy toward holding lots of cash because the fund manager feels that the market is going down. You might disagree with this and feel the market is going up. Again, you have the choice of selling out and investing with a fully committed fund.

Does a fund ever stick its nose into the management of a corporation in which it holds shares of stock?" The answer is a great big *yes*. If it doesn't get satisfaction it may of course sell out and buy the stock of another corporation, but if it sees something wrong or disagrees with the policies of the management, it may try to get things changed. Selling out would more likely occur if (1) it is unsuccessful in getting the desired changes made, or (2) from its standpoint the future of the company or industry is in doubt owing to factors beyond its control. A few funds are happy to have their directors also be directors of corporations the fund has a position in, whereas others eschew the idea.

In summary, it would be extremely unlikely that a fund would make a move intentionally designed to hurt the shareholders. In order to keep abreast of whatever it does you need to subscribe to a good no-load fund advisory service. (See Section 4.2.)

1.17. THE ORGANIZATIONS THAT PROTECT YOU

In an accurate sense there are no organizations that protect you—at least from the possibility of losing money if you buy funds when the market is high and sell them when it is low—but there are two that go a long way toward protecting you from being conned by unscrupulous managers or brokers. These are the Securities and Exchange Commission (SEC) and the National Association of Security Dealers (NASD). The former was set up by an act of Congress (the Securities and Exchange Act of 1934) to administer the Federal Securities Act of 1933. NASD is an organization to which most fund salesmen belong, which sets up qualification standards for mutual fund dealers and brokers, sets rules to prevent fraudulent practices, and administers the compliance of the people in the fund industry, much in the same manner that the American Medical Association decides what are and what are not ethical medical practices for doctors. The NASD levies fines that are "accepted" for minor infractions, and the SEC pursues the outright crook with an aim to incarceration.

A third organization, the Investment Company Institute, is a trade association to which most funds belong. This furnishes an organization such that the members can present a solid front in matters pertaining to the mutual fund industry. A fourth organization, the No-Load Mutual Fund Association, looks out for the interests of the no-load funds.

The SEC and NASD have an excellent record in their efforts to keep the skulduggery down, but unfortunately in their zeal to accomplish this they have in many instances restrained investors from learning all they should. For instance, a table showing the average compound growth rates of a specific mutual fund cannot be used by a broker to help sales, since a rule exists that brokers must not discuss the performance of funds in terms of compound growth rates. This is thought to imply that one may expect the same growth every year. If it did, I could agree with them. And I could agree that anybody discussing average compound growth rates should have the honesty to point out that the yearly growth rates may run from −52.7 percent to +184(!) percent. But to outlaw the use of compound interest tables is going a little too far. Tables comparing mutual funds to savings and loan accounts, rentals, real estate, and so forth are also forbidden. This would be a violation of the regulations because "A broker must not compare the performance of mutual funds with other types of fixed value investments." Why a client should not be advised as to his chances of making money in real estate, notes, or Las Vegas is beyond me. But as I said, the overall results from this regulation have been good. My biggest complaint is that it has kept lots of people (particularly *me*) from knowing about no-load mutual funds as soon as I should have.

Indeed, one could get nasty about the withholding of fund performance in terms of layman can understand and ask how many average people would be rich today if they had known that $100 per month invested in growth stock mutual funds almost certainly would grow to $1 million in 40 years. That kind of protection I could have done without. Current NASD leaders would do well to review some of their predecessors' restrictive rulings.

1.18. DISTRIBUTIONS ARE HOW FUNDS PAY YOU

Mutual funds make money from their investments in several different ways, and customarily they send their profits (less their expenses) to you as a shareholder once a year. The checks you get are properly called *distributions,* but many funds and many fund advisers call them *dividends.* This leads to all sorts of confusion because investors tend to equate fund distributions with stock dividends and there is no real way to compare them:

1.   Stock dividends are reasonably predictable; fund distributions are not. The latter arises because fund managers have no reason to be regular as to when or even if they take profits.

2.   You may request that your distributions be reinvested in more fund shares, or if you wish only the capital gains will be reinvested and the remainder paid to you. Or you may request that only the dividends and interest be reinvested, and the capital gains sent to you. None of these options are available with stock dividends or bond interest.

3.   The fund situation is different from the behavior of a stock when a dividend is declared. The day a stock pays a $1 dividend it "opens" down $1, but very probably the value of the dividend is lost in the trading that takes place that very day. It might make sense to buy a stock a few days before it goes "ex-dividend," and hope the market price movement of the stock doesn't reflect the dividend so that you get a little extra. This situation doesn't exist with a distribution from a mutual fund. When a fund makes a distribution of $1 a share (it could be from profits taken, dividends, or interest), and you order the $1 reinvested, *you are not one dime ahead because the price of the fund shares went down a $1 the day it was distributed.* Unless you have the distribution reinvested, you will end up with less money in the fund than before. In fact you will end up with less anyhow because you have to pay taxes on the distribution: full taxes on the part that came from stock dividends and interest received (less any exclusions allowed), full

taxes on stocks held less than 12 months, and reduced taxes on stocks held over a year.

It is worthwhile repeating the same thing using numbers. Suppose at the start of the year you have $1,000 worth of the Smith Fund. And suppose that during the year the stocks that the fund holds went up 30 percent. The fund still holds most of the stocks because the managers think they will go higher, but they sold $100 worth. If you asked the custodian bank to give you a statement on December 31, they would say, "Your account is worth $1,300; $1,200 in stocks and $100 in cash." By law the fund must distribute the profits taken. If $50 out of the $100 sold was profit they must "send" you the $50, and even worse, they must tell Uncle Sam they sent it to you, so Uncle Sam can catch you if you don't pay taxes on it. This applies, as we have said before, whether you ever see the money or whether they reinvest it for you. If you accept the $50 in cash your acount is now worth $1,250. If you have the custodian bank reinvest the $50 your account is still worth $1,300, but you must pay appropriate taxes. So in a way distributions are bad because they make you pay taxes, but good because they show your fund is making money. They don't show it to you very well because they say nothing about the additional profits they may be in a position to take. It gripes me to have a friend say, "My fund just paid a 20 percent distribution," and smile like he had made a great investment. I'm glad it made a profit, and sorry he had to pay taxes.

Aggressive funds often don't pay distributions because they are invested in stocks that pay small dividends, if any, and the other monies they make, plus the dividends, just about pay the fund expenses. Finally, they hope to take, and usually do take, big long-term capital gains.

Let me summarize what I just said: *After a fund makes a distribution, shareholders do not have a dime more than before it was made; in fact they have less because taxes are owed on the distribution.*

As I said before, if a mutual fund broker ever tells you to buy right now because the fund is going to pay a big distribution soon (he might call it a dividend), tell him to go jump in a lake because you want to avoid paying taxes on the distribution and you will be better off if you buy after the distribution (neglecting any movement of the share price due to the market). And get yourself another fund salesman. A no-load fund would never dare write you a letter to this effect. Come to think of it, a broker wouldn't either.

The following will enable you to understand how a fund figures a distribution and how you treat it taxwise.

Example 1.1.   Calculations for a distribution:
1. On May 1, 1977, you bought 1,500 shares of Fund Z at $9 a share for a total of $13,500.
2. On June 1, 1983, the value per share goes to $12.50 and your portfolio is worth $18,750.
3. A $2 per share distribution is declared, dropping the share value to $10.50.
4. The amount of your distribution is $2 × 1,500 shares, or $3,000.
5. You are credited with $3,000 ÷ $10.50, or 285.714 additional shares. You owe taxes on the $3,000 according to the fund's statement as to what fractions are dividends, interest, and capital gains.
6. The total number of shares in your account, assuming you asked that all distributions be reinvested, is

$$1,500 + 285.714 = 1,785.714$$
7. The total value of the account is, hence,

$$1,785.714 \times \$10.50 = \$18,750$$

In short, the distribution did nothing for you except make you pay some taxes.
8. Should the share price go to $13 in 1984 and you decide to sell, you will receive

$$1,785.714 \times 13 = \$23,214.28$$

Since you paid $13,500 originally and then added $3,000 when the distribution was paid, your cost is

$16,500, and your profit for tax purposes would be

$$\$23,214.28 - \$16,500 = \$6,714.28$$

See Section 3.11 for help in keeping your records straight.

As for taking distributions in cash or having them reinvested, there are several factors to consider. If you are in the accumulative stage, you should clearly leave them in to be reinvested; the charts of fund performance assume that you do this. The arguments for having them sent to you are twofold: (1) You are going to have to pay taxes on them and might as well be awakened to that fact, and possibly put the required amount in a money market fund for later use; and (2) the distribution check will wake you up to the fact that maybe you don't want to put any more money in that particular fund and prefer to invest it elsewhere.

There are three dates that are of great interest with regard to distributions: (1) the declaration date announcing that a distribution of a certain amount will take place on (2) a specific date, and (3) an unannounced date, frequently a *month* after the "X-date," when you will receive the distribution (assuming that you asked for a payment in cash rather than reinvestment). Reinvestment takes place the day after the X-date. You may or may not notice that a distribution is imminent, and you may or may not notice that on a particular day there is an X after the fund data in the newspaper which accompanies a sudden drop in price. In fact the drop could easily mislead you to sell because the fund price has dropped below a sell price selected by you. As for waiting a month to receive your distribution, this is really an annoyance and an expensive one at that. In Example 1.1 it might cost $30. You can beat the delay two ways. If you had planned to redeem all of the shares you own in the fund, and if the time period represents a long-term capital gain, by all means redeem *before* the Fund goes X. The distribution will surely be partly or fully taxed, and maybe you can make it 100 percent capital gains. If this is not possible for your situation, write or phone the fund the day after the X-date and request a check for the same amount as the distribution. This will only take about a week to reach you, or if you have a telephone switch the distribution can be making money for you in two days. I don't know why shareholders should have to put up with a one-month delay, but that's the way it is for many funds.

Load funds have a legitimate reason for not making the purchase of the new shares immediately: They don't know how many shares have been sold by brokers around the country because the money has not yet come in and they need a few days to get the figures right.

The various states are greatly confused about how the capital gains distributions should be treated taxwise. Eight say capital gains are income, fully taxed; 8 say they are not taxed at all; and 32 say that capital gains are taxed as capital gains. You will have to check locally to find out the most recent ruling in your state. See Section 4.3 to learn how plotting funds including the distribution really overstates how well they have done, and Section 3.12 to learn how distributions are taxed.

Now here's a question for you. What about being out of the market and hence missing a distribution? Wouldn't that clobber you? It wouldn't hurt a thing. If you knew—and you generally do—that the fund will make a distribution on a certain date, and you sell out the day before and buy back the day after, you will not be hurt directly by the maneuver, but you might be hurt by the side effects. It depends on when you bought the shares. If you bought them a week before, learned of the distribution and sold out, and then bought back after, you would come out ahead because you wouldn't have to pay taxes on the distribution. If you had bought months before, and sold the day before the distribution, everything could be capital gains.

1.19. TWO HARD QUESTIONS

There are two questions people ask about mutual funds that are very difficult to answer unless you have had time to think about them. Even though they are covered elsewhere, I'll answer them here and now. Here are the questions:

1.   If mutual funds are so good, how come some of them sell for as little as $4 a share?
2.   What dividends do they pay?

To answer the first question, it is very hard for investors to dissociate the price of a mutual fund share from its performance, but that's what we have to do. We agree that if, say, 100 people each buy 1,000 shares of Delta Airlines stock on one day, it will drive up the price per share and the last buyer will assuredly pay more for 1,000 shares than did the first. But if 100 people each buy 1,000 shares of Smith mutual fund, it won't change its price one bit. Why? Basically because buyers are not competing for a fixed number of shares. Suppose Smith Fund has issued 5 million shares and the total portfolio is worth $20 million. Obviously each share is worth $4. When the 100 buyers each buy $4,000 worth of shares, nothing has happened to raise the share price. The fund is now worth $20 million in stocks and has $400,000 cash. The manager of the Smith Fund will order the custodian bank to issue 100,000 new shares, but this isn't like issuing new corporate stock because the assets of the mutual fund have increased by the value of the shares issued. A corporate stock dividend or new issue makes more shares for the *same* corporate earnings or assets, and the price per share should go down.

The price per share of a mutual fund may also go down for the same reason as that of a corporation; there is a stock split. This is done with both mutual funds and corporate stocks because there is a widespread belief that lower price stocks have a better chance of going up than higher-priced stocks. I'll stay out of that argument, but there is no question as to the general belief. So from time to time you will have the share price of one of your funds cut in half and you will get a notice that you now have twice as many shares as you had before. But there is no change in the value of your investment. If you care to score the price ranges of mutual funds in your daily paper, you will find 55 percent under $10; 35 percent, at $10 to $20; 6 percent, at $20 to $30; and only 4 percent over $30 a share.

So the answer to the first question is that the price of a mutual fund share is determined by dividing the current value of the portfolio by the number of shares out, and the share price has *nothing* to do with the fund's performance. (This is not quite true for closed-end funds. They have a net asset value per share, but since the share prices are bid for in the public market, a share might cost more or less than it is really worth. Usually it's less.)

To answer the second question, "What dividends do they pay?" it is probably better if you just say, "They don't pay dividends." Once or twice a year, usually on about the same date, they distribute pro rata the dividends they have received plus the interest they have earned and the capital gains they have taken that year, less the costs of running the fund. Since the capital gains make up the largest item, usually, the size of the distributions vary all over the lot from year to year. Some sort of general assumptions can be made by looking at the distribution record. Table 6.1 has the distribution record for two well-run mutual funds with widely different philosophies about making distributions.

1.20. TAX ADVANTAGES

Investors in mutual funds may benefit from a number of tax advantages, some of which are not at all well known. As will be demonstrated, in some instances the tax benefits may be substantial.

1. Custodian wash sales.   The first tax advantage is rather special and applies most often to custodian accounts, those special accounts held for one's children under the custodian act. In many cases these accounts are small, say a few hundred to a few thousand dollars. But they grow with the years, and some day it may be necessary to sell them. At sale time capital gains taxes must be paid on the profit figured from the cost price. A way around this is to *switch the fund each year.* As long as the profit is less than the taxable minimum, and this is the child's only income, no taxes need be paid, and a new base is established from which future taxes may be computed. Possibly the switch, depending on the amount involved, may only be needed every few years. The proposed switch is most useful with no-load funds so that a new sales commission is avoided. A load fund owner sometimes is able to switch without a commission if he or she selects a fund in the same family.

2. The Keogh plan. The Keogh plan is covered in Section 7.6, and is mentioned here only for completeness in the tax savings section.

3. Very long term capital gains. Important tax savings come from the fact that in general the top-performing mutual funds make their profits from long-term investments. They may trade a lot, but they take their profits quite infrequently. A lot of serious investors make the mistake of separating capital gains into *short* and *long* term, feeling that they have done as well as they can taxwise when they hold a stock until it becomes a long-term capital gain. This is not so. Capital gains taxes should be divided into *short term, long term,* and *maybe never.* The periods for short and long term have been covered elsewhere. The "maybe never" comes about because capital gains taxes are never paid on appreciated stocks or mutual funds (or other items) if they are used in the manner of a gift. The monetary value of a gift bought before January 1, 1977, and made after January 1, 1977, is its purchase value or its value on January 1, 1977. If the size of the gift comes within the gift deduction, no taxes are owed. Similarly, if the capital gain does not put an estate into a taxpaying bracket, no taxes are paid.

Long-term capital gains are also apt to arise in the new municipal bond funds, since the price of bonds varies with the current rates, and often drops below their par or maturity values. It would be rare indeed for a bond fund to take a short-term capital gain. All of this is probably not news to most readers, but the point that has not received attention is that many, many funds are for the most part very long term profit takers. Although there is no guarantee that this will continue, the ratio of capital gains distribution to total capital gains is available for each fund, and should be considered in selecting a fund to buy. One will find the ratio varies from funds that have *never* taken a capital gain, and state they do not intend to, to those that essentially distribute all gains available each year.

4. **Withdrawal plans.**   Withdrawal plans are an arrangement with a fund such that it sends you a monthly check made up of dividends and capital gains. This means the total is more than just dividends, and the capital gains part is only partially taxed. These plans are covered in Chapter 6.

5. **Commission wash sales.**   This applies only to some load funds. Suppose funds A and B are in the same family and it is desired to buy $1,000 worth of A. Fund B is bought instead of A, and immediately switched to A for a transfer fee of (typically) $5. A short-term loss of the commission, say $85, is immediately established, and taxes on $85 saved for the current year. If the fund is later sold, the short-term loss is offset by a long-term gain on $85, so the final gain is somewhere between the full taxes on $85 now and taxes on four-tenths of $85 (at possibly a different rate) later on.

6. **Buying losses to offset capital gains.**   Mutual funds managers take losses from time to time, which in a bull market are more than offset by capital gains. However, before a bear market turns around so that capital gains can be made, a number of losses are collected. These will be used up in the ensuing bull market and until they are, you will not have to pay taxes on capital gains. Capital gains simply will not appear on your year-end statement. Losses and sometimes a schedule of years by which they must be used up appear in the prospectus. Other things being equal, buy a fund with the most losses.

7. **IRA funds and IRA programs.**   Funds especially managed for IRA plans are discussed in Section 1.13, item 14. The general subject of IRA programs is covered in Chapter 7. They are mentioned here only for completeness.

1.21. TAX DISADVANTAGES

Several examples have been given of tax advantages from mutual funds. Now we come to some "bad" tax features of mutual funds.

The first "bad" feature, I am happy to say, was eliminated in July 1973. This was the seemingly capricious ruling of the Internal Revenue Service that *for estate tax purposes, load funds must be valued at the asked price rather than at the bid price,* which is roughly 8.5 percent lower. The reason was that in theory at least your executor could sell the shares to another person at about the asked price because he is going to have to pay it anyhow, and he would just as soon pay it to you. There is a grain (Webster says a grain is 1/7000th of a pound, and he's sure right in this case) of truth in this argument but thank goodness the ruling was changed. Previously it presented an argument for owning no-load funds since their bid and asked prices are identical.

Another and really more serious consideration is the varied treatment that capital gains distributions receive from the various states. According to where you live, capital gains distributions may be taxed all the way from 0 to the same as income. Finally, it is true that funds can "make" you take capital gains in years when your other income is high and your income tax rate is at a maximum. This is a disadvantage you could reduce by owning shares in funds that greatly limit the capital gains they take.

1.22. HOW THE MONEY OF OTHERS MAY AFFECT YOURS

This month each fund you own will receive some new money from somebody else. If the managers hold it as cash and the market drops before it is invested, *you will make a little profit on somebody else's money when the market goes back up.* If the managers invest it as it comes in, it has no direct benefit to you, except, as we will see in Chapter 2, it is helpful for managers to have new money to invest. If the managers hold it as cash and the market goes up before they invest it, *you will make a little less than the case where no new money comes in.* In general, if the flow of new money is large relative to the size of the fund, it can explain why the fund has been and continues to be successful. The effect of money that comes after yours is almost always small.

1.23. HOW MUTUAL FUNDS AFFECT THE MARKET

Mutual funds hold about 6 percent of all available stocks, and enough of their holdings are concentrated in the stocks of the New York and the American stock exchanges that their trading currently represents about one-third of the shares transferred each day. Pension funds are even larger. They now own 15 percent of all stocks (about $450 billion out of 3.0 trillion) and in a few years will own 50 percent. What does that mean to you as an investor?

1. The knowledge that their pensions depend on the success of American business will finally soak through to various union leaders who currently only pay lip service to the need for profits. They will eventually want not only profits but a rising value to stocks, knowing that someday the stocks will be sold, and the proceeds paid to an insurance firm for annuities. Unions may actually join management to combat government regulation.

2. The insurance companies seek to have a dependable group of stocks and bonds to buy to provide the income for their annuitants. This inflow of money will prop up the high-grade stocks and good-to-top-grade bonds.

3. The increased income (now only a grand average of $250 a month) of an increasing group of retirees (now 20 million) will help stabilize business, but the main recipients will be food stores as retiree wants in clothing, shelter, travel, and appliances are minimal. Increased

pensions could slow the growth of Social Security and welfare, to everybody's benefit.

All three actions seem to point to a more stabilized and growing market.

1.24. *FINANCIAL SUCCESS FOR SALARIED PEOPLE*

In an earlier book, *Financial Success for Salaried People* (New York: Vantage Press, 1966) I wrote about mutual funds from the standpoint of the salaried person—one who presumably would have to start his or her fortune with very little each month. Earlier I mentioned the advantages of mutual funds as (1) having very great certainty of a high rate of profit; (2) having a negligible chance of failure; (3) furnishing a profit with a tax shelter; and (4) staying fluid, always readily available for collateral. They require only small continued effort on the part of the investor and inflict no liability on the owner such as is the case for property, rentals, businesses, or partnerships.

These are cogent arguments, and when you add the mutual funds may be started with little down and continued with little monthly payments, thus making them the *only* investment most salaried people could consider anyhow, well, you have quite a case. Fortunes have been made in land, ranches, or dozens of other investments, but never at $300 down and $100 a month. Even with such a minimal investment, the rewards are substantial. For instance, let us see what happens should you put $300 down and $100 a month ($1,200 a year) into a no-load fund that grows at an average rate of 10 percent a year. To make things easier (and still more conservative) let us assume that the 10 percent occurs at the end of the year and is applied only to what you had at the beginning. We start by putting down $300 on January 1 and $100 on February 1, March 1, and so on until at the end of the year, January 2, if you will, you would have made 12 more payments, a total of 13 or $1,500 the first year. We assume a profit only on what you had at the start of the year, $300 from which you net $30. Putting this in tabular form we get Table 1.11. Table 1.11 is continued to 40 years in Appendix B. Recognizing that funds do not grow at steady rates, let us look at some peg points and consider what they might mean to an investor.

1.   **The end of the first year.**   At the end of the first year the total should be shares worth $1,500. You may then (or really at any time) write the fund and ask them to send you a certificate for any sum up to the total you own. If you take this

Table 1.11.   Investing Results for a No-Load Fund That Grows 10 Percent a Year

1.	End of first year ($300 down and $100 a month for 12 months), profit only on the $300	$1,530
2.	Growth for second year	153
	Amount added	1,200
	Value at end of second year	$2,880
3.	Growth for third year	288
	Amount added	1,200
	Value at end of third year	$4,370

certificate to your bank or credit union you can borrow from 50 to 70 percent ($750 to $1,000).

The loan cost will be at the minimum rate on the unpaid balance, about one-half of what you would have to pay for store-financed time payments, or a charge card. This will add up to many tens of dollars each year. It could mean the end of high interest payments for appliances or other modest purchases.

2.   **The end of the third year.**   At the end of the third year the account should be worth about $4,300. The amount you can now borrow at a minimum cost could mean an outstanding vacation, or a down payment on a larger item.

3.   **The end of the fifth year.**   At the end of the fifth year the accounts should be worth about $7,800. Loans on this

amount could greatly reduce payments for remodeling your home or buying a new car.

What if we had bought a load fund instead at $100 a month and 10 percent per year growth? Well, there is a loss of the load, say 8 percent, and a loss of the growth earned on the 8 percent. All this adds up to about $600 in 5 years—six payments, if you will. Obviously a no-commission fund beats a commission fund if they both grow at the same rate. Well, how much faster must a commission fund grow to equal a no-commission fund? This is a fair and honest question, and the answer depends on the time you will allow for catching up. Let's pick 10 years. If you can find an 8 percent commission fund that grows 4 percent faster than a no-load fund (say 14 percent instead of 10 percent) it will equal the no-load in 10 years and beat it from then on out. The extra 4 percent is not easy to come by.

At the back of this book is Appendix B, which shows the amount accumulated for a wide selection of profit rates and number of years, starting with a $300 down payment and $100 a month. Look at it. The results are impressive. (It is assumed that you have extra money to pay the taxes as they come along, or are in a tax-deferred IRA account.)

4. Retirement with mutual funds. At retirement, the withdrawal plan can be used to obtain far more income than you can find in other investments not needing personal management. (See Chapters 6 and 7.)

1.25.   THINGS YOU CAN DO WITH YOUR MUTUAL FUND SHARES

Mutual funds are an extraordinary investment having many properties not found in any other type of equity or real property purchase, and there are a number of things you can do with the fund shares you own. Some of these are well known, others less well known. They include the following: You can (1) do nothing with them, (2) use them for gifts, (3) borrow on them, (4) sell them, and (5) make special provisions in your estate with them. Indeed, you can even sell them to your children in a manner that avoids both gift and estate taxes. You should know about these things, but please be well aware that laws differ from state to state and should any of the suggestions offered below seem to suit your circumstances you should check with your lawyer to align your actions with local conditions.

1. Do nothing with your shares. If you are frankly too busy to work on your investments, growth mutual funds are ideal because while owning your shares, you are paying managers to manage your money. You should at least watch the progress of your funds, however, and most investors should consider selling one a year (out of four or so) to try to stay in the most successful. The investor in load funds could let his broker make these decisions.

Mutual funds offer an excellent estate vehicle because when you die your money is still being professionally managed through the estate transition period, and possibly ad infinitum. No emergency decisions need be made to sell certain stocks. The money is already invested as you would want your executor to invest it. If you have been using the withdrawal plan, the monthly payments may be simply transferred to your spouse and/or children, and if you have them set at a yearly rate of 6 to 8 percent, experience says that growth-type mutual funds will pay out that much and continue to grow. Still further, there are no pressing reinvesting problems to get an income coming in.

2. Using shares for gifts. Gifts are made because you feel you should and/or because you may prefer to start the dissolution of your estate before you die. Mutual funds are particularly useful for giving, and indeed, in the several billions of dollars given each year, they are well represented.

Uncle Sam recognizes two types of gifts: those to "charitable" institutions such as schools, hospitals, colleges, museums, and the like (these are not taxed at all), and gifts to people. (Also see Section 8.2.) Should it be reasonable to make a gift of mutual fund shares, you need only write to inform your fund that you have given the shares to whomever you name, and for a few dollars transfer fee the shares are put in the new name. The transaction is reported to the tax people the same as other transactions and may or may not incur taxes, as described earlier. You would think that recipients of a gift would be happy to pay the taxes on the gift, but they're not liable—you are. In fact, if they pay them, the IRS considers the amount of taxes as income for you and you are liable for taxes.

All gifts of mutual funds will reduce your taxes in the sense that you will have less dividend interest and capital gains to be taxed, but some special applications may be very advantageous to you. For instance, if you give Uncle Louis $1,200 a year to help with his living expenses, you'll come out ahead if you give a trustee shares (say, worth $15,000) to furnish that income for life, with the remainder returning to you when Uncle Louis dies. Chances are that Uncle Louis' income will be taxed at a much lower rate than yours. However, it won't work to set up a trust so that your son or daughter has an income to eat on, as you can't "trust your way around" expenses you are socially obliged to handle.

One more point is of interest, not confined to mutual funds, but applicable to them. If you give to your church or other charitable organizations, you may either give more, or the same amount for less cost to you by using your earlier fund purchases. For instance, suppose you give $10 a month, $120 a year. Go through the fund shares you own and find some that have doubled in price. Ask the fund to send you a certificate for $120 worth of fund. For a small transfer fee you can transfer this to the church. You do not have to pay the capital gains tax, the church gets the $120 same as always, and you get to claim a $120 deduction for which you paid $60. If you had sold the mutual funds, and given the $120 to the church, you would have had to pay taxes (say $10 to $30) on your $60 profit. In either case you lose the income from the same amount, $120.

How does this relate to the mutual fund theme? Many shareholders who have had funds for a long period of time have some cheap shares that could be used and *should* be used as this sort of gift instead of giving to the church from current income.

Before closing this section on mutual funds for gifts, I should point out that mutual funds, both growth and more conservative types, have applications for widows, and for those needing an income, but planning to give substantial amounts to their church or other charitable organizations upon their death. For the gift case, you may give ownership of a fund away while realizing part of its income during the remainder of your life. You get to take a portion of the gift from current income according to a schedule worked out by the Federal Tax Department using life expectancy tables, and may in many instances realize *more income during your lifetime* than without making the gift. Let me give an example to show the principle, without going excessively into details.

Suppose you are 75 years old and have $10,000 in a savings account that pays you 5 percent. This is $500 a year on which you pay say $100 in taxes and have a net of $400 as income. If you give the $10,000 to your church, the arrangement states that (for age 75) 78 percent of the amount may be excluded from income. On the $7,800 at the 20 percent tax rate used, a net saving of $0.20 \times 7,800 = $1,560$ would ensue. This may be taken over a number of years if you desire.

If the $10,000 is placed in a no-load mutual fund selected for large payout each year by the church, one might get 3.5 percent from dividends. This comes to $350, of which according to tax laws the first $100 is nontaxable. The distribution from capital gains might also be 3.5 percent ($350), but this is considered as belonging to the recipient; that is, you don't get it.

A little pencil pushing will show that you net $290 from the dividend *plus* whatever fraction of the $1,560 you chose to apply against taxable income. This is large compared to the net spendable income of $400 from the savings account. The difference in the example is substantial and rises with income and hence income taxes, but the example is for a somewhat special case.

You may also set up the opposite type of trust in which the income comes to you, and the corpus goes to a charity. Why would you want to do this? Suppose you own a piece of property that has increased greatly in value but yields a small return. If you sell it you have a lot of capital gains to pay. If you transfer this property to a trust with yourself (and your spouse) as lifetime beneficiaries and a charity as remainderman, the trust can sell the property, pay no income tax, and reinvest the money in just about any situation you desire, such as a mutual fund. You receive the income from this investment and upon your death the property would go to the charity.

You avoid the capital gains tax on the sale of the property, you get income for life from the investment of your choosing, you get a tax deduction for the gift to charity in the year the trust is set up, and in some cases your estate taxes will be reduced. Use a good tax-and-trust specialist to set this up, as there have been rulings such that you may not invest in tax-free bonds or accept capital gains distributions from the funds.

Should you be in the happy circumstances such that you wish to convey some shares to your child and have already used up your tax-free gift allowance, you may *sell* them to the child and let the child pay for them using the withdrawal plan. Uncle Sam has ruled that a rate of 7.4 percent a year is acceptable and this is not unreasonable for a withdrawal rate. After payment your child has the shares without a gift tax or the shares being in your estate for probate and estate costs.

You do not have to redeem your shares in order to convey them to another person. You may simply sign them in the designated place on the back and the buyer may mail the certificates to the fund's custodian bank and have a certificate reissued in his or her name. There will be a nominal transfer fee, like $5.

3. **Borrowing on mutual fund shares.**   Mutual fund shares are excellent collateral for loans, and essentially any bank or your credit union will lend you money on them and at a much lower rate than on a signature loan or a much more lower rate than for typical time payments. The percentages you can borrow depend on the bank making the loan, and on whether you intend to use the borrowed money to buy securities. For the latter case, the Federal Reserve Board issues rules from time

to time about the amount that may be loaned on securities in order to buy more securities. Regardless of that, you may probably borrow up to 70 percent if you intend to use the money to pay debts, or add to your house, or buy a car.

Any time you borrow on securities you run the risk of having your shares sold to cover your loan should the market go down sufficiently. Thus, if you borrow $700 on $1,000 worth of shares and the value of those shares goes down, as it approaches $700 the lender will get uncomfortable about a further drop that might cause him to lose money if you fail to pay off the loan. He will then call on you to reduce the amount of the loan, or conceivably he could sell your shares before they drop below what he loaned on them. The way around this is not to borrow excessively on your shares, and to be available should a call for more margin be made.

There is a second minor irritation about using your shares for collateral. You might want to sell them in order to invest in another fund, but they are locked away in a bank. Your broker or bank can easily set up a *due bill* for you. In essence, the due bill says that when the new shares are issued they must be deposited immediately to cover the loan.

I would not recommend borrowing all you can except in the case where you set up a payment schedule such that in a few months the loan will be down to a more reasonable margin. Borrowing to some people is an admission that they can't handle their finances; for others, particularly in business, it is a way of life. Whatever the reason or the philosophy, mutual fund shares are excellent collateral, surpassing common stocks in that (a) they do not fluctuate as widely and are hence not apt to drop suddenly down to the loan value, and (b) you are not as apt to require the certificates to switch to another investment—which you may do anyhow.

4. **Selling mutual fund shares.**   Selling fund shares in order to purchase shares in another fund is covered in Chapter 3, as is the mechanism of selling and the taxes incurred thereby. If fund shares must be sold in order to raise cash, the procedure for selling is covered in Section 3.8.

5. Fund shares and estates. The use of mutual fund shares in your estate and how trusts may be set up are covered in chapter 8.

1.26.   INVESTMENT CLUBS

Another type of diversified investment program is the investment club. Here a group of amateurs pool their resources of money and stock market know-how and invest as a group. Why anybody would think that a group of amateurs paying relatively high commissions on their purchases and sales, lacking capital for reasonable diversification, lacking a good cash flow, and lacking extensive stock market experience can possibly beat the professional managers of mutual funds is beyond me, but that doesn't stop the fun and learning people get from investment clubs. It just stops me from being one of them.

The foregoing words aren't going to make me any friends among the tens of thousands of people who belong to some 30,000 investment clubs, so let me quit by wishing them good luck.

2

The Importance of Cash Flow

The mutual fund industry had its beginnings in England around 1860. It took a long time to cross the Atlantic; not till around 1920 did the first U.S. funds start, in Boston. These included the Massachusetts Investment Trust and the State Street Investment Corporation. For about 35 years additional mutual funds joined in, all operating in what may be termed a conservative manner. There were speculative funds, it is true, but only in the sense that they invested in smaller, unseasoned companies trying to see if on balance enough of the small companies prospered so that the average result was good.

Around 1960 and indeed every good year since then, a few funds showed enormous profits: 70, 80, and even 100 percent in a year. The managers of these funds were hailed as people who really understood the market and whose funds would make you a lot of money. And a lot of people put money in these funds. But for some (then) unknown reason, every single one of the red-hot managers lost his or her touch as the years rolled by, and the funds sank into obscurity. They had their three or four good years—usually less—in which they ranked in the top 10 percent of all growth funds, and then they sank, sometimes like rocks.

Now think about this for a minute. In every nonphysical

endeavor people emerge and *stay* at the top: surgeons, lawyers, merchants, artists, executives . . . but not fund managers. It's unreal. How can there be a nonphysical occupation at which people get worse over the years? You just have to conclude one of four things: The managers got stupider as time went on; their funds got too big to manage; what they were doing really didn't matter and their luck ran out; or something happened that stopped them from doing what they had been doing.

I reject as absurd that increased experience made them stupider. And a careful analysis shows that bigness has nothing to do with it. Funds drop out of the top 10 percent at all sizes. But size is nonsense anyhow. One could always cut a "too large" fund into five pieces and hire five managers, if being small meant anything.

It turned out that a combination of the third and fourth points was the culprit. The top managers originally had some luck, but something stopped them from what they had been doing. *They had been receiving steady large streams of new money, sometimes equal to the size of the entire fund, every year, and this had given them an enormous advantage*, which I'll discuss shortly. When it stopped, they stopped. How and why this occurred is the meat of this chapter. I am also happy to say that it was your author who first discovered and measured the importance of cash flow, although many others had sensed it earlier. A discussion of this discovery may be found in *Fortune* magazine (June 1, 1968, page 138). I am happy to say that the advantages of having a large cash flow are now accepted throughout the fund industry.

What is cash flow? It is the new money a fund manager receives to invest; the new money that comes into the fund and for which new shares are issued. If the total size of a fund (they call this the total assets) went up 100 percent in a year, and the stocks held went up 20 percent, then the remainder (80 percent) had to be the result of new money coming in. That's the cash flow. (There's other money coming in from dividends, the sale of some stocks, and the profits made on the new money invested during the year, and there is also the loss due to redemptions, but we can accomplish all we need using the simple definition.) If you wish to obtain the cash flow for a given fund, find out the total assets at the beginning and end of the period you are interested in, and compute the percent growth. (It doesn't have to be positive, of course.) Then subtract the profit for the same period as obtained from a fund advisory service or data book, and there you are. Here's an example:

Example 2.1. A fund had total assets of $1 million at the start of a year and $1.4 at the end. It made a profit of 22 percent that year. What was the approximate percentage cash flow?

1. The total asset growth was

$$\frac{\$1,400,000 - \$1,000,000}{\$1,000,000} \times 100 \text{ or } 40 \text{ percent.}$$

2. The cash flow was then $42 - 22 = 18$ percent.

The discovery of the effect of cash flow was almost accidental. Routine plots of performance against fund size for various 5-year periods showed no correlation at all. But when growth of total assets was used instead of fund size, the correlation was remarkable. Since most of the growth of total assets for the top performing funds comes from cash flow, this is the presentation currently used. Figure 2.1 is a typical plot. It

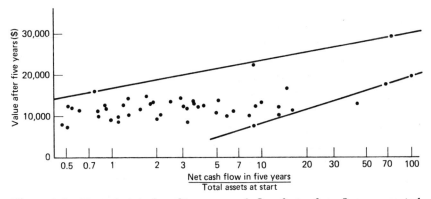

Figure 2.1. Typical plot of profit versus cash flow factor for a five-year period. Each dot represents a different fund.

shows the value of a $10,000 investment after five years plotted against the ratio of the total cash flow in five years to the starting assets. Note that some funds doubled or tripled their value in 5 years, and that the winners had cash flow rates as large as 100 to 1. The top fund, it so happens, grew from $1 million to $100 million. Note that the correlation isn't with cash flow per se; it's with cash flow ratio (or percent). Some of the enormous $2 billion funds may get $100 million in new money each year, but it is such a small percentage of the total fund (5 percent), that it isn't a big help.

One more thing about the correlation between percent profit and percent cash flow and Figure 2.1: About 96 percent of all the growth funds plot in an orderly fashion. The three or four (out of a hundred) that don't are of course important. They typically consist of a couple of funds that just had such a lucky year that nobody could account for it. They plotted well *above* the correlation group. There were one or two that plotted *well below* the rest. I dug into those and found they correlated, also, even though they weren't in the proper channel. How could that be? Well, to compute cash flow the first step is to compute the percent growth of total assets, and *assume it was due to profits and new money.* It doesn't have to be. *A fund can grow by merging with another fund.* In this case there is a great growth of total assets, but there *isn't any new money!* Sure enough, *every* fund that plotted below what its cash flow rate indicated its profit should be was involved in a merger. I remember one called the Gryphon Fund that amalgamated in 1971. I even bought it because my figures showed a big cash flow. When its performance didn't come up to expectations, I wrote to the fund and said "Hey, did you merge with another fund?" Sure enough, it had. So all this was a further corroboration that cash flow helps. Let's proceed with the cash flow discussion. I hope you find it interesting. *It is the only correlation ever found between a fund manager's temporary great performance and the reason for it being temporary.*

2.1. *FUNNEL CHARTS*

Funnel charts illustrate the amazing decline of a manager's ability as time goes on. Here's how you make one. Assemble a lot of old fund data and pick a year. Assume that you bought every growth fund that then existed, and compute the average compound growth rate for each for the next 2, 5, 10, 15, and 20 years. You will find, and it doesn't matter which year you pick to start, that a few funds had a very lucky 2 years and averaged a very high return. Some fund had to be the worst one, and possibly it averaged only a few percent per year, or even lost money. Turn to Figure 2.2. You will note that Fund A averaged 71 percent for 2 years, and Fund B averaged 3.5 percent. No matter which of all the growth funds you bought, the best you could do was 71 percent, and the worst 3.5. That's a spread of 67.5 percent, and a hasty (and wrong) conclusion would be that there sure is a lot of difference between managers.

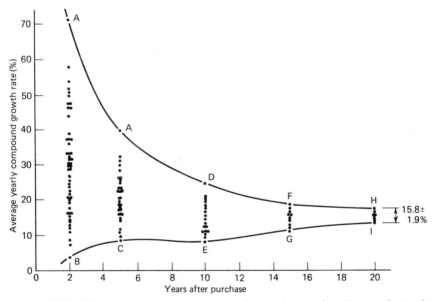

Figure 2.2.   The average yearly compound growth rate for all growth-stock mutual funds for 2, 5, 10, 15, and 20 years after purchase; one particular period.

Now let's consider the spread among all the growth funds for 5 years. We see that the best, which happens to be Fund A once again, averaged 39.6 percent, and that Fund B crawled up from the bottom and Fund C took its place with an average compound growth rate of 8.6 percent. (Changing relative positions is entirely normal, but only once in many funnel charts have I seen a bottom fund go to the top in 20 years.) The 5-year spread is only 31 percent. Continuing for 10, 15, and 20 years, the spread narrows until at the end of 20 years the total spread of the performance between the smartest and the dumbest managers is only 3.7 percent! That's 1.9 percent from the median of 15.8 percent.

No investor holding one or the entire number of growth funds that existed during the 20 years under consideration could have averaged more or less than 15.8 ± 1.9 percent!

I'll spare you listing a great string of 20-year periods, giving the average and the spread for each and just say that in all I have checked (hundreds) the best was the 15.8 ± 1.9 used as an example, and the worst was 10.6 ± 2.2 percent. The average of many periods was 12.8 ± 2.3 percent, and I generally use a simple 12 percent growth rate when I speak of average long-term growth fund performance.

Here's a point to consider: *I do not think an investor has grown up until he or she realizes that the best of the full-time managers averages 15 percent per year over the very long term, and any individual's chance of doing better is extremely small.* This applies to holding the same funds forever, and there is nothing wrong with a 15 percent average over the years. Much more money can be made, as we shall see later, by moving out when the market heads down.

The funnel chart in Figure 2.2 is typical and yet it isn't, if that makes sense. There may be big changes in the first 2 years if the chart is started during a down market. The worst I recall had about a 60-point spread, but it went from +10 percent to −50. Others only have a 45-point 2-year spread. But the end point is very typical, with a spread of only a few percent between the best and the worst when the 20 year period is considered. The different vertical positions of the best and worst funds are surely due to the market, but you can't blame the narrowing down on anything but the people who make the decisions. Size is a secondary factor. In all the funnel charts I have ever made (each takes 3 days of hard work and I wince at the thought) the top 10 funds for the first 2 years:

1. Averaged less than $10 million each in total assets.
2. Did not exceed $30 million in total assets at the start of the period.

The 10 worst funds, just to get the other side of the picture,

1. Averaged $100 million in total assets at the start of the period.
2. Included several small operations.

In short, being small doesn't make a fund successful; it just gives it a chance. Being large almost certainly eliminates any chance of meteoric performance. All this lines up well with the hypothesis being developed that a large percentage cash flow is helpful, and of course it is usually easier to get a large percentage if the fund is small so that the amount in dollars is small.

The fall of a top performer—let's say from 70 percent for 2 years to an average of 30 percent per year for 5 years—has a lot more to it than meets the eye. To have a 30 percent average for 5 years after 70 percent for 2 takes an average of only 8.7 percent for the last 3 years. This is a pretty low figure, and corroborates the proposition that when the top funds fall, they really hit the bottom. Thus, an aggressive investor buying from a list of the best funds for the past 2 years has missed the boat, although admittedly the top performer may go on for several more years. The important thing is not to be there when it finally drops.

Moving all the way to the 20-year periods, since luck and cash flow are pretty well out of the picture by then, we have to conclude that some managers *are* smarter than others and the 20-year periods show it up. They're not much smarter; the best have averaged only a few percent better than the median

(15.1 percent per year profit compared to 12.8 percent per year), but the difference is still a lot of money. An investment of $10,000 for 20 years at 12.8 percent compound interest is $111,000. At 15.1 percent it totals $165,000.

Following particular funds across a funnel chart shows that none hold the same rank over the years. Sometimes the worst for a 2-year period becomes the best for 10, and then it may be the worst for 15. The wandering around in position seems to strengthen the argument that good performance has a luck facet to it. There does seem to be a faint correlation in that the best funds for 10 years more often than not end up doing well for 20 years, but this does not help you decide which fund to buy, since you can't buy into a fund "after 10 years." You can only buy it *now*, and this is along the vertical axis of the funnel chart with the future unknown. If the fund you buy today is small, it has a *chance* of top performance (say 50 percent profit per year) for the next 2 years, and also a *chance* of averaging out the best for the next 5, 10, 15, or 20 years (say 15 percent per year). If it is medium or large now it almost certainly will not be a super winner for the next 2 years, *but it still has a chance of averaging the best for the next 10 or 20 years.* Read those last two sentences again; they have a lot of power if you are set on buying and holding a fund.

Wow. That was quite a dose on funnel charts, and how nobody stays smart in the market. I think by now you probably agree that cash flow helps, but let's see why.

2.2. HOW CASH FLOW HELPS MANAGERS

Here are 10 ways cash flow can help:

1. **It permits buying on dips.** Essentially all investors know that there is a mathematical reason why steady buying with a constant number of dollars each month will result in a tiny advantage. As discussed in Section 3.4, when the cash flow is constant it becomes such a

small percentage of the total that its effect becomes negligible. A constant *percentage* of new money of the size we are talking about (50 to 100 percent a year) will make "dollar cost averaging" work.

2. **It attracts the best investment ideas.**   Analysts are always coming up with investments they feel are superior. They seek out funds that *have money to invest* in order to solicit their business. In turn this provides the fund with a steady flow of new ideas to review and act upon.

3. **It erases mistakes.**   Consider a fund whose total value is $100,000, of which $10,000 (10 percent) is in a stock that turns out to be a lemon. To nongrowing funds (or most individuals), there will be a 10 percent loss. However, should the $100,000 fund grow to $10 million (a factor of 100) in the following 5 years, the $10,000 loss shrinks to 0.1 percent of the total, a quite inconsequential amount. How many investors would like to erase their mistakes!

4. **It eliminates forced sales of stock.**   There are always a few stockholders who get disgusted with funds or need their money for other reasons. These furnish a steady and usually small requirement for cash that rises to a sizable amount during market drops. If a fund has a flow of new money that meets redemptions, no forced sales at market bottoms ensue, and there results a consequent advantage for the fund. Market dips are times to buy, not sell.

5. **It keeps management alert.**   Managers of a static fund may and probably do study the market and make switches from time to time. But there is no "may" to the actions of fund managers who have a flood of new money coming in; they *have* to work to invest it.

6. **It enables the managers to take advantage of new situations.**   To a degree, this item overlaps items 1, 2, and 5, but it is worth mentioning anyhow. It is just that new money enables managers to buy without sell-

ing older holdings that need more time to come to fruition.

7. **It reduces the percentage drop during a market dip.** A flow of new money also helps during a drop as the stocks held become a proportionately smaller fraction of the total fund. For example, suppose a fund is worth $1 million and the market drops such that its portfolio goes down 20 percent. The share value shows a concomitant drop of 20 percent. Now suppose a second fund worth the same amount sells $1 million of shares during the same period and the manager astutely withholds the money from the market. At the end of the period this fund is worth $1.8 million and has only experienced a 10 percent drop, half that of the non-growing fund.

8. **It permits "bootstrapping."** If you or I buy 100 shares of United Overshoes each month there will be little effect on its price, but $1 million a month may indeed cause a price rise. This implies that a fund, or perhaps a number of funds, may benefit by the size and continuance of its purchases. Bootstrapping is largely responsible both for the success of a fund with a big percentage cash flow and for the correlation with percentage cash flow rather than with the dollar value of the cash flow. Turn to Table 5.1 if you want to see the extent of bootstrapping that occurred in one fund.

9. **It helps fund managers time the market.** In general fund managers do not practice market timing.* The *Harvard Business Review* once said, "We find no evidence to support the belief that mutual fund managers outguess the market." I have to agree, but I do note that the managers increase their cash accounts as a market drops. I suspect those managers with a large cash flow are greatly helped in this "hold back" maneuver. It is far easier to hold back new money than it is to sell to create cash. Indeed one manager with a

---

*Some do. See Chapter 4.

big cash flow said, "All I have to do is to do nothing, let the cash come in, and in a few months I'm one-third in cash."

10.   **It provides a manager with a psychological lift that instills self-confidence.** This is like item 5, but different enough to be put separately.

The interesting thing about cash flow is that a lot of very successful managers never realized what made them great. One, whom I'd rather not name, was an absolute whizbang during the bull market sixties. He was so full of how great he was that he quit his successful fund and decided to start a new one. Thinking that having enough money to "work the market" was essential, he let it be known that he wouldn't start the new fund unless he got $25 million. Well, his reputation was such that he got $250 million! That's the worst thing that can happen from a cash flow standpoint. And what happened? He bombed out. And he never understood why.

2.3.   *WHAT DO FUND MANAGERS SAY ABOUT CASH FLOW?*

One of the first things I did after discovering its effect was to write several managers to find out if they agreed. Some did, but others from their actions obviously did not. While they were riding at the top they thought they were all geniuses, and even today they keep waiting for "their kind of market." At any rate, here is what I got in personal letters:

"It very definitely is an advantage to the shareholder for new money to be flowing into the fund."

"A fund that receives a continuing flow of new money is helped to some degree in its performance."

"Does new money help? Yes, it does."

"It would be hard for me to say one could get performance without the inflow of new money."

Some of the funds have even published statements about cash flow. The New Horizons Fund said, in its quarterly report, "Several times in past stockholder letters the management of the fund has commented that, in its opinion, the rate of the inflow of new money to the fund is a more relevant problem than the size of the fund." And the Shamrock Fund went all out about cash flow in its letter to shareholders: "We recognize that a steady flow of new money into the fund gives the manager an advantage because it enables him to use his own judgment in timing portfolio purchases and sales rather than being forced to buy when large sums of money come in from heavy shareholder purchases or to sell when heavy redemptions occur."

Hasn't anybody come out with a statement *against* cash flow? Not that I've seen; it doesn't make sense. One manager did say, "I don't think it's cash flow, it's the stocks you hold." Probably he is both right and wrong. At any time a manager may luck into a good portfolio, and have an outstanding short term. For that, the stocks you hold are very important. But we have seen that the luck *never* continues over the long term. On the other hand, a large cash flow can be used to drive up the stocks that a fund holds.

Even those fund managers who don't think that cash flow is so all-fired good always agree that redemptions hurt. Since redemptions are negative cash flow, the implications are obvious. By the way, for further proof that negative cash flow hurts, consider that during the 1973 decline funds lost far more money in redemptions than they received from new buyers. And they performed *worse* than the stock averages.

The disadvantages of a high percentage cash flow are:

1. A high percentage cash flow cannot be continued forever, or a fund would own the market, so high cash flow funds have a limited time at the top.
2. When a large cash flow stops, it leaves the fund in a very poor position.

Note the world *flow* in *cash flow*. Inherent in advantages listed is the idea of a steady flow of cash rather than a single lump of the same total amount. The *flow* is better for several reasons:

1. It forces a manager to spread investments out, which is fundamentally a good procedure.
2. It results in more thought being applied than for a single large purchase.
3. All opportunities do not arrive simultaneously. Cash *flow* enables a manager to buy as they arise, or await a lagging growth.

Is the need for a high percentage cash flow an argument against no-load funds, since a load fund through a vast sales organization can surely bring in more money than no sales organization? I suppose it is, but it doesn't seem to hurt. Successful no-loads do generate a large cash flow. Apparently no-load buyers get a lot of help from advisory services in telling them which funds did best.

2.4. MEASURING THE EFFECT OF CASH FLOW

If cash flow is helpful, we ought to be able to measure its help and find out whether the effect is small, moderate, or substantial. This I have done by measuring the slope of many plots of profit against cash flow, subtracting the average profit of all funds, and assuming the difference is due to cash flow. Of course performance varies with the market, and I will simply summarize the findings:

1. Less than 10 percent cash flow doesn't help much.
2. A cash flow of 100 percent increases the fund profit by 10 to 14 percent over the market average.

There is a lot of meat in the second point. It was established earlier that fund managers average close to the market averages, which is a sneaky way of saying that they don't contribute a lot, maybe a couple of percent over the averages. Cash flow, when it is very large, is worth much more than a few percent. So, to put it bluntly, brokers who sell a lot of a commission funds, and advertisers who bring in a lot of money for no-load funds, contribute more than the managers who get both the kudos and the big money.

2.5. WHEN A BIG CASH FLOW STOPS, A MANAGER'S PERFORMANCE STOPS TOO

For this section I want you to put yourself in the place of a fund manager who has a large percentage cash flow coming in. Money is coming in very fast. It has to be invested. Anybody who has ever managed a portfolio knows that one puts new money on one's winners. Fund managers are no different than anybody else, but the amount of money they have may be quite different. When you or I buy our small amounts of stock, the purchase makes little or no difference to the stock's price. But our fund manager is dealing in millions of dollars a month—even tens of millions. This kind of money cannot help but push the winners still higher. Ultimately the fund's portfolio includes a high percentage of inflated stocks.

When the cash flow finally stops, or slows to where redemption requirements mean that some stocks must be sold, it becomes hard to find buyers of the inflated stocks at current prices. Down the stock prices tumble and the fund's share prices with them.

I have to go back a long way in time to demonstrate the worst real case of the "to whom"* syndrome, but here it is: Consider an investor in growth-stock funds who, at the end of 1967, bought the four funds that were to lead the list in 1968. Gibraltar Growth, Mates, Neuwirth, and Pennsylvania. At the end of 1968 that investor would have been happily sitting behind gains of 72.7, 72.6, 71.4, and 68.0 percent in one year. In

---

*The "to whom" phrase comes from one of the oldest stock market jokes I can recall: A broker found himself with an oversupply of OTC shares of a small company—"United Potatoes." He called a client and suggested a buy at $5 a share. The client bought, and as the weeks went by the broker sold him more at ever increasing prices.When he announced the last price at $20 a share the client said, "Sell!" After a long pause the broker answered, "To whom?"

1969, however, things turned sour for these four funds (run by the "smartest" managers in the country—in 1968) and they moved down in the list of growth-stock funds. This trend continued until by the end of 1970 they had essentially (see Table 2.1) *completed the move from best to worst.*

Losses are to be expected in poor years, particularly for volatile "performance" funds, but for two of the top four to become two of the bottom four is somewhat heady. And how did it come about? Let me quote the newsletter of one no-load fund: "The most highly publicized example of a no-load fund's performance being affected by heavy redemptions is the case of one which grew to about $100 million while it was the popular favorite of 1968–9 and then collapsed to $30 million during 1970 as the advisory services reversed their buy recommendations to sell. That particular fund was the *top* performer in 1968 but was ranked fifth from the *bottom* out of 466 funds for 1970!" (The difference between the quote and Table 2.1 results from giving the position relative to *all* funds, while the table is only concerned with growth-stock funds. "Heavy redemptions" is of course another phrase for "negative cash flow.")

2.6.   WHY TOP-PERFORMING FUNDS HAVE A LIMITED TIME AT THE TOP

I think that we have established that the really top performing growth-stock funds get a lot of help from a large percentage cash flow, on the order of 50 to 100 percent of the total assets per year. This is impossible to maintain or the fund would own the whole market. How limited is "limited"?

There is no firm answer, but we may hypothesize a start and a growth rate and come up with some sort of an estimate. First of all, a fund must have $100,000 in total assets to make a legal start. If we pick 100 percent per year as a large enough cash flow, a little arithmetic will show that in 13 years our fund will reach $1 billion, which we may assume is close to an end point for maintaining 100 percent per year cash flow. Thus

Table 2.1. Performance history of Four Growth-Stock Funds

Fund	Rank in 1968 (128 Funds)	Rank in 1969 (165 Funds)	Rank in 1970 (192 Funds)	Loss during 1969–1970 Dip (%)
Gibraltar Growth	1	60	190	−70
Mates	2	94	123	−77
Neuwirth	3	121	172	−52
Pennsylvania	4	131	192	−75

we can make the rough approximation that 13 years is a life-time for a top performing fund. Of course, it might not get money at 100 percent per year. Indeed, the chances are that things will go the other way and, if it is a top performer, it will get more than 100 percent per year and hence have a shorter life. In recent years only one fund has stayed in the top 10 percent of all funds for as much as 14 years, and for many a lifetime of 8 years has occurred. Others have had still shorter lifetimes.

This raises the question as to whether an aggressive inves-tor would be well advised to buy a fund with a lower rate of cash flow in order to hold it longer. The answer is *no*. Almost no situation can be found where it is not better to have the highest cash flow and the highest profit and sell most often in spite of taxes.

2.7. CLOSED-END FUNDS AND CASH FLOW

Closed-end funds, as mentioned earlier, consist of a fixed number of shares. No new shares are issued, and hence the managers have zero cash flow. This offers us a chance to see if these funds can tell us anything relative to open-end funds, which may have negative, zero, or positive cash flow. They certainly do have a message for us, but I must admit my statis-tically competent friends tell me the number of closed-end funds (25) compared to the number of open-end funds (790) makes such comparisons statistically unsound. I'll defer to these good people by telling you what I have done, without presenting a lot of averages and such. In a nutshell, if cash flow helps, we should find closed-end funds performing somewhere between those open-end funds that have negative cash flow and those open-end funds that have positive cash flow. I have done this for several 10-year periods. I used a convenient source of data and found that the 10 open-end funds with the highest percentage cash flow outperformed the 10 best closed-end funds. Similarly, the 10 open-end funds with the highest percentage of *negative* cash flow did *worse* than the 10 *worst* closed-end funds. This was true for several different 10-year periods, and it meant something to me—namely, it was a confirmation of the cash flow theory—even if the group sizes on which I drew were vastly different. I invite you to do this with the lastest fund data. It is not a hard exercise and would get you familiar with fund data sources.

2.8. MANAGER INCENTIVE PLANS

Manager incentive plans are special arrangements made by some funds that tie a manager's pay to one of the stock averages, so that if the manager beats the average, he or she receives substantial extra pay. Several studies show that bonuses *do not produce extra performance*. I take this as a sort of confirmation of many things I have said in this chapter about the surprisingly small contributions managers make to their funds. For a further case in point, the Competitive Capital Fund had a setup such that the worst of their five managers, each of who managed one-fifth of their fund, would be fired each year. Now there's another form of incentive: do great or you are out. It didn't work any better than the "more money" type of incentive, and I understand that the setup has been abandoned. Some say it pressured managers into taking great risks and suffering great losses. I say they couldn't do well over a long period without a large cash flow. Take your choice.

All of this is darn interesting. If you can't encourage managers with money, or by firing them if they don't do outstandingly well, it must be that being outstanding is not up to them.

2.9. SUMMARY OF CASH FLOW EFFECTS

I have given 10 reasons cash flow helps fund managers, and shown that there is a correlation between the percent profit and the percent cash flow that some funds enjoy. I have also shown that some very top managers became very bottom managers when their cash flow stopped, and that because cash flow can't continue forever in the large amounts needed, top-performing funds have a limited time at the top. Fund managers agree that cash flow is helpful.

I acknowledge that the contents of this chapter go against a fundamental tenet of the American character, namely that "If I had the time and enough money, I could make a killing in the stock market."

Not so. I could introduce you to 790 people (the mutual fund managers) who have the time and the money and the training who *can't* make a killing in the stock market—or at least for long. Some do better than others, it is true, but the spread between the best and the worst, as we have seen, is small—less than in any other endeavor. Managers *can* manage for particular objectives (growth, income, etc.) but in any one group they are quite close. It took me a long time to admit all this. I tried to prove that the loss in performance was fund size. It didn't check out. I even tried managers' ages, and that didn't work.

There is nothing wrong with trying for the best fund in a group. But don't believe that a 40 or 50 percent a year manager can keep it up. It's impossible.

Why hasn't the importance of cash flow been noticed before? Very probably it has. Indeed the SEC all but fell over it in its publication, *Public Policy Implications of Investment Company Growth*. On page 259, speaking of the smallest funds (under $1 million at the beginning of selected 5- and 10-year periods), it said that for both periods the funds that performed above average tended to grow out of the under-$1 million group. And on page 260, speaking of the largest funds, it said that, of the large funds, those that were smaller at the beginning of the periods had better performance records than the other large funds. In short, funds that got proportionately the most new money did the best.

Once again, cash flow theory does not say that all managers are the same; it just says that they are not as different as one would expect. It also says that cash flow is *not* what counts, it's the percentage cash flow. No matter how large the fund, it does fine as long as there is a large percentage cash flow.

In closing, although I have quoted studies that show no difference in performance between load and no-load funds, there is evidence that the cash flow situation is changing this. In 1981 99 percent of the new money going into stock and bond funds of all types went into no-load funds,* whereas the load funds were experiencing net redemptions. And guess what—6.6 percent of the growth and aggressive growth no-loads showed up in the top 25 funds, while only 5 percent of the load funds got the same ranking.

And now, I'm going to surprise you. Despite the arguments that a large cash flow is very important to the success of a fund, we won't use cash flow techniques in our fund selection other than as a secondary factor. Cash flow provides under-standing. *When* you buy a fund is a whole lot more important than which fund you buy. Timing outranks cash flow, and that's in Chapter 4.

*Handbook For No-Load Fund Investors, 1982 Edition, Editorial Staff, The No-Load Fund Investor, PO Box 283, Hastings-on-Hudson, NY 10706.

3

Buying and Owning No-Load Mutual Funds

Let's consider what should come first—a chicken-or-egg question—discussing how to buy a mutual fund or discussing how to select one to buy. A little thought should convince you that deciding to buy, say, a car does come before selecting which one to buy, and that is the route we will take. Chapter 4 will help in the selecting.

Let's not make something hard out of buying a fund. When you buy a car you can pay cash for it, buy it on time, buy it in your name or jointly with your spouse (or for your kids), keep it at home or in your garage, pick your dealer from advertisements or from a friend's recommendation. Same thing with buying funds. You can pay cash for them, buy them over a period of time, buy them jointly with your spouse or for your kids; you can let the custodian bank hold the shares or accept them and keep them in a safe-deposit box. This chapter discusses all these choices.

3.1. FUND SERVICES

Mutual funds are popularly known as investment devices *to make money*. They have many features that make them useful investment vehicles, even if they didn't do better than individual investors. These features include a saving of time and worry, special retirement plans that you could not hope to beat by individual investing (both from accumulating the money and from receiving payments upon retirement), substantial tax advantages, a chance to make money from other people's money, great advantage for those salaried people who have to buy their fortune on a time-payment plan, and advantages from estate and gift angles. Most of the various services are listed here. Since lists aren't much fun to read, I have italicized key words so you can just scan the list and stop where something catches your eye. Not all the funds do all the things delineated:

1. *Invest your money* in the manner described in the fund's prospectus.

2. Send you a *statement* after every transaction—not just one a month like a bank.

3. Issue *certificates* upon which you can borrow at a bank or a credit union.

4. After your account is established, permit you *to buy by telephone.*

5. *Accept continued additional monies* as per the prospectus.

6. Permit you to *redeem* any or all of your shares anytime—unlike with a bank certificate of deposit.

7. Accept a *telephone order* to send a redemption check to your bank. (Some funds guarantee 48-hour service.)

8. *Reinvest dividends,* interest received, and capital gains, no matter how small—unlike stocks and real estate.

9. Accept a *switch order by telephone.*

10. Provide a monthly or quarterly *withdrawal check.*

11. Provide a number of different *registration options.*

12. Provide a variety of *retirement programs.*

13. *Lend money on your shares,* directly.

14. Provide *free check service* (with money market funds).
15. *Send all profits* to you at regular intervals.
16. Arrange *automatic monthly investments* directly from your bank.
17. Permit *changing of specific services* anytime.
18. Send complete *tax forms* describing sources of distributions.
19. Provide *shareholders' meetings* annually.
20. Permit *transfer of share ownership.*
21. Handle *custodian accounts* for your children.
22. Handle certain types of *trusts.*
23. Provide simple forms for *IRA accounts.*

That's quite a list of services. We'll be examining many of them throughout the book. But first, let's talk about using a broker to buy commission mutual funds.

3.2. SELECTING A BROKER

This is a book on investing in no-load funds, and it may seem strange to talk about having a broker. Although I'm not a believer in needing a broker for buying mutual funds, and I hope you won't be either after reading this book, I *am* a believer in getting help from a broker for trust forms, stock powers, and other services that in most instances you could get from your fund. I keep in my broker's good graces by occasionally buying some bonds, and once in a while I splurge and buy a stock, for which I am usually sorry. The forms I mentioned cost brokers nothing, and they are usually happy to furnish them in hope of some future business.

Here's a list of what a good broker can do for you, and if you are a beginner there is nothing bad about making your first buys through a broker. This book, plus a good advisory service and a good market timing service, will enable you to handle all nine items listed. As you gain confidence, you can save commissions by operating on your own. A good broker can:

1. Help you select funds to buy.
2. Help you decide how to buy them.
3. Help you decide how you want to register them.
4. Call you from time to time with news of your investments.
5. Be available when you want some service performed.
6. Be available when you want some fund data or research.
7. Be available for general financial advice.
8. Furnish special forms as needed.
9. Sell your shares and pay you the same day.

I'll bet that any broker can come up with some more reasons, but that's all I can think of right now. Here's how to select a broker; Look in your phone book under "Mutual Funds" or "Stock and Bond Brokers" (or ask your friends if they know a stock broker) and call one up. (Nearly all companies have both men and women brokers.) Just as for a "salesperson" or "broker," and after ascertaining that the broker handles more than one group of mutual funds, ask for a convenient time to come in and talk about them. Chances are this'll be in the afternoon, after the market is closed, or maybe Saturday morning. There will be no charge. When you get there, you may get all sorts of reactions about mutual funds, from "Great investments" to "I can make you more in the market." If you ask for records supporting the latter opinion, I don't think you'll get them, as I know of nobody who keeps good, accurate records of how well they have done. I'm not implying any skulduggery at all. One normally collects dividends and spends them, or adds to or takes from an account, and very few people know exactly how they would compare with mutual funds.*

I don't think you will get a big argument to the effect that the broker can make more for you in the market, even before you mention that you are going to put a small amount down and make monthly payments, and this is extremely signifi-

---

*I do. They beat me for six straight years; the message finally got through. *Now I beat them* using timing.

cant. Even if he thinks he can make more than a growth-stock mutual fund, he doesn't think so with enough confidence to argue.

I will give you one check point. One of my neighbors is a stockbroker and I asked him point blank if he could beat mutual funds. He told me a customer had come to him a year ago with $10,000 and they had put half into a mutual fund and "maneuvered" the remainder in the market. "Well," I said, "who's ahead?" "Right now, the fund." This honest statement goes deeper than one might think, offhand. The customer paid 8.5 percent on his fund, and the account, closely managed by an "insider," must have been 8.5 percent worse than this to be below it. The fact that this was in a period of a rising market makes the point doubly piercing, as most funds are more stable than small accounts because of their diversification. I don't think much of taking one point and averaging the results, but I do believe this one is typical.

When you get to talk with the broker, say you have been reading about mutual funds and would like guidance in selecting what to buy. Explain your circumstances, and do not feel the slightest embarrassment about not having a lot of money to invest. The broker will be glad to help you get started. Do not feel you must buy from this broker. You can just say you'll think it over and walk out. And when he makes a suggestion there will be some bias involved; he may know the dealer, likes the fund group, and so forth. I'm sure he will recommend a good fund, but I'm just about as sure that he won't recommend the very best one he knows. Sorry about that.*

You are not locked in to the broker who starts you in a particular fund. At any time you may authorize a new broker to have the account, either at the same firm or at another, and *he* will get subsequent commissions. A transferral of the account to a new broker will be made automatically by the manager of your

---

*According to Bob Levesque, a survey of subscribers to his *Prime*, a no-load fund advisory service, less than two percent gave their brokers a grade of "A" or "B". I guess this is another argument for doing it yourself with no-load funds.

current firm should "your" broker leave it, or he may ask you to transfer it to him in his new location.

Now we come to an odd question, which we can discuss as well here as anywhere: "Why does anybody put money into the less successful funds?" It works out like this: Fund XYZ has a good year, and its owners tell friends about having an investment that "went up 30 percent this year." Said friends buy XYZ on a "Joe told me" basis. The truth is that said friends never looked into other funds, and possibly didn't know they existed. My own case was very much like this. My at-that-time broker told me that I should have some funds, that I should put all new money into funds, and that I should put whatever money I made on stocks into funds. Well, in all three of these recommendations he was right, and when he recommended one particular fund (a quite new one) I took his word and bought it. I have never regretted all this, but now, knowing a bit more about funds than then, I would do a little more studying. Nor would I put money into a specialized fund, which the recommendation turned out to be.

Why did he recommend this particular fund when it was new and had no 10- or 20-year record? There were several reasons: He knew the group that ran the fund and respected their judgment; the prospectus looked sound; and right or wrong (wrong in this case) he had a hunch this fund would be very successful. It has been successful, but not *very* successful. Also, the fund was just starting and I suspect some special concessions in the commissions had been set up.

An amusing follow-up comes to mind. Apparently I talked a fellow worker into buying this fund because a year or so ago he said, "Do you remember telling me to buy such-and-such a fund?" I said, "No, but I still have some." "It's worked out fine for me," he said, "I put $50 a month into it and now my $4,500 is worth $8,000." This is a compound growth rate of about 13.5 percent and nothing to complain about, but for the same period my other funds did much better.

Don't fall into the trap that it doesn't make any difference which fund you buy, and don't believe the oft-repeated statement to "buy the fund that is right for you," which implies that every fund is right for somebody. This is not so. Some funds go up less in bull markets and down more in bear markets, and the idea that these are right for anybody is pure hokum. Also, the few percent difference in compound growth rates over 20 years amounts to a lot of money. I think the proper conclusion from a funnel chart is that so far *all* growth-stock funds have done pretty well, and if you buy several you will have a successful investment. And if you *time* your investment, you will have a very successful one.

3.3.   DIFFERENT FUND-BUYING PLANS

Since commissions for load funds vary according to the size of the present investment (or sometimes according to how much you have in the fund—a big difference), there is a covey of different buying plans: voluntary, contractual, letter of intent, and so forth. We will look at these in a minute so you will know what people are talking about. No-load funds charge no buying commission and they, hence, have no "plans" except to meet the required amount for the first payment (usually $1000) and subsequent payments (usually $100). A few no-loads will waive the $1000 down payment if you sign up for scheduled investment, but they can't hold you to it.

Let's look at the charges made by the commission-type funds and see what the no-loads save us. And let me make a point: I'm not against load funds at all. I just think no-loads are better for most of us. If you need a broker to talk things over with, buy a load fund, but make sure you buy one that can be switched. Indeed, I know brokers who will *only* sell load funds that can be switched. Commissions typically run as shown in Table 3.1.

Let's examine that table. Although the percentages might not look so bad, the actual dollars sort of grab you. How a man can earn $15,000 by filling out a piece of paper is not clear. It certainly does not compare to the work done in selling a house or other real estate and should be reduced. On the other hand, 8.5 percent for a $50 sale is not a profit-making procedure for

Table 3.1. Typical Commissions for Load Funds

Amount	Sales Charge		
	As Percentage of Offering Price	As Percentage of Amount Invested	Actual Dollars for Top Amount
Less than $10,000	8.5	9.3	.850
$10,000 but less than $25,000	7.5	8.1	1,875
$25,000 but less than $50,000	6.5	7.0	3,250
$50,000 but less than $100,000	4.5	4.7	4,500
$100,000 but less than $250,000	2.5	2.6	6,250
$250,000 and over	1.0	1.0	10,000

a broker if he is involved, but he *may not be and get the money anyhow.* That is, the broker gets his commission on monthly payments made by a client, without him actually doing anything at all. This is similar to the situation for an insurance salesman who gets commissions for payments made long after the first sale. Also notice that whoever set the table up was not too bright, as the percentages overlap. For instance, the commission for $249,000 is $6225 and that for $250,000 is $2500. If they make profits, and they usually do, most funds do not charge you a commission to reinvest said profits. A few charge a commission to reinvest dividends. The rate for this investment is then based on the size of the dividend, which almost always puts it in the 8.5 percent category; with some funds it may depend on the size of your investment. Thus, if you had $100,000 in some funds *they* would reinvest dividends at the 2.5 percent rate.*

Before you buy, however, let me ask you to divorce yourself from thinking about the number of shares you will buy; think about the number of dollars you will invest. Unlike stocks, which must be bought in whole shares, mutual funds accept *dollars.* If your dollars work out to equal 13.146 shares, fine. That's what you'll get. And divorce yourself from being at all concerned about the price per share of your funds.

Here are the different ways you can arrange to buy *load* funds:

1.   **Single payment.**   If you have the money, you may simply buy as many shares as you can afford.

2.   **Voluntary plan.**   Here you pay the minimum initial amount that the fund you have selected will accept (or more), and add to your investment at your convenience. Of course, each payment must be as large or larger than the minimum subsequent amount the selected fund will accept. These additions should be on a regular basis. Almost all fund buyers, both load and no-load types, are on voluntary plans.

---

*Some funds permit the sales commission to be set by the total value of the shares owned by members of your family. It is your responsibility to point this out at the time of the purchase; the funds can't keep up with it.

3.   **Contractual plan.**   Only the commission-type funds have contractual plans, for reasons that will become obvious in a minute. Here the minimum to start is waived if you agree to make monthly payments for 10 years. On the other side of the fence, the fund takes out half of all the commissions for 10 years, the first year. You may get a refund of all the commissions if you change your mind within 45 days, and 85 percent anytime within 18 months. Eight states have ruled that these plans are illegal because only about half the buyer's money is working for him or her at first. The funds claim that the compulsion keeps people putting in their money, and this is good for them.

Some contractual plans have a number of special features, and I'll mention some. For instance, part of the dividends paid early in the plan are tax exempt; sometimes you may draw your money out and reinvest it later without paying a second commission; commissions are typically smaller for larger investments and your contractual plan may get you into a smaller commission rate; dividends will always be reinvested without commissions; you are protected against an (unlikely) rise in commission rate; sometimes you can get cheap insurance with a contractual plan; and sometimes you can name beneficiaries in the event of your death in a manner such that executor fees can be avoided. You may also borrow on a statement from the fund that you have so many shares in the contractual plan. I can't make much of a good case for contractual plans, nor can a number of brokers.

4.   **Letter of intent.**   Somewhere between the voluntary and contractual plans lies the letter of intent. This semilegal document (it is nonbinding on the buyer) permits prospective buyers to say they "intend" to buy, say, $10,000 worth of funds during the subsequent 13 months,* and in the expectation that they will do so the fund extends to them the $10,000 commission rate, say 7.5 percent instead of 8.5 percent. Now you would think that the early purchases would be at the 8.5 percent rate

---

*Why 13 months? This is a convenience for those lucky people who get a yearly bonus. It enables them to achieve their letter of intent by putting together bonuses for 2 years.

with a grand adjustment made when the total amount is finally brought up to $10,000, but that isn't how it works. It would be too easy. Instead, you get the 7.5 percent rate (in our example) from the beginning, but 5 percent of your shares are held in escrow to pay the difference in commissions in case you do not complete the plan. There is almost no reason not to use the letter of intent unless you are really sure you have no intention of putting in the required amount. With some funds it gives you the added profit (or loss) from the extra shares. With others, you are not permitted to make a profit on the extra shares if you don't complete the plan. A possible disadvantage of having a letter of intent is that if you have to liquidate your shares during the period of the letter, it may take two or more weeks to get all of your money. Since you may have called out 95 percent of your shares, this isn't too tough.

Well, that's enough about the load funds—just educational in case you already own some or might want to buy through a broker. We now go back to no-load funds, which can be bought on margin. Most stock market investors know that you may buy all stocks on the New York Stock Exchange and the American Stock Exchange and a few over-the-counter stocks on margin, putting up the required fraction of money and borrowing the rest through your broker. However, it is also possible to give no-load funds to your broker with a stock power and use them as collateral for the purchase of stocks, or for that matter more mutual funds. Shareholders doing this must forgo using the reinvestment-of-distributions plan. This is only partially stupid. When you give your stock or fund shares to a broker for a margin account he puts them in "street name" (his name), collects dividends (or distributions), and credits them to your account. It just gets extra complicated if distributions are in shares, so you will be asked to take them in cash.

You may always take your certificates to a bank and borrow on them to buy more (within existing Federal Reserve Board restrictions), but that's a little different from buying on margin. Incidentally, in England you may borrow 100 percent on funds, like buying something on the installment plan with nothing down.

3.4. DOLLAR COST AVERAGING

Every book on mutual funds are probably every mutual fund salesman (and your author, too, when he was younger and stupider) have at one time or another discussed a buying technique known as *dollar cost averaging.* According to this, an investor can make money by continuous buying even if a stock (or fund) doesn't go up—it just oscillates.

For a simple example of how this is supposed to work, suppose you bought $300 worth of a $10 stock (30 shares), and its price subsequently went up and down 20 percent in a year, finally returning to $10 a share. I believe it is obvious that if you bought at $10 a share and after a year it is at $10 a share, there is no profit. OK?

Now consider an investor who split her money three ways. She bought $100 worth when the stock was $10 a share (10 shares); $100 worth when it was $12 a share (up 20 percent), when she got 8.33 shares; and $100 worth at $8 a share (down 20 percent), when she got 12.50 shares. When we add up her total (10 + 8.33 + 12.50 = 30.83) we find she ended up with 0.83 shares more than you. At $10 a share that's $8.33 on a $300 investment, or 2.77 percent. (It's not exactly 2.77 percent, because the whole $300 wasn't invested all year, but let's neglect the difference.)

What happened? Well, she got more shares when the price was down than she lost when the price was up. Seemingly, a person would make more money by buying over a period of time than in one lump sum. That is really true, and that's dollar cost averaging.

But now let's go on to the next cycle, same as before. During the second cycle our investor doesn't make anything on the $300 she put in during the first year, but she again makes $8.33 on her new money. Since she now has $600 in her fund, the profit is roughly half as much or 1.38 percent. The cycles continue, until after 10 years of 20 percent cycles dollar cost averaging has netted our investor about one-tenth of 1 percent more than what she would have had if she invested all the money in the beginning. This isn't large enough to even consider.

Watch out for phony examples of dollar cost averaging. I remember an author explaining that had you dollar cost averaged in the Dow Jones industrials starting at the peak of the 1929 boom right through the worst depression this country has ever seen, by 1939 your capital gains and dividends would have netted you a 30 percent profit, whereas if you had simply put the money in the same stocks in 1929 and held them through the same period, you would have had 22 percent loss. That wasn't dollar cost averaging profit—it was just the result of continuous buying through a dip. Not having all your money invested while the market goes down is always good. I did it myself in 1970–1971; and again in 1972, in 1973–1974, and in 1981–1982. Chapter 4 tells how to do it.

Now, as I am running for cover from all those who have pointed out that dollar cost averaging is glorious, let me remark that there really are some benefits from *continuous buying:*

1.   Continuous buying will at least permit you to put money into whatever fund is currently doing best, and this can't hurt.
2.   Continuous buying, at least during the first few years, works toward buying at the average price, which may be good or bad.
3.   Continuous buying may be the only way a lot of us can invest, so let's accept it.

Continuous buying by investors can be a big help to a fund manager by supplying a good cash flow, which can actually make dollar cost averaging work. In the example given earlier, we invested $300 the first year. In later years the same investment made the same dollar profit, which progressively became a smaller percentage of the whole. Now if we had invested $600 the second year and $1,200 the third, the "drag" of the earlier money would have become less and less. In the real world, with reasonable oscillations, a fund with a great big cash flow probably makes an extra 1 percent per year. It is small, but we are happy to have it.

3.5.   THE CUSTODIAN ACT

Buying through the Custodian Act may not be a "plan," but it is so important that it rates a separate section. In a nutshell, if you seek to start building an estate for your children, don't buy funds for them in *your* name. All states, the District of Columbia, the Canal Zone, and the Virgin Islands have a law that permits you to buy mutual funds (or stocks, for that matter) for a minor by having them registered as "John Doe, Custodian for John Doe, Jr.," under the state's Uniform Gifts to Minors Act. In some states it is called the Gifts of Securities to Minors Act, and in others, the Uniform Gifts to Minors Law. No matter what it is locally called, it permits the dividends and capital gains distributions to go directly to your child so that you do not have to pay taxes on the money as you would if it came to you. The child does not have to pay taxes on a low income limit of $3,300 per year.

The custodian may still sell the funds and reinvest the money in a different manner for the child, or use a switch fund, but all of it must be used for the child, and must not replace monies that would ordinarily be spent for the child. Thus you can't use the child's dividends to pay for food or pre-college schooling. College comes outside of "ordinary" expenses and a custodian account is an ideal way to prepare for the cost of college. (A few states have ruled that if you "can afford it," you can't do this.)

The money you put into a custodian account is the property of the minor and is kept out of your estate, with the following exception: The courts have ruled—quite erroneously, in my opinion—that if you as custodian die within three years after making a gift to a custodian account, the gifts you have made to your children are part of *your* estate, and must be included when the executor figures the estate tax. How gifts made to your child return to become your property is one of those wonders of our judicial system, but the way out is easy—make your lawyer or a relative the custodian, or don't die within three years. Should the outside custodian die before the child becomes of age, the value of the fund shares is not added to his or her estate. Of course John Jr. must then get a new custodian. Parents may be tax-free custodians if the money comes from grandparents.

The paperwork of a custodian account is unusually simple. No trust instrument need be worked up by a lawyer; you simply open the account as a custodian account. When the minor becomes of age, securities are his without a formal accounting or even the payment of transfer taxes or fees. No gift taxes are involved unless you exceed the exemptions described in Section 8.2. The parents still get the normal dependency exemption as long as they supply most of the support of the child and the child is under 19 or a full-time student. Since the child does not have to pay taxes unless his income exceeds his exemption, the custodian plan may be considered a way to get an extra exemption.

You may want to start the custodian account by using some of your money currently invested in stocks. If so, how you handle it depends on whether you have a profit or a loss in the stock, as follows:

1. If you have a *loss* in the stock, sell it, use the loss against *your* income and buy mutual funds using the custodian plan with the remainder of the money.

2. If you have a paper *profit* in the stock, have your broker* get it transferred to you *as custodian for your child*, then sell it and buy the funds with the remainder after taxes. If the child's income including this sale is less than his exemption, there will be no taxes. If it is more, the taxes will be less this way than you would have had to pay had *you* sold the stock while it was in your name.

*Or do it yourself.

When your child becomes 21 years of age you will want to transfer the fund shares entirely into his name. Here is how you go about this:

1. Write a letter to the fund requesting reregistering the shares in his name.
2. Enclose a stock power signed by you with your signature guaranteed by a national bank.
3. Enclose a copy of your child's birth certificate.
4. Enclose a statement that the transfer does not constitute a sale. You will then only have to pay a transfer fee (typically $5) and a transfer tax if the fund's state of registry has a stock transfer tax. In New York the transfer tax is $0.025 per share.
5. Enclose a new application completed in the name of the child and signed by him.

If the fund involved is a load fund, your broker will be glad to handle all this for you. Some funds do not require everything just listed.

Some day your child may want to sell his shares, and he will then need a "cost" to subtract from what he gets for them in order to figure his profits (or loss) for tax purposes. Each purchase or transfer of your shares to his account was a gift and hence their cost was their value when you made the gift. In most cases this is the same as what you paid for the shares. Since no taxes are due for the distributions until the child's yearly income exceeds his exemption, his total cost will be what you paid for the shares plus all reinvested dividends and capital gains. Individual share cost is their price when you bought them for your child, or whatever he paid when a distribution was reinvested. At any time the distributions must be added to other income, and if the total is more than the exemption in one year some taxes will be due—at the child's rate because it is his income, not yours.

If you want to be "smarter than the average bear" you will each year sell enough shares to bring the total profit to the exemption mentioned earlier, and then reinvest the money you get for the sale. This raises the base on which final taxes are due. Indeed, it would really make sense to sell *all* the profits to reduce ultimate taxes because any taxes that have to be paid later on will almost certainly be at more than the child's *current* rate.

Suppose your child needs to sell some of his custodian acquired shares, and they show a loss, but he doesn't have enough income to take the loss. Is the loss lost? No. He files and carries forward the loss until he can use it. There is no way you could get the loss; you don't own the shares.

How hard is it to change funds as a custodian? Nothing to it.

1. Get a substantiated signature ("stock power") from a national bank—it's free.
2. Write a letter to the fund asking for redemption of the number of shares you want sold, and enclose the stock power.
3. The day you get the check, buy shares in a new fund for the same amount. This is not the time to add to the account. (You *could*, but the same amount in and out of your checking account on any one day is easy to audit.)

3.6. HOW YOU ACTUALLY BUY NO-LOAD FUNDS

After you have decided which fund you want to buy (see Chapter 4) all it takes is one letter, as follows, to your selection:

Dear Sir:

I enclose a check for ____ dollars [the minimum required or more], for which please buy me shares in your fund. My Social Security number is ____ I would like all distributions reinvested [add other instructions, from Section 1.18]. Please hold all certificates. I would like a prospectus.

Yours,

Unless you add special instructions, the shares will be registered in your name.

If you live in Virginia, your letter may bounce and you will be given a Virginia address to send your letter to. This comes about because Virginia has a law that firms seeking to do business in Virginia must have an office therein. Some funds use a broker's office, and that broker may get some stock trading business in return for the help. Other funds have set up their own offices in Virginia. I think future additions can be sent directly to the custodian bank.

Some further details on the housekeeping decisions you will have to make follow:

1. **Check Chapter 4 for information. Time to invest and fund selection.**
2. **Prospectus.**   Regulations say that you must have been given a prospectus before you are allowed to invest in a fund, and it would make sense to write for one before you send your money. Most funds send a prospectus along with the statement of your account, or if you have one already you could include that fact in your letter. I have a hunch you'll get another prospectus whether you want it or not because when your name goes into the computer as a new account, it sends you a prospectus.
3. **Form of registry.**   There are eight ways to register your mutual funds, many irrevocable. So take several minutes to go over this and check with your lawyer to make sure that what I tell you applies in your state. Here are the different registries:

   a. **Individual ownership.**   ("John R. Doak.") The shares are in your name. You own them and may sell them or give them away, exchange them or do as you will. They are *yours*. When you die they go into your estate to be disposed of according to your will. The fund will need your name, address, and Social Security number. You may also buy shares in another's name provided he or she is 21 years of age. (If not, see Section 3.5.) Such purchases are gifts and subject to the limitations given in Section 8.2.

b.   You as a trustee.   ("John R. Doak, in trust for Mary S. Doak," under declaration of trust dated . . .) When you die, the shares go directly to the person you have been holding the shares for. They are part of your estate, but not part of the property described in your will. This arrangement, in most states, moves the shares around probate and saves a few percent of your money. You are called the *creator, settlor,* or *donor* for initiating the trust, and a *trustee* for managing it.

While you live, the shares are still yours, and you may cancel ("revoke") the trust at any time. The slightly sticky part is that each purchase is a separate account, and you must execute the simple trust form furnished by the fund for each purchase. (Each is identified by having a different date.) I usually recommend this form of registry to save probate costs, and if the trust is being used as a withdrawal plan, your spouse's income will continue (in most states) right on through the execution of the will. You will have to furnish your name, address, Social Security number, and those of the recipient (called the "beneficiary") of the trust.

c.   Another agent as trustee.   ("Bank of Weehauken, in trust for Louis Doak.") You may designate your bank to hold shares as a living trust *(inter vivos)* to provide for mother, father, grandchild, grandmother, uncle or aunt—anybody you don't *have* to provide for, such as wife and kids. Dividends from these shares belong to the beneficiary and he or she must pay taxes according to normal income tax tables, but usually the tax rate will be substantially less than yours. Capital gains are treated differently in different states. The living trust may be for a specified number of years (more than 10) or until the death of the beneficiary, when they revert to you. You will have to furnish your name, address, and Social Security number, and the same for the beneficiary.

d.   Joint tenants with right of survivorship and not as tenants in common.   ("John R. Doak and Mary S. Doak as joint tenants with right of survivorship but not as tenants in common.") The effect of this registration is the same as for the trust, in that when you die the shares automatically become the property of your spouse without going through probate, and they revert to you should your spouse die first, but there is joint ownership and both must sign when redeeming shares, which either may request. The joint tenancy is not revocable. Both tenants must furnish name, address, and Social Security number.

e.   Joint tenants in common.   ("John R. Doak and Mary S. Doak, tenants in common.") This is similar to (d) except that if one tenant dies, the shares go into the estate of the deceased for allocation according to his or her will. While both tenants are living, both must sign ballots or redemptions, and the fund writes checks with both tenants as bearers. Both tenants must furnish name, address, and Social Security number.

f.   Trust under court order.   ("John R. Doak under will for Peter J. Smith.") One would not ordinarily be concerned with buying funds under court order, but the existence of this type of purchase should be understood. It may be as a court order (CO) for a person ruled incompetent, as directed under a will (UW), or for other legal reasons. The point is that the mutual fund, being accepted as a legal vehicle for trust investment, has, in my opinion, a 30-year record of doing a lot better than the typical bank management, which seems to be overly concerned with "safety."

g.   Custodian.   ("John R. Doak, custodian for John R. Doak, Jr., under the . . . state gifts for minors act.") This arrangement enables a minor to "own" shares. It is tax free within gift laws and is irrevocable. (See Section 3.5 for much more detail.)

h.   Guardian.   ("John R. Doak, guardian for Peter A. Smith, June 10, 1982.") This type of purchase may be made if you are the legal guardian of a minor. It was useful when some states did not have a custodian act, but is not often used now.

And how may you *not* register your shares? You may not register them as "John or Mary Doak." This would be a way around estate taxes, as the survivor could simply pick up and handle the shares as he or she wished, without going through an estate settlement. It is, hence, not legal.

4. Sending the money. Whether you start off with the suggested letter or wait until you get a prospectus, you will have to spend an initial amount according to the fund's rules. Essentially all of the stock and bond funds require $1,000 or more, and the money market funds require $5,000 or more, with a few as low as $1,000. A few funds will only handle accounts in even shares and since the dollar amount almost certainly won't come out exactly, you may get a small check back for the remainder. Send the letter by some sort of mail that gets you a receipt from the fund, and if big money is involved, send it through your bank. They will bank wire any amount directly to the custodian bank for about $10, and you won't have to trace a lost registered letter. There isn't any hanky-panky going on—no one's holding back the purchase of your shares while the market is going down and telling you that you bought at the high. No way. First of all, the money doesn't go to the fund; it goes to the custodian bank, which cashes your check, uses the most recent price per share, computes how many shares you get, and makes out the paperwork. In a few days the bank mails you a receipt. There is no way a fund manager could tell a bank to fudge the paperwork. Any time you worry about this, look on the back of your check and see the date on which it was processed. Incidentally, I have kept a careful record of my purchases and sales, and it completely confirms this. The trade date is within a day of mail time. Confirmation takes 2 to 3 days more. With a weekend in there, it frequently takes 10 days to *hear* about your trade, but there's no hanky-panky. Normally you can't open an account by telephone unless you do it through a broker. You can call and try.

Must you always send money? No. Many funds will accept your stock certificates, provided:

a.   The fund already owns the same stock.
b.   The stock being traded was on the open market the same day the certificates were received. (This is to determine the price for the swap.)
c.   The size of the swap is not above certain size limits.

Why would anybody trade certificates instead of selling them and sending money? Just to save the commissions.

5. Telling the fund how you want the distributions handled. Mutual funds do not pay dividends; they make distributions, and they need to know whether you want those distributions reinvested or sent to you.

6. Buying more shares. When a fund acknowledges your first order and sends you a little form saying how many shares you bought, it also sends along a form with your name and account number typed on it, which they hope you will use when you send in more money to buy additional shares. If you lose the form, send your account number; if you lose that, they will find the account. They also send you an addressed envelope.

3.7. STORING YOUR SHARES

You may ask the custodian bank to hold all of your shares for you, send certificates each time you make a purchase, or hold shares until you order them out. Even if you have no intention of ever using your shares for collateral, I recommend that you get a safe-deposit box and order some certificates sent out. The reasons are twofold: First, should you die the existence of the account is made known immediately; it could be several months before another routine statement from the fund came to the executor's attention. Second, if you want to borrow on your certificates you are all ready. There is no charge for having the custodian bank hold your shares—indeed they won't even exist in certificate form just as an entry. When you do ask for certificates, order them out in 50- or 100-share certificates. If you just ask for one big certificate, you may end up like a friend of mine who only had a certificate worth $25,000 when he wanted to borrow $6,000 to buy a car.

3.8. THE MECHANISM OF SELLING OR SWITCHING FUND SHARES

Selling mutual fund shares (it's also called *redeeming*) is easy to do. Just write a letter to the fund telling them what you want done. You may ask for a given number of dollars or of course you may redeem the whole account. (To make paying taxes easier, you may select the sale of exactly the number of shares you bought on a certain date and ask that *they* be redeemed.) You should include your account number. Most funds require that you also include a form called a *stock power* if the redemption is for over $5,000. Your bank or broker has stock-power forms and you will have to sign them in the presence of the bank officer, who will then sign and stamp them as a veri-fication of your signature. Your broker is probably not quite so picky, knowing you and having seen your signature many times. In most cases you may sign a stock-power form at home and send it to him and he will verify it. I suggest that you not attempt to fill out the form—let the fund do that. If you mess it up, you'll have to go through the whole thing again. I gener-ally get a number of stock powers signed and verified at one time and simply clip one to a fund certificate or include one in a redemption letter. A signed stock power does not constitute a hazard should one get lost. When you send the certificate by mail, use registered mail and require a receipt—in fact, I generally use registered or certified mail and a return receipt any time I write a fund. Your request may get a little more attention and in the case of a delay you have data for a complaint.

Don't expect a redemption check by return mail. It will take a couple of days for your letter to reach the custodian bank— more if you make the mistake of sending it to the fund address because *they* then have to send it to the bank. It is acted on the next day, but the bank is not required to send you a check until 7 days have passed. (Some funds just send the check and don't worry about making a little interest money on your money.) Then of course it takes another 2 days for their letter to reach you, all of which adds up to 12 or 14 days. Most funds register the letter if a large amount is involved, and somebody will have to be home to sign for it. There's more. If you are redeeming a large dollar amount, and the custodian bank is out of town, as it almost always is, your bank may not release the money until the fund check clears—another week. If you are reinvesting the money in another fund, add another 3 days. (You can, without much chance of embarrassment, use the money immediately for a new fund, as there is a time lag for them to clear, too.) Thus there is a substantial delay during which you do not have the use of your money, nor do you earn interest on it. The way around most of the problem is to invest in funds that have a telephone switch or telephone redemption.

If a fund does not have a telephone switch, there is a way to set one up by yourself. Essentially all funds have telephone redemption, whereby upon your call the fund will redeem according to your instructions and send the money to your bank. They are just as willing to send it to a money market fund, by wire. This gets your money out by telephone. You may arrange with the money market fund to set up a telephone redemption whereby instead of sending your redemption to your bank, they send it to the custodian bank of the fund you want your money to be in, and they in turn put the money in your fund account. This is about a day or so longer than a direct telephone switch, but a whole lot faster than mail and a lot more convenient.

Starting about 1976, several funds responded to the delay problem by making arrangements with money market funds such that a client could order her shares to be sold and the money put into a specific money market fund, or vice versa. They probably hoped that this procedure would help keep the money in their fund at least part-time, rather than have a "market-timer" take the money out when she felt the market was headed down, and then put it into another fund later. At any rate, telephone switching has been a boon to no-load fund investors. (Most load funds permit almost free switching among their own group, if a group exists.) However, through increasing the paperwork at the fund end through much more switching compared to the old letter-writing route, it has raised costs. Several funds have added a 0.5 percent switch charge. A switch is a sale, and must be so treated taxwise.

Even with telephone switch there is still modest delay. When you call and ask to move your money from the fund, it is moved out at today's closing price (sometimes tomorrow's closing price). If you call to move *from* the money market fund into a mutual fund, the swap is usually made at today's closing price. It may be a week or 10 days before you get a notice of the switch. Despite the delay, the telephone switch is far faster than mail redemptions. This can mean quite a bit of money from interest payments.

Since there is no way for the custodian bank to identify who is calling, you may authorize another person to do it for you: your investment counselor, broker, or whoever you wish. All that person needs are the numbers of your mutual fund and money market fund accounts, and the phone number of the bank.

If you are moving money out of a fund family, then you will have to face the almost two-week delay before it is back in the market.

If you have fund shares pledged against a bank loan, you may still sell them to make a switch, and then use the shares of the new fund to replace the missing collateral. The procedure is a little sticky, and I suggest that you see your bank manager for details on how it must be done.

3.9. KEEPING TRACK OF MUTUAL FUND PERFORMANCE

When you buy, say, 100 shares of a stock, it's generally not too hard to remember what you paid for it, and on a daily basis note from your newspaper how your investment is doing. If it's up 2 points, you've made $200, and that's about all there is to it.

I wish I could say the same for mutual funds, but I can't. You can no more keep track of your investment by its price in the daily paper than you can tell, accurately, by what percentage one fund is outperforming another. One reason is the distribution of dividends and profits, which are usually taken in additional shares. Thus the chances are even that if you buy 100 shares of a fund, a few months later you may have 105, and possibly you have a profit even if the posted price of a share is below what you paid for it. A second reason arises from the commission and taxes you may have paid while holding one fund compared to another. For instance, suppose you own two funds, A and B. You have held both a year and both have gone up a healthy 20 percent. If Fund A received no dividends and took no capital gains, the full 20 percent is available profit. But if Fund B distributed 3 percent dividends and 17 percent capital gains, then you have to come up with several percent to pay the taxes. Nor is there any validity in saying, "Oh well, I might as well pay taxes as I go along—I'll have to pay them some day anyhow." Not so if you keep the fund and use the withdrawal plan. (See Chapter 6.) Here you can enjoy the profits on money you *never* paid taxes on. I like it.

Turning back to what you can do on a slightly longer basis, there are several mutual fund advisory services that keep track of the performance of the various funds on a monthly basis, and on a three-month, six-month, and yearly basis as well. Read the fine print carefully, because some services include the reinvestment of capital gains in their statistics but not the reinvestment of dividends. None, of course, include the effect of your taxes on any distributions, because they don't know your tax rate.

Unfortunately, you can't learn as much as you might like from the daily paper, which carries price data on about 540 funds including 200 no-loads, because capital gains and dividend distributions* are omitted; only the net asset value per share and the offering price are given. The change in the net asset value since the last day the market was open may also be given. The net asset value per share is just what you'll get if you sell. The offering price is what you will have to pay if you buy in small lots and pay the maximum commission. If the two price quotes are the same, then the fund in question is a no-load fund. Sometimes instead of an offering price, you will find the letters *NL*, which stand for no-load, as we saw earlier.

What do I do? I keep running plots (see Section 4.3) of the funds in which I am interested, and meld my thinking with that of several advisory services.

Barrons lists distributions.

3.10. STATEMENTS AND MISCELLANEOUS LITERATURE

Although I have promised you that minimum effort would be required for your investment in mutual funds, that minimum isn't zero, nor is it much. An annoying part of the correspondence is that it won't come in an envelope marked "Smith Fund." Rather, there will be some mysterious letters in the name of an outfit you never heard of. The answer is that there are several companies that specialize in handling fund correspondence, and they put their own letterhead on their envelopes. I wish I had a dime for every envelope I nearly threw away because I figured it was a dun letter, only to open it and find the data from my latest fund transaction. Anyhow, here's the list of things you may expect:

1.   **Statements.**   When you start in a fund, every time you make a purchase, or the custodian bank makes one for you as it reinvests dividends or capital gains distributions, you will get a statement. It looks baffling at first, but a little scrutiny will clear it up. Basically, it will say eleven things:

a.   Your name and address.
b.   If it is a load fund, the name of the dealer from whom you originally purchased your shares and to whom commissions will go each time you put in more money. The name of your broker will also appear. He gets part of the commission paid the dealer.
c.   The date of the transaction.
d.   The amount of the transaction in dollars. This will be identified as new money from you, called *amount received;* long-term capital gains distribution from the fund; an income distribution from the fund; or (rarely) a short-term capital gain distribution.
e.   The applicable price per share. For load funds it will be net asset value for the *capital gains distributions,* or the offering price for new money. It depends on the fund as to which price is applicable for *dividends* reinvested.

f.   The number of shares received for the amount of the transaction: (d) divided by (e) should yield this number, in case you want to check their arithmetic.

g.   The shares held by you in certificate form, sometimes called *certificates issued.*

h.   The shares held by the custodian bank in trust for you. You may order out certificates for these at your discretion.

i.   The total number of shares you own, which should be the sum of (g) and (h).

j.   Your account number. Usually a form is provided for you to use when purchasing more shares. It has your name, address, and account number on it. If you don't have such a form and want to purchase more shares, it helps to state your account number.

k.   Summary of capital gains and dividends invested for you so far this year. This gives you a hint of how much money to hold back at Christmas to pay the taxes on your mutual fund profits.

Keep every statement you receive. You will someday need this information for tax purposes. There may be mysterious abbreviations on the statements. Here's what they mean:

ATIC	As tenants in common
DRO	Dividend reinvestment order
FBO	For benefit of
JT TEN	Joint tenants
SER	Self-employed retirement (plan)
SIP	Systematic investment plan
TR/UDT	Trust/Under declaration of trust
TR/UW	Trust/Under will
UCO	Under court order
UDT	Under declaration of trust

Table 3.2 shows a slightly simpler cumulative statement form. Note that the redemption number of shares matches an earlier buy. This really makes tax computations easier.

Table 3.2. Example Fund Statement

XYZ Fund 1982 Cumulative Statement

Name: *Social Security Number:*
Address: *Account Number:*

Trade Date	Transaction	Dollar Amount	Share Price	Shares This Transaction	Total Shares Owned
1/1/82	Beginning balance				132.329
1/11/82	Income reinvested	69.68	12.35	5.642	137.971
1/11/82	Capital gains	323.47	12.35	26.192	164.163
2/3/82	Purchase	100.00	12.13	8.244	172.407
2/16/82	Purchase	100.00	11.71	8.540	180.947
3/16/82	Redemption	316.40	12.08	-26.192	154.755

2. Notice of annual meeting of shareholders. By law each fund must hold a meeting of the shareholders once each year, and you would be astounded to see how many shareholders elect to stay away—I'd say 99.99 percent. Usually the meeting is held contiguous with the board of directors' meeting, and *they* will be there along with representatives of the management group. The fund officers will have the proxies you have filled out and returned so that a quorum is assured. Four items are always taken care of: Electing the board of directors; approving or rejecting continuance of the management group; ratifying or rejecting the auditors; and "transacting such other business as may properly come before the meeting or any adjournment thereof." I don't know why they have to put in that part about the adjournment, but they always do.

If you are in general satisfied with the performance and operation of the fund, I'd suggest you vote yes on the proxy. And I'd recommend that you arrange to go to a shareholders' meeting sometime.

Also in the notice of the annual shareholders' meeting you will find the names and addresses of the directors and how many shares of the fund they own. (It is assumed that directors have enough confidence in the fund to put some of their money in it, and I'd be uneasy if several had token positions. It is also fun to notice who the rich guys are.) The balance sheet is of minor interest to most of us. Things that are a little unusual will get a comment or explanation in the literature. There is no reason to keep old meeting notices.

3.   **Quarterly, semiannual, and annual reports.**   The reports are little folder-type things that start off with a letter from the fund president saying things have been pretty good considering the state of the market, and they hope to do better next period. Then, there will be a lot of statistics about the performance of the fund and the changes in assets. There will also be a list of securities now held, generally broken down into bonds (even the growth-stock funds will hold short-term bonds or speculative bonds from time to time) stocks, cash and "other." The stocks will be divided into industries and if you are curious you may note that your fund managers evidently think airlines, or motor freight, or some other industries are due for a rise. Some fund managers will list the 10 largest holdings, and perhaps the 10 stocks that went up the most and the 10 that went down the most. The item, "Cash," is quite clear— either they do not have enough to invest right now or they think the market is headed down for a while. Sometimes the report includes a list of stocks added or eliminated since the last report.

I always glance at the tables showing the growth of total assets. If a lot of new money is coming in, everything is fine, even though the market may have gone down and the share price with it. There is no reason to keep old periodic reports.

4.   **Prospectus.**   Once a year you will receive the latest prospectus. You will also have received one when you started in the fund. A prospectus is a fairly boring 30-odd-page description of the fund, who runs it, and the many details of all its many facets. The only way to read a prospectus is to glance at the table of contents (see Table 3.3) and run down the data presented to see if you are interested in any of the items. You may not learn a whole lot after you look the item up,

Table 3.3.   Typical Table of Contents Prepared for a Prospectus

Condensed financial statement	The fund's shares
Performance	How to purchase
History of fund	Net asset value
Investment objectives and risk	Redemptions
Investment strategies	Retirement plans
Options	Dividends, capital gains, and
Leverage	tax status
Turnover	Principal shareholders
Restrictions	Transfer agent
Lending securities	Custodian bank
Directors and Officers	Financial statement
Investment adviser	Accountant's report
Brokerage	Share purchase application

but you may indeed have some fun from this very serious and ponderous document. For instance, I once got curious and looked up "Principal shareholders." The answer was succinct: "There are no principal shareholders." Or you might turn up a gem of wisdom, such as this one: "The fund will earn dividends or interest received to the extent of dividends and interest received on its investments." You can't argue with that. And I couldn't fail to be impressed when I noted that an investment of $100,000 made in one fund on May 23, 1973, would be worth, 9 years later, $617,780, provided the investor came up with the taxes for each reinvested distribution. That's an impressive average growth rate of 22.25 percent.

You will not get a lot of nourishment from the list of stocks held, but the percentage in each group might be intriguing. It is interesting when the cost of stocks is presented along with their current value. Fund advisers make mistakes too.

Sometimes I forget whether a fund I own can go on margin or do other things, so I keep the most recent prospectus for reference. Most people throw them away, probably without reading them.

5.   **Reinvestment notices.**   Even though you have told the custodian bank to reinvest your dividends and capital gain distributions, it has found it expeditious to make a distribution notice a plug for reinvestment. Thus, typically once or twice a year, you will get a notice that the fund has declared certain dividends and capital gains distributions and will shortly issue checks. The statement is also made, "If you want the distribution reinvested, *do nothing. If* you want a check for the distribution, make a cross here. My advice used to be to do nothing, so that your investment would grow at the maximum rate. More recently, I lean toward accepting the distributions, for two reasons: (a) They alert me that some taxes will be due, so set money aside, and (b) I may prefer to put the money in another fund. (See Section 1.18.)

6.   **Year-end summary notices.**   Every January each fund you have owned at any time during the past year will send you a statement of how much profit and dividends they made for you during that year. A duplicate of this form goes to the IRS, so they may check your return against that of the fund.

3.11.   *KEEPING RECORDS*

It is necessary to keep proper records on your fund investments whether they be load or no-load types. The records *must* exist for tax purposes, and you must keep them for the life of your investment and several years after you close it out. You should also be interested enough in your investments to keep some sort of eye on whether you are making money, and if so, how much.

There are as many ways to keep records as there are people keeping them. So do not feel you have to agree with me—you may well have a better system. Here's what I do:

1.   I keep all statements I receive from each fund in a separate envelope. I have drawn a series of lines on the front of each and made columns for (a) the date I send money, (b) the date they act on it, and (c) the date I hear from them. I circle the

dates when they become 1 year old to draw attention to the possibility of a long-term gain. Then come some columns for (d) how much I put in this time (and of course distributions go in like any other purchase), (e) the total I have in, (f) the price of a share, (g) the number of shares I bought, and (h) the total number I now own. Finally I have a column (i) for the total value at the time I made the last buy or sell, and (j) a column for my running profit. You may not want to do all this. It is just something I have found that suits me. Distributions are entered the same as new money so the record is complete.

You could probably construct the same sort of list by pasting together a number of statements. Either way a complete list is essential in order to be able to sell one lot of the right amount every time you want to raise or move some money. This makes figuring the taxes as simple as any sale of stock, and gets away from the LIFO (last in, first out—see Section 3.12) and other laborious computations. Maybe I should add that it makes absolutely no difference to the custodian bank whether you redeem 2,000 shares or 2,134.456 shares. The number is punched into the computer either way, and I'm sure it doesn't care. In fact it might like the extra exercise.

2. Separate from the envelope I keep a running list of all "sells" in the form Uncle Sam wants it. Then when April 15 comes around I just copy it. This table also has a running column for profits or losses, so I can see at a glance whether I should make any year-end moves to reduce taxes.

3.12. HOW MUTUAL FUND PROFITS ARE TAXED

Mutual funds make money four different ways as far as the tax man is concerned: (1) long-term capital gains; (2) dividends qualifying for the current exclusion amount ($100 in 1982, $200 for a couple); (3) dividends not qualifying for the exclusion amount; and (4) nontaxable distributions. You will know what kind of monies they are sending you (or reinvesting for you) because at the end of the year they send you a Form 1099-DIV with the total amount and the amounts of each type spelled out. We will use the same headings as the Form 1099-DIV because you can't enjoy the show without a program.

   1.   **Gross dividends and other distributions of stock.**   This is simply the total of the following four items without regard to how each will be treated for taxes.

   2.   **Dividends qualifying for exclusions.**   For many years you could deduct $100 ($200 for a couple) from the total dividends you received, but interest was not included as a deductible item. In 1981 the numbers were changed to $200 and $400 and interest was included. Currently it looks as though the new numbers of $100 and $200 for both interest and dividends will continue. Incidentally, there is a basic reason for treating the two differently. Dividends are paid by a corporation with after-taxes-are-paid money. Interest is an expense that is paid with before-tax-money. Since there are many people who get a little interest from a savings account but who don't own any stocks, giving both an exclusion seems fair.

   At any rate, dividends qualifying for exclusions include those from domestic corporations, and the interest that qualifies comes from U.S. bank accounts, credit unions, savings and loans, and interest paid by domestic corporations on bonds and notes. The fund itself keeps the dividends it receives from the stocks it holds in a special account, and when it sends you your share, that share is identified so that you may claim your $100 or $200 deduction. Sometimes a corporation may send a few shares of stock instead of a cash dividend. When this happens to a fund the equivalent amount of money must be set aside and sent to you.

   3.   **Dividends not qualifying for exclusions.**   Nonqualifying dividends include those from foreign corporations, and interest paid by individuals. Short-term capital gains are also in this group. Many countries take out a percentage for taxes, and whatever the amount it is subtractable from your income taxes—not a write-off—through the use of tax Form 1199.

   4.   **Capital gains dividends.**   Capital gains are profits made by your fund by selling stocks at prices higher than they paid

for them. Sometimes it doesn't work out that way, of course, and the fund must take a loss. At the end of the year, or perhaps more often, the fund balances the gains against the losses and, if it has come out ahead, sends you your share of the gains. If it ends up with a net loss, the loss is used in future years to offset capital gains, and shareholders will benefit from capital gains that are untaxed until the loss is used up. If the gains are made in less than a year, they are called short-term gains and you must treat them taxwise the same as income. If the profits are made in stocks held longer than a year, they are called long-term capital gains and you pay taxes on less than half. In either case, profits or losses do not exist until the fund sells the particular stock. The value of your fund shares could go way up without any capital gains being made because no sales were made. This is actually a good feature about funds: Most of them hold profitable stocks 1 year or more—sometimes many years. As a result you will probably pay less on the capital gains you make from mutual funds if you hold them than from those you make with stocks bought for yourself. This is especially true if you are active in the market. (If you use market timing, you get to pay the maximum taxes. Can't be helped.)

There are two special cases that concern how to treat distributions when you sell your shares in less than 31 days but have received a distribution during the period in which you owned the shares.

a.   Capital gains distribution.   Suppose you buy $400 worth of a fund on September 1, receive a $40 long-term capital gain distribution the next day, and sell the fund on September 20 for $350. (The value of your shares went down $40, and the market went down $10.) You treat the $40 distribution as a long-term capital gain because that was how the fund made it. However, the sale of the fund shares in less than 31 days made you a short-term loss of $50. Taxwise you balance the loss against the gain and end up with a $10 short-term loss. If you had not sold the shares, there would have been a $40 long-term capital gain to pay taxes on.

b.   Tax-free distribution.   If you received tax-free distributions during the 31-day period and sell the shares, any loss on the sale up to the amount of the dividend is not allowed. The 50 states come close to treating mutual fund distributions in 50 different ways. For instance, should you have your fund send you both capital gains and dividend distributions, you will find they spend just the same. You won't get two checks, just one with a card saying that the total represents so much capital gains and so much dividends and interest. There is no argument from the states about the dividend and interest part. This money is called income and is fully taxed. But there is a whale of an argument hinging on whether the capital gain distributions is not taxable at all, treated as capital gain, or considered income.

5.   Nontaxable distributions.   Nontaxable distributions are monies earning from investing in tax-free bonds, or (rarely) return of capital. In the latter case, an equal deduction should be made in the cost of the shares you own, spread out over all earlier purchases.

If there is one area where mutual funds become a chore, it is figuring out what you owe taxes on after a redemption. You have three choices:

1.   **LIFO (last in, first out).**   Redemptions are made from the most recent purchases, working your way back until the proper number of shares are accounted for.
2.   **FIFO (first in, first out).**   Redemptions are made starting with the first purchases.
3.   **Redemption of specific lots.**

An example of LIFO and a discussion of the other methods follow.

Example 3.1.   Mr. Jones bought shares of Fund X as follows:

Date	Amount of Purchase	Price per Share	Number of Shares	
November 25, 1977	$2,000	$4.00	500.000	
December 16, 1977	3,000	2.25	1,333,333	
January 15, 1978	42.41	2.33	146.957	(distribution)
March 14, 1978	4,000	2.50	1,600.000	

On August 13, 1979, when the fund sold at $2.75 a share, he requested a redemption of enough shares to make up $4,500. What did he owe taxes on?

1. The total redemption of $4,500 at $2.75 a share comes to 1,636.364 shares.
2. The first 1,600 shares come from the March 14 purchase, which cost $4,000.
3. The next 36.364 shares will come out of the January 15 distribution of 146.957 shares at $2.33 a share. The amount received was $100 for shares that cost 36.364 × $2.33 or $84.73 (profit, $15.27).
4. The total profit was $415.27, on which long-term capital gains tax must be paid.
5. Subtracting those shares sold from the January 15 distribution we see that 110.593 remain at $2.33 a share, as well as the other shares bought earlier at $2.25 and $4.00 a share.

Mr. Jones could have saved himself a lot of trouble if he sold the shares in the share blocks that he had bought them in. For instance, suppose he needed about $1,200 for some purpose on August 13, 1979, when the shares sold for $2.75. If, instead of asking the fund to sell enough shares to send him $1,200, he said, "Sell 500 shares and mark the statement, 'Shares bought November 25, 1977,' " he would receive a check for $1,375 (500 shares at $2.75) and have a $625 long-term loss. That would wipe out the November 25, 1977, entry. This procedure is much simpler than fighting through the purchases until the books are balanced, as is shown in Example 3.1.

Taxes may also be paid on a first in, first out basis, where a method similar to the one just used is set up but you begin with the shares purchased first. This is almost never worthwhile, as the shares bought first are usually the cheapest, and taxes the most. When you have finally used up all the dollars you have paid, the remainder is all taxed.

If you have a large profit in a fund, and are in a high tax bracket, it might be advantageous to sell your shares on the installment plan, possibly to a relative. This spreads your profit over several years, and probably will save some taxes. It also might make it possible for your child to buy an estate. Here's how it works:

1.   It must be a "casual" sale, for more than $1,000, and you must get less than 30 percent in the year of the sale.

2.   There must be at least two payments at any time after the year of sale, and you must have made a profit.

Under this arrangement you may hold the fund shares as collateral until they are paid for. If you wish you may let your son or daughter use the withdrawal plan to buy the shares. Currently, a rate of 7 percent per year is acceptable to the tax people.

At first blush this type of sale seems like an arrant dodge to transfer money to your children without paying gift taxes (see Section 8.2), which might be involved if the sums are large enough, and to reduce your taxes by spreading the capital gains out over a number of years, and I guess it is. But the same thing happens when you buy a business with a small down payment and use the profits from the business to pay it off.

Before closing this section on taxes, let me remind you not to pay taxes twice. This can easily come about if, say, you bought $4,000 worth of Smith Fund years ago and sold it recently for $6,000, and write down a $2,000 profit. No such thing. The chances are that the Smith Fund made some distributions during the years you owned it, and you paid taxes on this money the year it came in. So, *all distributions should be added to the original cost* in determining the base on which a profit is to be figured. Just for fun, if the Smith Fund sent you $2,200 in distributions, you took a loss when you sold it for $6,000. Right?

4

Selecting Funds to Buy and Manage

This is a most important chapter, not so much because it deals with the meat of buying and managing no-load mutual funds, but because it encourages—no, *requires*—you to take a look at yourself and make sure you know why you are investing. In previous writings I had always assumed that all people want more money, either for spending now, or later, or leaving to their kids. Since they had a reason for more money, I assumed (and took a lot of lumps for a wrong assumption) that they would be glad to do a little work for it. Not so. Not so at *all*. There are tens of thousands who (1) either have lots of money and just want to park it in a safe, productive place, or (2) don't have lots of money and don't want to take any risks, but need more income. The latter are the hardest to talk to. Keeping your money in dollar bills would have lost you over half your buying power in the last 10 years. Government bonds would have been as bad or worse. Gold or gold shares would have given you a ride you couldn't believe in 1979–1980, and clobbered you in 1981–1982. Investments are like a garden: You *have* to give them a little attention, even if you just plant trees.

So I have divided all investors into five groups, which I define shortly. But first I have some more words to say about neglecting one's investments, or requesting that your broker or adviser or trust officer run a program of neglect. Many of them have had clients come up with some money and say: "I don't want to trade. I just want to get some income and forget it." I don't know how many of these poor chaps put their clients in good quality stocks or funds in the early 1970s or in AAA bonds in the late 1970s only to watch in dismay as their gilt-edged investments lost value and, in the first case, income as well, while in the second case the bonds went down as interest rates went up, and the fixed income bought less and less as prices rose. A personal example comes to mind of a widow friend whose husband left her a bundle of General Motors stock ("Never sell your GM stock") and a large amount of bank certificates of deposit (CD's), then paying 4.5 percent. The GM stock has gone from around $70 a share to around $45 and dividends have dropped from $3.80 a year to $2.40. The bank CDs have been rolled over (renewed) automatically by the bank at the *same* rate of 4.5 percent for 15 years while interest rates have gone above 16 percent! My friendly savings and loan tried the same thing with me, offering to roll over a 7.5 percent CD I had with them, and to continue the 7.5 percent rate!*

So, what I am really saying is that there is no "forget about it" investment. During an inflationary period you should have some of your money in a gold share fund. During a deflationary period some should be in a government bond fund. During a rising market most of your money should be in growth mutual funds. During a falling market most should be in money market funds. All this isn't as easy to do as it is to write about, but that's what this book is for.

What would I do if I were a broker or trust officer and had someone ask me to recommend a permanent investment? I'd say "There is no such thing as a permanent investment. The best I can do is recommend a mutual fund with a record of

*What's a dyed-in-the-wool no-load advocate doing with a 7.5 percent CD? Well, it's hard to believe but only seven years ago 7.5 percent was a pretty good rate for parking money. When interest rates went up I of course borrowed 90 percent of the CD from the bank at 8.5 percent (1 percent over their rate) and bought 16 percent bonds, so I really only had 10 percent locked in at the pitifully low rate.

doing the right thing as times change. But the manager may die, or the fund get too huge, and we may have to make some moves whether you want to or not. And that's the only way I'll handle your money."

4.1. INVESTOR TYPES, AND THE FUNDAMENTALS OF INVESTING

Here's my list of investor types. Which one are you?

1. **Beginner.**   A person who has been meaning to get started in an investment plan, but hasn't quite gotten around to it.
2. **Aggressive investor.**   An investor with a little experience in the market, intrigued with the idea of actually using timing techniques.
3. **Long-term investor.**   A more conservative investor than the aggressive investor, who probably will buy mostly growth funds, and only use timing for holding back new money.
4. **Withdrawal-plan user.**   The withdrawal plan is a retirement program discussed in Chapter 6.
5. **Preservist.**   A person who is possibly so wealthy that neither growth of capital nor low yield are problems; this type belongs in bond or money funds.

Doesn't being one of these types determine *what* you should invest in? No, there was a time when it did, the preservists for instance being limited to bonds. But the destruction of the bond market through various government policies has changed investing, so that now the different types of investors correlate with *how* they should manage their money, meaning when it should be in the market and when not in. And, by the way, you don't have to be any one of these types; you can manage part of your money with one objective, part with another.

In the following paragraphs I will discuss some things that

all investors should do. Later on I will discuss the important actions that relate to each type of investor.

1.   The tools to work with.   I really do not see how anybody can be a serious investor, managing a growing portfolio, without getting some outside help through a mutual fund advisory service. Despite the fine long-term record of some funds, changes occur, new funds arise, your situation changes, and you will need more than just the daily price data from your paper. A list of several services is given later in this chapter. The cost runs from $40 to $150 a year, and there is no reason why you cannot share a subscription with several people. For the aggressive investor, both data services and timing services are essential. See Section 4.2 for more about advisory services.

2.   Charts.   A lot of fund studies involve charts, both reading them and sometimes drawing them yourself. Since I have received more questions about charting than any other subject, I have described the dos and don'ts in Section 4.3.

3.   Diversify, even in funds.   No matter what type of investor you are, or how big or small your "poke," you have no business owning only one fund. The minimum is four—as soon as you can afford them. It is *extremely* rare, but still possible, for an entirely honest staff to make an error of judgment and get closed down pending settlement. If this occurs during a falling market there is no way to get out, and you will have to ride the market down.

Here is an example of this type of trap. For years many no-load funds took the position that since they were incorporated in, say, New York, and they received their mail in New York, the sales they made were in New York. Accordingly, they decided that (a) they did not have to be licensed in all 50 states, and (b) as long as they did not pursue sales in other states, accepting unsolicited orders from everywhere would be permissible. Actually this point has never been settled. Funds usually accept your money from a state where they are not licensed provided you started the account in a state where they were. One fund that I owned a few shares in accepted money from lots of Texans, a state where it was not licensed. All would have been fine except (a) the market went down and (b) some sharp-eyed Texan found an obscure law that said if somebody sells something in Texas illegally, the buyer can get his money back, plus 6 percent per year. This is called a *recission*, in case it matters.

Well, Texans by droves sued for their money back. It was a hopeless suit as the money no longer existed, nor would it have been equitable to take it from other shareholders for malfeasance (if that's what it was). So the fund closed down, and as a shareholder my money got locked in while the fund went farther down. Finally, it did reopen, and indeed this was a lesson to all fund managers to tighten up their sales practices. Investors who put *all* their money in this fund would have been most unhappy. Don't put all your eggs in one fund basket.

4. Forget the cost per share. When a new corporation is started it is difficult to convince people that they should pay, say, $50 a share for an untried stock. Consequently, new issues usually come out at from $1 to $10 a share. As the corporation prospers, the price of a share goes up to $20, $40, or more. Stocks with high-priced shares are frequently called *quality issues*, even though there may be little basis for that remark. The small investor doesn't want to own a very few shares of a high-priced stock because somehow it seems "easier" for a $10 stock to go to $15 than for a $100 stock to go to $150. In recognition of this, corporate managers often split a stock in the hope that a lower price will attract more buyers and push up the price of the stock. All of this makes the usual irrational sense that motivates the stock market.

This sequence of events is *not* true with mutual funds in general, although some of the logic (?) creeps through. First of all, you may buy fractional shares, so there is no point worrying about high-priced ones; just buy a tenth of a share. Second the public cannot run up the price of a share by fevered buying; price is based solely on the value of the portfolio owned by the fund. If a fund owns $4 million worth of securities and has issued 1 million shares, each share is worth $4. Had it issued 500,000 shares, each would be worth $8. It is distressing for somebody who knows something about funds to hear "I bought the $4 fund. Boy, when it takes off it will really go?" The truth is that if the stocks in its portfolio go up 10 percent, the fund share will go to $4.40; had the fund issued half as many shares, the $8 shares would go to $8.80. There is no difference to the shareholder.

Despite all this, enough uninformed people think a low-priced fund is more speculative than a high-priced one, to make fund managers give in and split their shares so the price remains around $12 a share. Indeed, the daily newspaper reveals that this is true for some 60 percent of all funds. The cost of this paperwork is borne by the shareholders, and really adds nothing to their investment unless a low price attracts a better cash flow so that the fund's performance is improved.

The closed-end funds have a different situation. Splitting their shares can raise their value slightly if more market interest is aroused, since *their* price per share is the value the market puts on it, usually 10 to 20 percent below the actual worth of the shares the fund owns.

5.   Understand your fund's portfolio.   The portfolio, of course, is the stocks that are held by the fund. A copy of this list is readily available from the fund—indeed, once you are a shareholder you will get a copy at least two but probably four times a year, along with a few words on changes. The list not only includes the names of the stocks, but their present value, and, if it isn't too embarrassing, what the mangers paid for them. You will learn that professional managers make mistakes, also.

Usually there are subheadings for various categories or groups of securities such as science and technology, consumer and services, preferred stocks, corporate bonds, corporate notes, U.S. government securities, cash, and "other." Typically the percentage of the total fund represented by each group is stated, as is the exchange on which it is listed, if any is given; sometimes an asterisk is used to designate that the particular stock currently pays no dividends. There will also be a grand total, which, of course, is the total assets of the fund. If you wish to get a good feel for the risk in a portfolio add up the total dollars in stocks listed on the New York Stock Exchange, the American Stock Exchange, over the counter, and the amount in bonds and cash and figure the percentage in each. The more conservative the fund, the more it will have in preferred stocks and bonds and in stocks listed on the New York Stock Exchange and, secondarily, the American Stock Exchange. If the sum of the bonds, and preferred and common stocks, listed on the New York Stock Exchange is less than 50 percent of the total, the portfolio is possibly a volatile one, becoming increasingly volatile as the percentage decreases. The volatile funds are a little more worrisome, even when market timing is being used.

An interesting portfolio item is "other." Mutual fund managers pay attention to what *other* managers are buying, and knowledge that a successful manager is buying XYZ stock could well entice other managers into buying it, with a concomitant increase in price. Accordingly, the SEC permits a fund to list 5 percent of its assets in the "other" category to hide from the competition the identity of stocks it is accumulating. Any particular stock can only remain in this category for 12 months, usually an adequate time to acquire as much as the fund desires.

Another parameter we can look at in the portfolio is the average price-to-earnings ratio (P/E) of the stocks it holds. You get this ratio by taking a recent price of a stock and dividing it by its per share earnings. Thus if General Electric sells for $80 a share and earns $8 a share the P/E is 10.

Price-to-earnings ratios vary like mad according to the state of the market, as well as according to how the market judges a stock. In "normal" times stable stocks (such as utilities) sell at price-to-earnings ratios of around 10 to 12, the supergrowers such as Xerox are up to 50 or more, and stocks with a poor future at 6 to 8. After the 1973–1974 decline some price-to-earnings ratios got below 2 for a few stocks, Xerox fell to a P/E of around 13, and stable stocks were in the 6 to 8 ballpark. Since P/E values obviously mean little by themselves, one has to judge portfolios by the percentage of stocks held that have high P/E ratios relative to the current average, rather than try to affix specific numbers to them. The higher values of course usually mean more volatile issues—more rise in a rising market, and more fall in a falling market. Going back to "normal" times again, fund managers used to say they would pay a P/E of 15 for stock whose earnings were going up 15 percent a year, or 20 for a stock whose earnings were growing 20 percent a year, and so on.

The *difference* between the cost of holdings and their current value represents a profit that could be taken and on which you would then have to pay capital gains taxes. I suspect that rather than preferring a fund with *no* untaken gains (paper profits), most investors would prefer to buy a fund that has shown its ability to make profits. Ideally, one would prefer to buy a fund that has demonstrated that it *can* make profits and has already taken all it can. This point suggests that large purchases in funds that have undistributed capital gains *not* be made just before a distribution is due; that is, not in December or January, depending on the fund. A broker for a load fund who says to buy "because the fund is about to make a distribution" is both dishonest and violating the NASD code of ethics.

Additional data are in the prospectus, but in general the prospectus tells us what a fund *may* do; the portfolio tells us whether it is doing it or not. A good advisory service will keep you advised as to portfolio changes in the funds that it follows.

6.   **Funds in a large fund group.**   Since we have seen that a large percentage cash flow is of immense benefit to fund managers, it is logical to conclude that a fund that is a small member of a large fund group would accrue several advantages. First of all the organization is already set up to sell the fund; second, there will be a continuity of management no matter what happens to one particular individual; and third, a very small percentage of the cash flow from the other funds invested in stocks held by the small fund could be a substantial help pricewise.

7.   **Stock powers.**   Any no-load fund will want a stock power whenever you ask them to send you some money. This is a verification of your signature, and you get stock powers free from any bank. Keep three or four on hand at all times. I wouldn't leave them around, signed, but there really is little hazard in doing so.

8.   **A special time of the year.**   Just as there are certain sales that occur the same month each year, December is a critical month for funds. Here's why:

a.   Most funds make their distributions in December. If you are planning to buy, write the fund and ask if a distribution is imminent. If so hold your purchase until it is made. As covered in Section 1.7 and elsewhere, you'll owe taxes on the distribution even if you haven't made a profit.

b.   If you plan to switch funds, and have a profit, consider making half the switch this year and half next year—or use some other plan to keep taxes down.

c.   If you plan to switch a fund, a distribution is imminent, and you live in a state that considers distributions income, switch before the distribution. This preserves your profits as capital gains.

9. **Avoid funds having very large shareholders.**   There are a few funds that have a large fraction of their total assets owned by a big investor. These funds suffer from the added risk that such owners can upset the fund's investment program if they suddenly liquidate their holdings. It doesn't help that they may have made an agreement to accept their holdings in shares of stock rather than cash as the only reason the holding company would want out is that they do not like the fund's performance. One could be fairly sure that they would sell the stocks as soon as they got them, and this would depress their value as much as if the fund sold them.

10. **Size of first and subsequent payments.**   Most funds require that the first payment be $1,000 and subsequent payments be $200 or more. A few are below this, and some wildly more. You will find this information in your fund advisory service, or in the fund prospectus. Check whether you can afford to start in a fund and make subsequent payments before you put a lot of study into whether you *want* to invest in it or not.

11. **Stoplosses.**   Some funds will let you place a stoploss if you so desire, and many will move your money automatically into a money market fund when the stop occurs. I don't do this because I watch the market daily. Should I leave the country for a vacation I might well tell the fund to move if its shares go below a certain value that I establish.

12. **Accumulated losses.**   After there has been a substan-

tial market decline, many funds will accumulate losses such that they do not have to distribute capital gains until, of course, later gains exceed the accumulated losses. You will find statement on accumulated losses (if any) somewhere in the fund's prospectus. After the 1973–1974 decline many funds had many millions in losses that benefited later purchasers, but most have been used up by now. Just for an example, imagine a fund that bought all its stock at $12 a share and had the same number of fund shares as stock so that it sold at $12 a share. Next imagine that the stocks and the shares dropped to $4, at which time the fund sold the stocks and replaced them with other stocks, creating a loss of (say) $2 million. The current owners don't get to use those losses taxwise unless they sell the fund shares at a loss. However, if they stay invested until the fund makes $2 million in capital gains, none will be distributed, and they will owe no taxes. Now suppose that additional people bought into the fund anytime before the $2 million in capital losses have been offset by capital gains. They will share in the accumulated losses because capital gains will not be distributed until the losses are used up. It is thus quite an advantage to buy shares of a fund that has a backlog of accumulated losses, and similarly a disadvantage to buy into a fund that has accumulated gains. Both of these actions are discussed in relation to other factors elsewhere in this book.

4.2. NO-LOAD FUND ADVISORY SERVICES

There are nearly a dozen no-load fund advisory services, and every one I have seen is both helpful and professional. There are two types: data services and action services. Data services present data such as gains or losses over a large number of periods, cash position, and often many charts for a very large number of funds—all aimed at giving you the data to make your own decisions. The action services furnish data for a selected number of funds and give concrete recommendations as to what should be bought, sold, or switched by the various types of investors. I suggest that you write to a number of services and subscribe to their short-term offers and then see which seems to suit your needs best. You might then subscribe to one or two on a long-term basis, possibly sharing the cost with a few friends. If you do this, keep the old issues for future reference.

There is one big difference between *stock* advisory services and *fund* advisory services. When you get a fund advisory service and they recommend that you buy Fund X and the same recommendation goes out to several thousand subscribers, you *won't* find a big bulge in the fund price when you send in your money, as you most surely will if a few thousand subscribers get the word to buy a specific stock. Many of us have had some sad experiences along that line, not only for the "Monday morning price rise" but an *earlier price rise* that was produced when the boys in the back office bought *before* they published their recommendation.

Another service that many advisory services offer is a free telephone hot line, which enables you to call for their latest revised recommendations. This is particularly helpful since most services come only once a month, and new situations require new actions. If you time your calls for the off-hour rates, calls are less than half a dollar. I might add that you won't get personal attention, just a recording that revises what had been proffered before, thus bringing the advice up to date.

Make sure the advice is in a form that isn't hedged. The services I prefer give specific buy and sell prices for those following an aggressive portfolio management, and I like that. Others just keep lists telling each type of investor what fraction of their money they should have invested and the preferred funds to buy. Also helpful is general knowledge about changes in the fund situations: new managers, changes in the cash position, unusual amounts of cash flow, and possibly a list of portfolio changes if they seem to have special significance.

Once again, I do not see how anybody can be an astute investor in no-load funds without the help of one or two of the various services. A number of them are listed in Table 4.1.

Table 4.1. Mutual Fund Advisory Services

Fund Data Services
  Growth Fund Guide
  Yreka, CA 96097

  Investment Companies
  Wiesenberger Company
  One New York Plaza
  New York, NY 10004

  Johnson Charts
  545 Elmwood Avenue
  Buffalo, NY 14222

Fund Action Services
  Dick Fabian
  Telephone Switch Newsletter
  P.O. Box 2583
  Huntington Beach, CA
    92647

  Fundline Newsletter
  P.O. Box 663
  Woodland Hills, CA 91365

  Investors Intelligence
  2 East Avenue
  Larchmont, NY 10538

  Mutual Fund Scoreboard
  Hirsch Company
  6 Deer Trail
  Old Tappan, NJ 07675

  No-Load Fund-X
  DAL Investment Company
  235 Montgomery Street
  San Francisco, CA 94104

Lipper Distributors
74 Trinity Place
New York, NY 10006

Donaghue Corporation
P.O. Box 540
Holliston, MA 01746

No-Load Investor
P.O. Box 283
Hastings-on-Hudson, NY
  10706

Prime
P.O. Box 8308
Portland, ME 04104

Retirement Fund Advisory
Switch Fund Advisory
8943 Shady Grove Court
Gaithersburg, MD 20877

Systems and Forecasts
185 Great Neck Road
Great Neck, NY 11021

United Mutual Fund Selector
210 Newberry Street
Boston, MA 02116

4.3.   CHARTING FINANCIAL DATA

I am particularly concerned that many readers have been looking at charts practically all their lives, and might have a tendency
to skip over this section, which admittedly will start at a beginner's level. Don't do it. Not one person in a thousand has ever
sat down and really thought about financial charts and what
they *don't* tell you, and I guarantee you are going to be surprised.
Just to pique your curiosity, can you imagine a chart going
down when what is charted is really going up? I'll talk about
one in a minute.

The usual type of financial charts (also called *plots* or *graphs*)
shows the price movement of stocks, indices, or mutual funds
as time goes on; "time" being days, weeks, months, or years
depending on how detailed the presentation is (see Figure 1.2).
The idea is that one picture is worth a thousand words, and
you as an investor can, with just a glance, compare a whole
bunch of data with another whole bunch of data. This is not
necessarily so. Unless the charts are on a special type of graph
paper that keeps an equal vertical movement for the same
percentage changes, and unless you know what has gone into
the data, you can be far, far wrong. And believe me, a lot of
people are.

1.   **Linear plots.**   Linear plots are those that have equal
vertical spacing for equal dollar amounts, say, half an inch
equal to $10. This seems to be a straightforward procedure,
but it is actually extremely misleading. On linear graph paper
a $5 movement from $5 to $10 (up 50 percent) is the same as
a $5 movement from $50 to $55 (up 10 percent). Well known
to all investors is that different scales may be selected from one
chart to another. To see how misleading these two factors can
be, let us look at the *Wall Street Journal* for May 10, 1982. As
seen in Figure 4.1, it is "apparent" that since the bottom in
mid-March the industrials have been going up faster than the
utilities, while the transportation stocks have enjoyed only a
slight rise. Many investors would therefore put new money into
the industrials. Hold on a minute. All three plots are linear

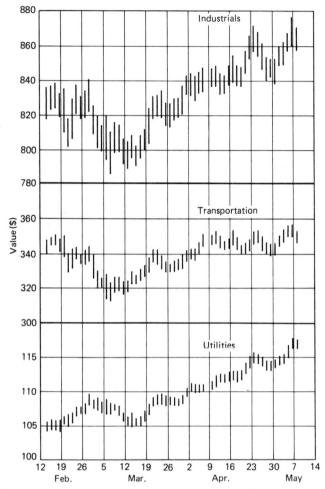

Figure 4.1.   Variation in ranges and scales of linear charts.

scales in different ranges, and indeed two of the scales are different. If the *actual* increases of the three indices from the bottoms to their end points are computed as a percentage, it was not the industrials that did best. The transportation stocks went up 12.2 percent; the utilities were next with 11.5 percent, and the industrials were the *worst* with a gain of only 9.6 percent! Part of the difficulty arose because the utilities are plotted at $10 an inch and the industrials and transportation stocks are plotted at $40 per inch (in the actual newspaper presentation), and part is due to the different ranges of prices involved: $40 per inch is about 5 percent per inch in the $820 range, but 11.8 percent in the $340 range.

> *Lesson 1.*   Before linear plots are used for comparison, be sure they are plotted to the same scale and are in the same price range.

2.   Semilog plots.   There is a type of graph paper, well known to many investors, called *semilog* or *proportional* graph paper, which can cure the problems of linear plots. Two commercial types are Dietzgen 340-L110 and Tekniplat R-78. This type of graph paper has the vertical scale so adjusted that a 5 percent change in price is, say, a half-inch no matter what the price level. This solves the range problem of linear paper. The compression of the scale for higher numbers enables one to get more on the page than with linear paper and hence a single scale can often be used for a very wide price movement or a wide range of prices for different stocks. By the way, when you are making a plot, do not be concerned about how accurately you need to estimate the proper location for a point between two lines. Just put the point for, say, 25.3 about a third of the way from the 25 line to the 26 line, and it will be accurate enough. Another point: When you use linear paper (I hope you won't), you may select any horizontal line and assign it any digital value you want; 5, 9, 14 . . . it makes no difference as long as you follow upward with consecutive digits: 6, 7, 8, or 9, 10, 11, and so forth. When you use semilog paper you do not have that privilege. The engineering semilog graph papers (Dietzgen 340-L110 and 340R-L220) have numbers 1 through 10 along their vertical scales and you should stick with those numbers. (If you wish you can make them multiples of 10 like 10, 20, 30, and so on, but don't call the bottom line 4 and continue with 5, 6, 7, and 8. Your plot won't be accurate.) The financial semilog papers (Tekniplat R-78 and K&E 476490) have the "control line" in the middle of the page and you can make the middle line any number you want as long as the bottom line is half of the control and the top line double the control. Thus if the middle line is 10, the bottom line must be 5 and the top line 20. If the middle line is 20, the bottom line must be 10 and the top line 40. If you try values other than multiples of 2 the lines in between won't work out. The simple check for *all* semilog plots is that the vertical distance from 2 to 4 should equal the vertical distance from 3 to 6 or 4 to 8. The same percentage must be the same vertical distance.

The foregoing may seem trivial to some and complicated to others. But aggressive investors either must make their own plots or read plots made by others, and it is essential that they know what they are looking at.

Figures 4.2 and 4.3 have been prepared to show the difference between the apearance of a linear plot and a semilog plot of the *identical* data. Figure 4.2 shows an apparent increase in performance in the most recent years as the curve is getting ever steeper. Actually the item being plotted went up a constant percentage each year, as shown in Figure 4.3, line *A*. The slope of a semilog plot (provided some sort of a straight line can be laid in) is the average percentage growth rate, in this case 15 percent per year. Once again, semilog plots keep a constant percentage of the price per inch regardless of the price range.

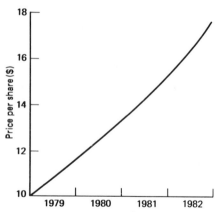

Figure 4.2.   Linear plot of 15 percent growth per year.

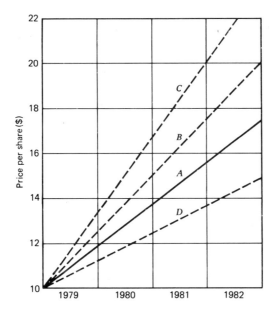

Figure 4.3. Semilog plot. Line A is a plot of 15 percent growth per year. For a description of lines B, C, and D, see text.

Lesson 2. Semilog plots using the same scales may be used directly for comparison regardless of the price range.

I feel so strongly about the misrepresentation shown by linear plots that when I get an advertisement for a service and its charts are linear, I just throw the thing in the wastebasket. To figure the average compound growth rate from semilog charts:

a. Read the starting value in which you are interested, X.
b. Read the end value you are interested in, Y.
c. Note the number of years involved, N.
d. Divide Y by X, getting Z.
e. Multiply Z by $10,000.
f. Read the average compound growth rate from Appendix A. If the exact value needed is not found, make an estimate from the two nearest values.

Example 4.1. From Figure 4.10, what was the average compound growth rate for the 44 Wall Street Fund from January 1, 1976, to January 1, 1981?

1. A = $7,000.
2. B = $35,000.
3. N = 5 years.
4. C = B/A = 5.00.
5. 5.00 × $10,000 = $50,000.
6. From Appendix A, read on the five-year line that $50,000 is almost exactly 38 percent.

   3. What's included in the data? Besides equal scales and, for linear plots, equal price ranges, it is extremely important to know what you are looking at. By convention, different pieces of an investment are omitted or included in plots of common stocks, closed-end mutual funds, and open-end mutual funds. This means their plots are *never* comparable. Let's see why.

   Assume that three separate plots have been made, one of a common stock, one of a closed-end mutual fund, and one of an open-end mutual fund, and by great coincidence they all come out to look like line A on Figure 4.3. Admittedly, price plots are never straight lines, but on the other hand many times a straight line can be laid in that approximates an oscillating one, and by starting with the same chart for each, we can show very clearly what data have been left out and whether the omission is significant.

   a. Line A as a stock plot. Graphs of common stocks leave out dividends, which may vary from zero to, say, 10 percent a year. Hence common-stock plots *understate* the worth of an investment by the amount of the dividends less the taxes paid on said dividends. A more accurate presentation would include this, although the different tax rates for different people make this impractical. For our example, which shows a constant growth rate of 15 percent, we might add 4 percent (6 percent for dividends less 2 percent for a 33 percent tax rate). Line B is laid in at a 19 percent rate (15 percent + 4 percent).

Stock splits would have changed the level of the curve, but not its slope. Neither do they change the value of the total investment.

b. **Line *A* as a closed-end mutual fund plot.** By SEC regulation, mutual funds must distribute all income (certain exceptions were noted in Section 1.12, item 12). This includes dividends, interest, and capital gains taken, less fund expenses, and by convention plots of closed-end funds simply show the price given each day in the newspapers. These also understate the true performance of the investment. It would be possible for a closed-end manager to take and distribute *all* of his capital gains and keep his losses so that a downward-sloping curve could actually hide a rising investment!

For purposes of discussion we will assume that the closed-end fund had a capital gains rate of 22.5 percent, and that a third of that (7.5 percent) was actually taken each year so that the increase shown (that not taken) is 15 percent. The tax on the capital gain taken, again at a 33 percent rate, comes to 2.6 percent, leaving a remainder of 5 percent. Dividends again are assumed to be 6 percent less 2 percent taxes, leaving 4 percent. The interest earned is assumed to equal the operating expenses. Hence we construct line *C* with a slope of $15 + 5 + 4 = 24$ percent.

c. **Line *A* as an open-end fund plot.** As discussed, mutual funds must distribute all net profit. The convention for presenting open-end fund performance is to add the distribution back in, despite the fact that taxes had to be paid on the distributions. This is equivalent to adding to the account each year, and for comparable representation, since no money has been added to the stock or the closed-end investment, the open-end plot should be reduced by the total taxes. Again assuming a 22.5 percent capital gain with one-third distributed, dividends of 6 percent and interest enough to balance the operating costs, we construct line *D* with a slope of $15 - 2.5 - 2.0 = 10.5$ percent.

If the closed-end fund and the open-end fund earned the same total, why is it that curves *C* and *D* are so far apart in

Figure 4.3? They *didn't* earn the same amount. They both, through convention, *plotted* the same. But the distributions were *left out* of the closed-end fund plot, and *left in* the open-end fund plot, and it was even assumed that somebody paid the taxes. So really, for this example, the closed-end fund did a whole lot better than the open-end fund, even though the plots of each (with different inclusions) ended up the same.

In the foregoing discussion, the assumed capital gains, dividends, interest, and fund operating costs were completely arbitrary, but the conclusions stand firm.

> *Lesson 3.* If semilog plots of a common stock, a closed-end mutual fund, and an open-end mutual fund are made to the same scale, both the common stock and the closed-end fund will have their performance understated, and that of the open-end fund will be overstated.

I have little doubt that the discount one usually finds for the closed-end funds is brought about by the omission of distributions from their charts, as is done for the great majority of open-end funds.

Commissions have so far been ignored, but should not be. Possibly the plots of the common stock should be shifted down 1 to 3 percent of the buying price and 1 to 3 percent of the selling price, as should the plot of the closed-end mutual fund. Open-end commission funds should have their plots shifted down 8.5 percent of the buying price, a significant amount. No charge is customarily made for selling, so no change is needed there. No-load funds would require no vertical adjustment.

For an actual example of the difference between plotting a fund's performance with and without the distributions reinvested, let us consider Figure 4.4. The bar chart shows the monthly range of values of 1,000 shares of Mathers Fund bought on January 1, 1972, assuming that all distributions have been reinvested. The average compound growth rate for the 10 years is 15.2 percent a year, and for the 6 years of the 1975–1980 bull market, 27.0 percent a year. The dots shown are the prices

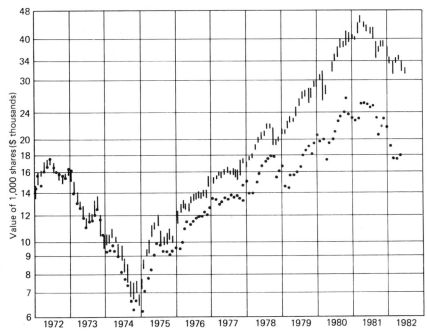

Figure 4.4. The value of 1,000 shares of Mathers Fund bought January 1, 1972. The bars show the value including reinvesting all distributions; the dots are without reinvesting the distributions. (Data from Growth Fund Guide, Yreka, CA 96097.)

given in the daily paper for the same time period. They illustrate the fund's performance without reinvesting the distributions (the usual method of presenting the performance of closed-end funds). The dots show an average compound growth rate for the 10 years of 5.7 percent a year, and a bull market average of 16.4 percent a year. We can draw the following conclusions for this particular fund for this particular time period:

1. An investor could have withdrawn 8 percent a year each year for living expenses and still had a nicely appreciating investment.
2. Including the reinvestment of distributions in a chart results in a far more attractive presentation than leaving them out.

Two items not apparent from the chart are

1. This fund for this time period did not quite keep up with inflation, but far exceeded it during the bull market phase.
2. Simply plotting the daily price shown in the paper by no means presents the true performance of a fund.

4.4. SWITCHING NO-LOAD FUNDS

Switching, which means moving from one fund to another, or moving out of the market during a slump, is a fairly new concept. As my friend, Dick Fabian (Telephone Switch Newsletter, P.O. Box 2583, Huntington Beach, CA 92647) points out, "Funds can provide pooling resources, diversification, professional management, and so on, but fund managers cannot take their shareholders completely out of the market. Switching provides that capability." It has become practical, he says, because of "(1) the increasing number of no-load funds, (2) the emergence of the money market funds, and (3) the telephone switching privilege between them." Truly this triad has changed the world of investing, and for the better.

I appreciate that many readers simply want to buy into a good fund and do nothing except spend the distributions or let them accumulate (and we will accommodate them later, as best we can). However, there are five good reasons to switch from one fund to another. I hope the "stand firm" investors will at least read the reasons, because there are times when switching makes sense for everybody. Here are the five:

1. Rarely, maybe once in a lifetime, a fund you own will go up so much that one day you realize that you have too large a percentage of your investment monies in one place. The prudent thing to do is to sell half, put enough money to pay the required taxes aside in a money market fund, and reinvest the remainder in a new venture. After a few weeks, or whenever you feel the time is right, more can be moved from the lucky fund as

needed to balance your portfolio. (I keep six funds, more or less, with equal amounts in each.)

2. Also rarely, and I hope never, you may find yourself at the opposite end of the spectrum, holding a fund that has gone down a substantial amount. Unless you are holding a specialty fund that is invested in a currently poor area, this will be after the market as a whole has declined. We have all done this with a stock, and after it has fallen too far we wonder whether the fall presages the end of the company, or whether the stock is just out of favor. Nobody knows, but this is one problem you don't have with a mutual fund. Holding maybe 100 different stocks, believe me, the fund will recover when the market does. And, with no-loads, you don't have to worry about incurring any commission to sell and buy back in. It usually makes sense to take the loss and have it available to use against another, more fortunate venture. If you will check the prospectives of several funds, you may buy into a fund that has accumulated as much in losses as the one you are leaving, so you will benefit by not having to pay any capital gains until those are used up.

There is a second point about the action of a stock that has gone down compared to a fund that has gone down. A stock that has progressively gone down from $8 to $7 to $6 and lower, had buyers at $8, $7, and $6. A number of these buyers have taken the vow, "If that thing every gets back up to what I paid for it, I'm out!" Thus there is great resistance to a rise after a fall, which is why a rise usually takes longer. This situation is not true with a mutual fund. It may well now be in new issues that have *never* sold at a higher price, and, as we have seen, distributions cloud the picture so that the share price is no indicator of performance. In short, there is no pronounced resistance to recovery.

Finally, when the market does recover, you will want to be in a volatile fund to gain the maximum rise. Once again, a decline in the price of a fund share does not mean that the management has goofed as often as it means that the market as a whole has gone down. It is not at all like the fall of an individual stock.

3. Most of us have decided to wait a while after the indicators and the advisory service we follow suggest a switch to a money market fund, and most of the time we wish later that we had heeded the signals. I have no argument with, say, moving half out, and completing the move if the downtrend continues. But when a system with a good record or an advisory service of similar ilk says to get out, I suggest you move at least part. Remember, it takes a 100 percent rise to overcome a 50 percent drop.

4.   I suspect that most of the switching between stock funds is simply due to investors noticing that one or two of the funds they hold are not doing as well as the others. This can occur in any kind of a market. The big question is, "For what period have they not done as well?" I use three months; any fund I own that has lagged for three months—not gone up as much as the others in an up market, or gone down more in a poor market—gets a hard look from me. Remember, though, that if you have a profit there will be capital gains taxes to pay, and you will have less money to put into the new fund than you had in the old. I would not let this be a big item. When a fund becomes a laggard for any of a number of reasons, I suggest switching.

5.   I hope you will pay attention to this one because the situation I am about to bring up occurs frequently and I have been bitten several times by just not staying alert. Here it is: Suppose you make a substantial investment in a fund and in a few months it is still at about the same price *and* it announces a substantial distribution to be made, say January 5. By all means, sell the fund January 3 or 4, and if you wish, buy it back a few days later, or pick another fund. There is no reason for you to be stuck with a substantial tax bill for which you get no benefits at all. Distributions can be as high as 30 percent of the total assets, and 20 percent is not at all rare. Don't pay for something you never got. (If the price is now different than what you paid, consider the taxes when you make your decision.) A way to avoid unwanted taxes on a sudden distribution is to look at the fund's distribution record before you buy.

Don't switch just because a fund has gotten too large, and

particularly not if the cash flow is continuing. I remember when the Dreyfus Fund, a big winner in the sixties, got to $1 billion. "They'll never continue the cash flow," I predicted. They sold $1 billion worth the next year and did fine, but they slowed the year after. Selling $2 billion worth was just too much. And don't set a target profit as you might with a stock and get out when you hit the target.

You may of course make your switch by mail or by phone. If your fund does not have a telephone switch, don't forget to include a stock power with a guaranteed signature; keep several at home. If you use a telephone switch, don't be upset if the phone is busy. *Keep dialing.* Don't wait a few minutes; you just increase the odds that somebody else will get on the line. Be ready with the account number of both the account you are leaving and the one to which the money is to be moved, and both accounts, of course, must be in the same name. The transfer clerk doesn't know who you are—in fact if you give someone else the relevant account numbers they can do the switching. (This is how advisory services manage your money. It stays in your name.)

For any of these switches, remember two items: distributions and short- or long-term gains. The following applies if an expected distribution is large. If it is small, the extra effort isn't worth it:

1. If you have a *long-term* profit in a fund and a distribution is imminent, sell right away because some of the distribution will be taxed as income. You can make it all capital gains.

2. If you have a *short-term* profit in a fund and a distribution is imminent, hold if the market is steady or up. Part of the distribution will be capital gains. If the market is trending down, sell right away as the market move could easily overcome the small saving.

3. If you have a *long-term* loss, and a distribution is imminent, there is probably some small advantage to holding to get the distribution with part of it being fully taxed.

4.   If you have a *short-term* loss, sell before the distribution.

Now for the effects on your taxes:

1.   **If you have a profit in a fund,**   selling it and switching to another fund will involve paying taxes so that you will end up with less money invested in the new fund than you had in the old one. How much less depends on your profit and your tax rate. One bright spot is that federal capital gains taxes can't go over 20 percent of your profit, and that is much less than 20 percent of your whole investment. However, an investor usually thinks in terms of total investment rather than percentage of profit.

Table 4.2 has been prepared to show this effect. You can use this table to get an idea as to whether or not you can afford to switch. For instance, suppose you invested $100 in a fund and its current value is $140, a profit of 40 percent. The maximum you can owe on the profit (provided you owned the fund a full year or more) is 20 percent of $8, leaving $132 to be rein-

Table 4.2.   Percentage of Pre-sale Value Lost to Taxes by Making a Switch When a Profit is Taken

Profit (%)	Value Lost to Taxes[a] (%)	
	Long Term	Short Term
0	0	0
20	−3.3	−5.8
40	−5.7	−10.0
60	−7.5	−13.3
80	−8.9	−15.6
100	−10.0	−17.5
200	−13.4	−23.4
300	−15.0	−26.3

[a]Long-term data are figured on the maximum 20 percent tax; short-term, 35 percent.

vested. The $8 represents a loss of about 5.7 percent of the original $140.

The third column shows the loss incurred through switching should the gain be short term and your tax rate 35 percent. It is apparent that short-term switching can be very expensive. If you wish to withdraw short-term profits (for any reason), sell the most recent purchase, as this will permit the earlier purchases to become long-term soonest.

For either column, add 8.5 percent if the switch involves a commission fund. It will become apparent that the use of no-load funds opens up a whole new door for investing.

If you have a profit in a fund, you will only come out ahead if in the years to come the new fund makes up the costs of the switch by outperforming the old one. Conceivably you might have a loss in another investment that would balance out the gain made in the fund sale. In this case taxes could be avoided.

2.   **If you have a loss in a fund,**   well, darn it, it is the basic tenet of this book not to have a loss. Losses are bad. As I said earlier, it is a galling fact of simple arithmetic that after a fund (or stock) goes down 50 percent, it has to come up 100 percent to get even. See Table 4.3 for other loss ratios.

Refer to the section on timing (Section 4.5) to see how reducing losses most of the time turns big losses into gains. But if you have hung on while a fund went down you can

Table 4.3.   Gain Needed to Get Even After a Loss[a]

Loss (%)	Amount Left (%)	Gain Needed To Get Even (%)
0	100	0
10	90	11.1
20	80	25.0
30	70	42.9
40	60	66.7
50	50	100.0
100	0	No way

[a]Help from taxes is not included, nor are commissions.

always switch to another fund and save a part of your current taxes. You thus end up (through applying the tax dollars saved to the new purchase) *with more money in the new fund* than you had in the old one.

Suppose, for instance, you have invested $100 in a fund and its current value is $60. The potential loss is $40 so that if you sell you may deduct the whole $40 from your income, with a resulting saving dependent on whatever your income currently is. If your tax rate is 25 percent, then your saving is $10, and you will, by applying the tax saving to your investment, have $70 to invest.

The percentage saved is $10/$60 = 16.7 percent. Had your tax rate been more, you would have saved more. If less, you would have saved less or even lost money in the last case. (See Table 4.4.)

Unfortunately, there is a limit to how much tax loss you can take—$3000. The rest must be carried forward and used in later years. The only way a switch that makes an immediate saving could turn out to be a mistake would be if the fund sold subsequently had a better performance than the one bought.

The foregoing discussion makes no provision for the taxes levied by the various states. Some states treat capital gains as income, which of course is their right, but not very encouraging for business. A few, incomprehensibly, *treat a capital gains*

Table 4.4. Savings Gained Through Making a Switch When the Present Value of Your Shares Is Less Than Cost

Loss (%)	Percentage of Pre-sale Value Saved[a]	
	25 % Tax Rate	50 % Tax Rate
0	0	0
−20	+6.2	+12.5
−40	+16.7	+33.4
−60	+37.5	+75.0
−80	+100.0	+200.0

[a]No commission.

distribution as income if accepted in cash, but as a capital gain or not taxed if reinvested! A good, smart, six-year-old girl would surely instruct her fund to reinvest her distributions, and a day later (if she needed the money) ask them to redeem an equivalent number of shares.

Decisions for switching for all five of our different type investors will thus be governed by both market timing and whether they have a substantial profit, which makes it hard to sell and costs a lot in taxes, or whether they have a substantial loss, which makes it easy to sell and saves taxes. This brings out the true situation that a particular fund may not be simply classed as a buy or sell. One investor may have bought a fund at a different price than another, and a fund that is a hold for one may be a sell for another. And of course, the two may have different objectives.

Finally, let me make a point and a few enemies at the same time. Many fund salespeople point out how an investor can use *growth* funds to increase capital and later switch to *income* funds for the most income when the money is needed for retirement. This procedure is hard to support in real life. The switch incurs taxes, if the investment has been successful, and the income fund furnishes income mostly of a taxable type.

Again, the telephone switch is the easy way to do it, provided your fund has the privilege and you have signed up for it. A count shows that about half the money market and stock and bond funds have a telephone switch; about half will redeem by telephone (they send a check to your bank); and about 40 percent will take a telephone order provided you already have the account. Checking on the six funds I currently own, none have telephone switch to money market funds, three will take telephone orders if an account has been established, and four will redeem to my bank by phone. The three money markets I own will all switch to certain stock funds and all will make redemptions to my bank. None will take telephone orders. (I hope I haven't said somewhere in this book to buy only funds with a telephone switch privilege!) Table 4.5 has a list of fund groups you might call.

Table 4.5.   Fund Groups That Permit Telephone Switching

Babson Funds
2400 Pershing Road
Kansas City, MO 64108
1-800-821-5591

Dreyfus Funds
600 Madison Avenue
New York, NY 10022
1-800-223-5525

Fidelity funds
82 Devonshire Street
Boston, MA 02109
1-800-225-6190

Founders Funds
1300 First of Denver Plaza
Denver, CO 80202
1-800-525-2440

Lexington Funds
580 Sylvan Road
Englewood Cliffs, NJ 07630
1-800-526-4791

Price Funds
100 E. Prett Street
Baltimore, MD 21202
1-800-638-5660

Scudder Funds
345 Park Avenue
New York, NY 10154
1-800-225-2740

Stein Roe Funds
150 S. Wacker Drive
Chicago, IL 60606
1-800-621-0320

United Services Gold Shares
   Fund   .
P.O. Box 29467
San Antonio, TX 78229
1-800-531-5777

Value Line Funds
711 Third Avenue
New York, NY 10017
1-800-223-0818

Vanguard Funds
P.O. Box 876
Valley Forge, PA 19482
1-800-523-7025

How each type of investor should look at switching is covered in the relevant sections to follow.

4.5.   TIMING THE MARKET

A number of financial advisers have developed their own proprietary methods for estimating whether the market (it may be the Dow Jones industrial average or the S&P 500 average) is headed up or down. Some methods use financial data, and others are based on the movement of various indices. To a degree this is of interest to us, because when the main market indices go up, most mutual funds do too, and vice versa. However, it is of more interest to us to time the mutual funds we are invested in, as covered in the next section. For an example of how funds didn't follow the Dow Jones industrial average, we might look at 1977–1981. During this time the Dow Jones went from about 800 to 1,000 and in between. The American Stock Exchange average for the same period went from 150 to 350, and a lot of money was made in funds that were largely invested in these stocks.

Two long-term timing systems that are of interest to us in a general way are mentioned in *The Handbook for No-Load Fund Investors*, 1982 Edition (P.O. Box 283, Hastings-on-Hudson, NY 10706). The first is a very simple rule to be out of the market for the first two years of a president's term, and in the market for the last two. The rationale for this seemingly unrelated-to-anything method is that for the last two years the president spends like crazy to make things seem good so he can get reelected, whereas during the first two years he is battling the damage done during the previous two. A sad commentary on our political system, the success of this timing system has been confirmed by a number of studies reported in the above mentioned *Handbook*. The second, called the "elves" on the TV program "Wall Street Week" is far from being a joke. It is the arithmetic sum of ten indicators selected by Robert J. Nurock, President of Investor's Analysis, Inc., of Paoli, PA 19301. When five or more of these give an UP signal, a BUY is indicated; conversely a SELL is given when five (or more) give a down signal. The 10 indicators, above the level of this book which concerns no-load funds, are also discussed in the *Handbook*. The "elves" have a good longterm record, averaging less than one move per year.

A list of market timing services is given in Table 4.6. You might write each for information and get a few trial subscriptions. In summary, market timing is interesting but of only modest use to mutual fund owners. Since we have managers who work full time to determine which stocks are of growing

Table 4.6.   Some Advisory Services Known for Their Market Timing Advice

The Cabot Market Letter P.O. Box 1013 Salem, MA 01970	Market Logic 3471 N. Federal Highway Fort Lauderdale, FL 33306
Consensus of Insiders P.O. Box 10247 Fort Lauderdale, FL 33305	Professional Timing Service P.O. Box 7483 Missoula, MT 59807
Indicator Digest Palisade Park, NJ 07650	Zweig Forecast 747 Third Avenue New York, NY 10017
Lowrey's Market Trend Analysis 350 Royal Palm Way Palm Beach, FL 33480	
Master Indicator P.O. Box 3024 West Palm Beach, FL 33402	

companies, most of the time we will make money when the market is level. So let's move on to when to buy, sell, or change our investments in mutual funds.

4.6.   MANAGING AND TIMING A MUTUAL FUND PORTFOLIO

In Sections 4.7 through 4.14 we will consider how to select funds to buy according to how you feel about investing. The problem we have before us in this section is this: You own some mutual funds. You have some money to add to them. Is this the time? Or even more serious, are the funds headed down and is this the time to get out and put your money in money market funds? You could of course act on the advice of an action advisory service, particularly one with a hot line you can call to get the latest word. Or you can, if you prefer, do the timing yourself. At the very least you should have an idea of what the advisory service is doing to generate the advice being given out.

To give you a feeling for what we are talking about, look at Figure 4.5. It shows the wandering price of a mutual fund over a one-year span. The fund started the year at $9.20 a share and ended it at $11.25, and had we simply held it, our profit would have been a nice 22.2 percent. But had we paid some attention to the dashed line (whose origin will be a mystery for now) and sold when the fund price dropped below our guideline and bought when it moved above the guideline *and* the guideline was rising, we would have made 55.6 percent. Now some of you readers are not interested in this, but some are. And all should know something about how timing is done; or better yet, several ways to do it.

To start with, one advantage that mutual funds have, and I have never heard this discussed before, is that they are amenable to timing techniques. The smoothing caused by owning, say, 100 stocks makes for a smooth curve compared to individual stocks that jump all over the chart and are too volatile to handle. Thus, timing our sales and purchases is possible. And note that good predictions are more useful to us as small investors than they are to a fund manager. This comes about because we can take our money out of the market for a week or month or whatever, but a fund owns such huge quantities of each stock that rapid switching isn't feasible. This leads to the intriguing conclusion that, again as small investors, we can do better than the funds we own!

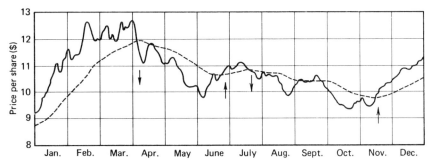

Figure 4.5. Illustration of using a 40-day exponential moving average for one particular fund in 1976. The share price of the fund is shown solid; the EMA-40, dashed. Sell signals are down arrows, buy signals are up arrows.

Here are two simple timing systems:

1.   The double-percentage system. Here is how you combine a fund investment with a money market fund so that you will *always* be out during a severe market drop.

a.   Note the price of the fund on the first day of each month.
b.   If the fund's price has gone down by, say, 1 percent, redeem 2 percent of your shares and put the money in a money market fund. If the price has gone up 1 percent, figure how much 2 percent of your portfolio will cost and move that amount from your money market fund to your stock fund.

A little thought will reveal that you will be easing out as a downtrend continues, and moving in when the trend is up. I know of fund managers who use the double-percentage approach to move their fund into cash or back into stocks. It works, but for individuals managing mutual funds it generates a ghastly number of trades and endless paperwork for taxes. On the other hand, there are no decisions to make; the system is completely mechanical. Table 4.7 presents the value of an account managed for 11 years by the double-percentage system. Note that it stayed above its starting amount (actually, not shown in the table, at one time it was a few dollars below) as measured at the end of each year while the unmanaged account dropped from $12,000 to $7,220. The end results are very close, but there never was the risk of a large loss had a sale been required for some extraneous reason.

2.   Moving averages.   A moving average is a curve-plotting technique that may be used to smooth the price curve of a mutual fund into a series of hills and valleys. This technique often tells the way the price of a share is trending and may be used either to get in or to get out, or simply to hold back new money when the trend is down. I use moving averages and they have greatly helped my investment success.

First of all, what is a moving average? An average is the sum of several values divided by the number of items. Gasoline at

Table 4.7.   Comparison of an Unmanaged Mathers Fund
Account and an Account Managed by the
Double-Percentage Method[a]

| | Number of Shares | | Total Value | |
Date	Double Percentage	Unmanaged	Double Percentage	Unmanaged
1/1/71	1000	1000	$12,000	$12,000
1/1/72	969	1016	14,671	14,945
1/1/73	850	1038	15,927	16,662
1/1/74	296	1118	12,615	10,419
1/1/75	211	1146	13,203	7,220
1/1/76	307	1211	15,269	11,480
1/1/77	425	1251	18,398	16,738
1/1/78	490	1282	20,947	19,111
1/1/79	597	1345	21,915	20,175
1/1/80	1321	1576	28,714	30,259
1/1/81	1550	1644	40,366	42,794
1/1/82	1054	1780	34,961	36,490

[a]The increase in the number of shares in the unmanaged account is due to reinvested distributions. The value of the double-percent account includes money in a money market account.

$1.00, $1.10, and $1.20 totals $3.30, the sum of all three prices. Divided by 3, the average price is $1.10 a gallon. The average of a fund's price for 10 days would be the sum of 10 days' prices divided by 10. What's a *moving* average? Well, today you take today's closing price and that of the last 9 days, add them all up and divide by 10, and plot that point for today. Tomorrow, you use tomorrow's closing price and that of the previous 9 days, and plot that point at tomorrow's date. These points generate the moving average curve.

Now, had the stock or fund been rising steadily for the past 10 days, the previous prices would all be *below* today's price, and their average—say the fund sold at $20 today—would be a number less than $20. Similarly, had the fund been falling for the past 10 days, today's moving average point would surely be *above* today's price. Thus when the moving average curve changes direction, a change of trend is indicated, and if the fund is headed down, one gets out. When the trend changes again, one gets back in. It is the nature of the moving average curve that a change in trend is usually accompanied by the price curve piercing the moving average curve. If the moving average curve and the price curve stay level, stay in if you're in. Stay out if you're out.

Let's interrupt our discussion of constructing moving average curves by looking at Figure 4.5, and I apologize that the figure does not have a vertical log scale that I have said is a necessity. It is, but it so happens that the year 1976 makes a particularly good year for an example, and the original data have been destroyed and the figure can't be redrawn. So be it, the plot still does nicely, and what you learn may encourage you to go to the trouble to make them for your funds. Figure 4.5 shows the price movement of Fund A (a real fund), along with a 40-day exponential moving average (explained subsequently), shown dashed. The year 1976 was selected because for this fund it tells us just about all we need to know to make use of the moving average technique.

We start the year invested because the price curve is above the rising moving average curve, a buy situation. On April 8, the share price crashed through the 40-day moving average as it bends over, indicating a sell. We get out, and shortly our money is in a money market fund at a good rate of interest. The share price stays below a falling moving average until mid-June, when it rises above a downward sloping average. This is more an *alert*, rather than a real buy signal. But about 10 days later the price does rise above a now rising moving average and a buy is indicated. The "being invested" signal is short lived because the moving average turns over and is pierced in late July for a sell signal. There is a "maybe buy" signal generated in late September, but the moving average is level, and we choose not to buy. A clear buy is generated in mid-November, and we are still in at the close of the year.

Since this fund went up in 1976 from $9.20 to $11.25, had we held firm, we would have made 22.2 percent. Not bad, but

Table 4.8.   Results of Making the Moves Shown by Arrows in Figure 4.5

In Fund A, 1/1/76 to 4/8/76	+32.3%
In Money Market fund, 4/12 to 6/30	+1.6%
In Fund A, 6/25 to 7/20	−0.7%
In money market fund, 7/26 to 11/15	+2.6%
In Fund A, 11/16 to 1/1/77	+13.6%

let's refer to Table 4.8 to see how we fared using the 40-day exponential moving average (EMA) to get in and out.

Multiplying the percentages in Table 4.8 as $1.323 \times 1.016 \times 0.993 \times 1.026 \times 1.136$, we get 1.556 or a profit of 55.6 percent against 22.2 percent had we just held. Even though holding firm for this year and this fund made a 22.2 percent long-term capital gain, 55.6 percent gives a lot more after-tax money. This isn't necessarily so. If both made, say, 10 percent, the hold fast long-term capital gains would have been better than 10 percent fully taxed. That's the tough part about market timing. Very often it results in short-term gains. The selection of a system that doesn't move you out more than every 13 months would be a great boon to investors, but the market isn't that nice to us. The losses you occasionally get from being whiplashed (taken out at one price and put back in at a higher price) plus those that arise from higher taxes are the insurance you pay for not being in during a long slide.

In the foregoing I used the trending up or down of the 40-day EMA as our buy or sell indicator. It is amazing how difficult the rule is to apply. It is very natural to see what you want to see and wait too long to make a move. A good way around this indecision is to add a column to your EMA calculation table for "Price/EMA" and buy when it exceeds 1.05 and sell when it drops to 0.95. Now you have a numerical target and won't have to agonize over minute changes in slope. After a year or so of plotting a particular fund, you may want to change your targets to, say, 1.06 and 0.94, or 1.04 and 0.96.

We could have used a slower moving average and maybe made one less move, and possibly with a "tighter" moving average, made more moves. The big, big point is that we were never exposed to a large loss. This is vital. Using EMA's for other years you may make more, or more probably less, but you never ever will sit by and see your investment money drop to 25 percent of what you started with. Moving averages are tremendously powerful tools. So now let's see how all this is done with the minimum effort. First, some observations:

1. A 10-day moving average is too close to normal market aberrations and would have us moving in and out at a frantic rate. I recommend 20-, 40-, or 100-day averages.
2. The 20-, 40-, or 100-day moving averages can't be started until you have collected the price data for the past 20, 40, or 100 days, a nuisance for sure.
3. The simple moving average gives equal weight to data for 100 days ago and for yesterday. It would be nice to give a little more weight to the most recent data.

The answer, is to use exponential moving averages rather than simple moving averages. They are far easier to compute and you don't have to know anything about exponents to use them. To give them a name, since they approximate simple moving averages, we call them by the number of days simple moving average they simulate. Here are the formulas for computing exponential moving averages:

1. 20-day EMA = 0.9 × yesterday's EMA + 0.1 × today's price.
2. 40-day EMA = 0.95 × yesterday's EMA + 0.05 × today's price.
3. 100-day EMA = 0.98 × yesterday's EMA + 0.02 × today's price.

Where do we get yesterday's exponential moving average so that we can get started? Simple—just start with yesterday's price. In a few days you will see the EMA move out above the

Table 4.9.   Table for Starting and Continuing Computations of an EMA (in dollars)

Date (1)	Price (2)	YEMA[a] (3)	0.95 YEMA[a] (4)	0.05 Price (5)	EMA (6)
1/29	14.22	—	—	—	14.22
2/1	13.85	14.22	13.51	0.69	14.20
2/2	13.97	14.20	13.49	0.70	14.19
2/3	13.75	14.19	13.48	0.69	14.17
2/4	13.69	14.17	13.46	0.68	14.14
2/5	13.84	14.14	13.43	0.69	14.12
2/8	13.28	14.12	13.41	0.66	14.13
2/9	12.92	14.13	13.42	0.65	14.07
2/10	13.19	14.07	13.37	0.66	14.03

[a]Yesterday's exponential moving average.

price curve if the price is falling, or ride along underneath it if the price is rising.

Table 4.9 and Figure 4.6 illustrate how this works. In Table 4.9 column 1 is simply the date. Column 2 is the price per share as published in the newspaper for the date shown. Column 3 is yesterday's exponential moving average, left blank for the

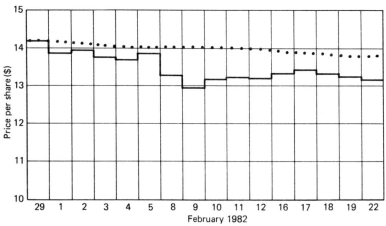

Figure 4.6.   Starting an exponential moving average.

first day because we don't have yesterday's data. Column 4 is 95 percent of yesterday's moving average, also blank for the first day. Column 5, 5 percent of today's price, is blank because it is not yet needed. Column 6 is yesterday's exponential moving average, which we hypothesize is the same as today's price, realizing that it will take a couple of weeks to get everything on track. The rest of the calculations may be simply checked out. They are shown plotted in Figure 4.6, where it is seen that a downtrend is in force. Money should not be added at this time. When you make your actual plot, just use one space for each day. I made the spaces wider than needed in Figure 4.6 so you could see the dates and how Saturdays, Sundays, and holidays are left out.

You can get an insight into how the EMA works by considering a simple 100-day moving average. For this you take the last 100 prices and divide the sum by 100, making the most recent data contribute 1/100 or 1 percent of the total. The EMA for 100 days, as we see from equation 3 above, uses 2 percent of today's price. Thus it gives the most recent data added weight.

Now I suggest you refer to Figure 4.5. Look at the movement of the curves, but do this one important thing: cover the *right* side of the plot as you consider it, all the way back to the day you are looking at. This is how it is in the real world—you don't have a full-year plot, only a plot up to yesterday. Moves that look obvious when you have a view into the future are real brain squeezers when you don't have that advantage, and there is money on the line. There *is* a way to apply a little foresight: If the fund price is close to the EMA and the market is down today, in all probability it will pierce tomorrow if the market continues down. Then if the market opens down tomorrow, call in a sell. You will be getting out before the home office computes the fund price!

The preceding paragraphs make timing funds sound easier than it really is. Let's look at a real case (Figure 4.7). In September 1979 the 20th Century Growth Fund was rising nicely above its 40-day exponential moving average, hitting a new high of $7.99 on October 5. That was a Friday. On Monday October 8 it dropped to $7.84, no cause for alarm. On October

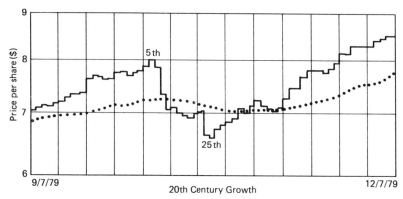

Figure 4.7.   Timing problems.

9 the market made a substantial drop and the price of 20th Century Growth fell to $7.33, close to its 40-day EMA. It crashed through by going to $7.05 on Wednesday. Now the $7.05 price didn't actually show in the newspapers until the next day, Thursday, October 11, which those who plot their funds daily would plot that night.* If the fund had a telephone switch (20th Century does not), one might have gotten out on Friday at $7.12—more likely the following Monday at $6.95, or maybe by mail Tuesday, October 16, at $6.94. By October 23, 20th Century was down to $6.51 and our market timers were pretty happy. Then the fund started back up, and on Friday, November 2, it was up to $7.23, above a level 40-day EMA. One could buy back in there, or more likely wait for the price to be above a *rising* slope. This occurred Friday, November 9 at $7.29, or Monday November 12 at $7.48. Selling at, say, $6.95 and buying back at $7.29 is a loss of 4.9 percent of the shares; at $7.48 the loss would be 7.1 percent, and two days after that, buying in at $7.68 would be a 10.6 percent loss. It takes only a couple of these small oscillations to wipe out a year's profit. Go through the exercise again. It cost me a lot of money to learn. What's the answer? After you have-plotted a fund for a year or more, you get a pretty good feel for the size of oscillations that can be

*People who live in small towns may be a day later on all this if their paper doesn't carry mutual funds.

ignored, and so you ignore them and are wrong now and then. Going to a 20-day EMA would have been a big help for this particular oscillation, but it would have gotten you into a bunch of smaller ones. But bear in mind that had the fund price continued down, the market timers would be out and very happy. In a nutshell, you have to work at making the most money in no-load funds, or, I guess, anything else.

I know that some of you have no desire at all to spend the time to plot your funds on a daily basis, and admittedly it is a drudge in a falling market. Plotting is a decision each person must make on his or her own. If you do decide to give it a try, let me make the point that plots are almost useless unless they are made using semilog scales, and unless all of the funds you are interested in are plotted to the same scale. If you don't have the time, or the inclination, there are a number of money managers who will do this for you. Usually they charge 2 percent of the total per year.

Now would be a good time to go back and reread Section 4.4 on telephone switch. It's a big help when you are using moving averages.

There is no law that says when you move in and out you must move the total you have in the fund. I frequently move half, and wait a while to see how things are going before I move the other half. When you do move half, do a little thinking first. If one half is six months old and the other is nine months, it might make sense to sell the six months half first because maybe the nine months part will be a year old before you want to sell it, and there's quite a savings in capital gains taxes. Also make sure you know whether the fund has a 1 or 2 percent fee for early redemptions. You might be able to avoid it.

We have just seen how using moving averages can result in a loss, albeit in this case a small one. The important thing is not to be in during a long slide. As I say elsewhere, after a fund drops 50 percent, it has to rise 100 percent to get even.

There are just about as many timing predictions as there are advisory services. For the really aggressive investor, nothing beats the daily decisions of your own charts using a 40-

day exponential moving average. For a slower but quite reliable indicator as to which way the general market is trending, I like the Cabot Market Letter and Switch Fund Advisory. Market Logic is also fine for long-term trends.

Keeping charts can be quite a chore, although 15 minutes a day is sufficient for a half-dozen funds. As mentioned earlier, semilog chart paper is a necessity. I use Dietzgen 340-L110 or Tekniplat R-78. Charting individual stocks is not too difficult, other than the nuisance of changing the fractions to decimals, but charting mutual funds over the long haul is a problem indeed. Each time the fund declares a distribution, its price drops and all of a sudden there is a break in the curve. The right way to treat this is to have the scales on a piece of transparent paper and simply shift the scale to match up with the new fund share value. I don't go this route. If the distribution is, say, $2 I drop the price of the fund to its new and proper value, and drop the moving average the same amount. (This is argument for using exponential moving averages rather than arithmetic moving averages, which would require changing the earlier values in the computation.) Usually I run the new curves back a couple of weeks so I can see trends better, but that's it. Of course you *can't* go to some tables and use a predistribution share price for any sort of a study.

It wouldn't hurt to reiterate that mutual funds move smoothly enough that trend watching is very helpful, and that the decisions are worthless if you have to pay commissions to get in and out.

I'm afraid there's no such thing as taking a vacation from your charts if you are serious about obeying their signals, and I take mine along wherever I go, along with a pocket computer. (Few of us note that the computations described in the preceding paragraphs could not have been done 15 years ago, when slide rules were all we had to work with.)

And now we come to something very, very important. In Section 1.7 I "proved" that funds, through their wide diversification, beat individual investors, and in Chapter 2 I pointed out that some funds get an extra advantage through a large cash flow. This section, through pointing out that aggressive individuals can beat funds through market timing techniques not available to fund managers, is a real clincher. *Moving in and out of no-load funds has many advantages over other ways of investing in the stock market.*

In recent years the procedures for implementing timing have been greatly enhanced through the advent of the money market funds, described in Section 1.13, item 16. A number of these have made arrangements with specific no-load mutual funds (or are part of their family) so that it is possible to switch either way by a telephone call using a free 800 number. The transaction to get out is made the same day as the call if it is early in the morning, and the new purchase is made the next day. This replaces writing a letter, getting a stock power at your bank if you don't have a few in your desk, mailing the letter, waiting seven days or more to receive your redemption check (if you are moving out of the market) and then putting the money in a money market fund. Moving back in is almost as bad—the total in-out move takes close to two weeks, including mail time. The switch funds are obviously a tremendous help.

A number of funds that do not have a telephone switch with a money market fund *do* have a telephone redemption to your bank account, usually a 48-hour service. This is almost as good as a telephone switch, as you can order money sent to your bank and then use it to buy another fund in a total of three days.

An ominous note, which may greatly reduce the benefits of the telephone switch, was the 1982 announcement by a few funds that, though they would accept a telephone sell and execute it the same day, they would wait the allowable seven days to make the accompanying buy. Although this is acceptable for getting out of the stock portfolio, it is by no means acceptable if the move is *to* the stock portfolio. Also some funds limit the shareholder to four switches a year with a $50 charge for the fifth switch and $40 from then on. We will have to wait and see if these unfortunate changes become the general mode of the no-load fund market.

4.7. SELECTING FUNDS FROM CHARTS

In the sections that follow this one we will look at tabular methods of selecting funds to buy for the various types of investors. In this section, I'll present a system that is very useful for all types of funds—aggressive, growth, balanced, or whatever. It is a chart method suitable for use with the charts in *Growth Fund Guide* (Yreka, CA 96097) or other charts that cover several years and are also plotted to log scales. Here is the philosophy: Some funds go up the most in a bull market and they are usually among those that go down the most in a bear market. But this doesn't always happen. Some funds go up the same as others but go down *more* when the market goes down, and some even go up less and go down more, and we certainly don't need to invest in these. You can tell a lot from just looking at charts, but here is a more graphic way to see performance, at least for me:

1. Draw a horizontal line on a piece of paper.
2. Using a scale or a pair of dividers, measure the growth of the fund you are considering for any particular period, say three years, and plot it as a vertical line above the horizontal one.
3. Measure the largest decline during the period and plot it as a continuation of the growth line, but below the horizontal line.
4. Do the same for a number of funds.
5. Select the funds that went up the most and down the least.

Figure 4.8 shows the ups and downs for four funds. Once again, the ups are for a three-year period, and the downs are the largest dip they made during that period. As we can see, Fund A went up more than B, which went down more than A. We surely don't want Fund B. Funds C and D offer a fielder's choice. D is more conservative than C, and if you don't mind the wider oscillations, then buy C for the greater gain.

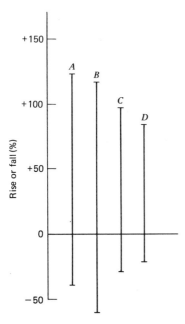

Figure 4.8.   Comparing volatility and gain.

The comparison of profitability and risk (or volatility) is a valuable tool, provided you have the charts to obtain the needed data.

4.8. SELECTING FUNDS TO BUY AND MANAGE FOR BEGINNERS

It has been almost 40 years since I first walked into a broker's office and bought my first stock, and I can still remember the feeling of awe and "Who needs me?" I chanced on a fine fellow who became my friend, later became the top man in the firm, and finally retired. For years I bought and sold stocks. Finally I learned about mutual funds. They beat my stocks even including the 8.5 percent commission, as I will describe elsewhere. And then I learned about no-load funds—you might say the hard way. There wasn't any book about investing in no-load funds written by a man who didn't sell anything or have an axe to grind, and no place to look for help. I hope this book fills the gap, *especially* for beginners.

As a beginner, here's what I would like you to do. Read this book through all the way to get a flavor for investing. Next ask around work and locate a couple of no-load buffs and ask if you can join their advisory service group. If there isn't one, write the services listed in this book and get some free copies and show them around and organize a group. Next, make up a table of growth funds such as Table 4.11 and select one whose performance you like and whose starting payment isn't too large. Or, if you wish, and the group takes a timing service, select a fund with a money market fund partner. If you have to, borrow the starting payment from your credit union. If you do, don't make any more payments to the fund until the debt is paid off. Adopt a philosophy that each month you will put off buying something you want, and buy it 30 days later and use the money held back for your fund. Or, once the credit union is paid off, leave the plan in force and use the payment for your fund.

As soon as you have enough accumulated, split your money and use two funds, putting new payments into the one that did the best last month. Take a second look at Section 1.24 and Appendix B to inspire yourself to stick with your investment plan. The time to get started is now.

4.9. SELECTING FUNDS TO BUY AND MANAGE FOR AGGRESSIVE GROWTH

The aggressive investor endeavors to make the most money he possibly can through market timing and, when he is in the market, being in the most aggressive funds, which he constantly upgrades. When he is out, his money is in a market market fund. Being able to get out is an advantage for us little investors. Although funds can lighten up over several months, we can get out today. Table 4.10 lists the essential data on a number of very, very good aggressive funds. Every time I put together a table like this it boggles my mind. Imagine owning 100 stocks that go up an average of 50 percent in a year! How do they do it? Well, you start with a good manager, who gets a good staff and good computers and a good cash flow. And some people want to compete with that by buying individual stocks? Unbelievable.

So let's suppose we have some money to invest, and we have elected to buy aggressive growth funds.

Let's take a minute to remember what a table of data tells us and what it doesn't tell us:

1. Again, the table is for no-load funds. Had you bought load funds during any particular year, the 8.5 percent commission would come out of that year's gain. This point is never shown in tables comparing funds of both types.

2. The movement shown is the difference between the start and the close of the year. If the net is a +23 percent, that says nothing about how high it might have gone at one point, or how low it might have gone. A drop of −15 percent might hide a −35 percent maximum drop sometime during the year.

3. If you want to know the total rise for several years, don't add the percentages. That won't work. You treat them as decimals, add 1.0, multiply, and subtract 100 percent to get the gain. See Section 1.14. The average profit of all seven aggressive growth funds for the first (rising) four years in Table 4.10 was a sparkling 253 percent; when you include the last two "bad" years, the average profit drops to 183 percent. You'll be fascinated when we compare that performance with that of the growth funds in the next few pages.

The selection procedure requires 11 steps, which are given here. You will do well by doing the extra work required.

Step 1.   The first step before putting any money (or any *more* money) into funds is to determine if this is a time

Table 4.10. Percent Profit Made by Aggressive No-Load Funds

Fund	Total Assets ($ millions)	1977	1978	1979	1980	1981	1982 estimated	October 1, 1982		
								Last month	Last 3 months	Last 6 months
AG-1	32.0	−3.6	+21.6	+76.8	+74.5	−17.4	−18.4	+3.6	+9.6	+3.5
AG-2	101.0	+25.1	+38.0	+46.3	+47.5	−1.8	−1.4	−1.4	+2.7	+11.5
AG-3	135.0	+16.5	+33.0	+71.4	+36.4	−24.0	−18.4	+3.1	+4.1	+1.7
AG-4	28.0	+23.7	+15.6	+35.6	+21.7	+0.7	+3.8	+4.6	+13.2	+13.4
AG-5	277.0	+13.8	+47.4	+74.5	+73.3	−5.6	−11.5	+3.3	+11.1	+9.7
AG-6	363.0	−4.0	+12.0	+60.0	+52.0	−15.7	−12.9	+0.6	+6.4	+4.5
AG-7	39.0	+18.7	+26.7	+50.3	+65.5	−12.2	+1.6	+4.2	+14.4	+17.6
Average		+12.9	+27.8	+59.3	+53.6	−12.0	−8.2	+2.6	+8.8	+8.8

to be in or out. This we learn from our *market* timing service or our regular advisory service, or the price location of the fund we plan to buy relative to its moving average line. If the signal is buy, proceed with the following steps. If not, leave the money in a money market fund.

Step 2.   Check the items in Section 4.1.

Step 3.   Find a service or use data from various sources such that a table of aggressive growth no-load funds can be constructed for a few years back and for the last month, three months, and six months, as is shown in Table 4.10. It wouldn't hurt to code each fund (I have called them AG-1, AG-2, etc.) so that your comparisons are more objective. Use the table and your own judgment to decide which time periods are the most important. Your choice is really not vital, as by buying several *of the best* for whatever periods chosen you will end up with an excellent average.

Step 4.   Running down the total assets column, we arbitrarily drop out funds AG-5 and AG-6 as being too large. A limit of $200 million is probably about right for starting in a new fund. There is no reason to dump a fund because it grows over $200 million unless its performance goes down, but I wouldn't start in one that big. I prefer to "test" funds below $50 million when I start in one.

Step 5.   Is the present price of each fund satisfactory chartwise? This requirement means you have to have an advisory service that keeps up plots for you, along with a moving average. We have already hypothesized that the market is moving up, or we wouldn't be studying funds to buy. The chart comparison really compares each potential buy against the market timing system.

Step 6.   Are any of the potential buy funds too risky? Some funds are only invested in a half-dozen or so stocks, and some are too heavy in the over-the-counter smaller companies for me. This might be fine with you. For some numbers to look at, I don't touch a fund that has more than 10 percent of its assets in one stock, or more than 30 percent in any four.

Step 7. Is the fund on margin? Many funds have the right to go on margin, to borrow money on the stocks they hold in order to buy more. When one of the funds you own does this, watch it like a hawk and sell in a week if it diverges downward from the others. Margin is a good way to make big money, and a way to lose big money.

Step 8. Do any of the funds have telephone switching arrangements? It turns out that AG-3, AG-4, and AG-6 do. However, all of the others have telephone bank wires, which will get you control of your redemption in about two days. We can settle for that.

Step 9. This is a special situation in funds, but if you are entering the market after a long decline, give special consideration to buying funds that have suffered the most, for two reasons: (1) they are the most volatile and should come up the fastest (one fund climbed 184 percent in 1975 after a drop of 81 percent in 1973–1974) and (2) they have accumulated a lot of tax credits from the losses taken.

Step 10. Review the group of potential buy funds and make sure that data are available on those you are serious about. This is an indirect way of saying "Is it large enough?" To be in the daily paper a fund must have 1,000 shareholders. Mutual funds average about $6,000 per account, so to be in the daily paper a fund must have total assets of about $12 million. Investing only in funds posted in the daily paper is a good practice.

Step 11. Buy the funds that most often surpass the average of the funds in the table. We have already selected very good funds; we'll invest in the best of the best. It so happens that AG-5 does the best and most continuous job of staying above the averages, but we have thrown it out as being too large. I would be inclined to buy AG-1 and AG-7. Maybe next month will turn up other outstanding aggressive funds.

It is, by the way, far easier to select aggressive growth funds to buy during a rising market than at the end of a declining market. At market bottoms the most aggressive of the aggressive growth funds will have gone down the most, and whether the managers have gotten their nerve back or have become timid about comitting vast sums of money is an unknown. There is no rush; wait and watch for a few months and place your money on those emerging as the best.

It might be instructive to close with what does not need to be looked at by aggressive investors. Don't spend time trying to rate the management; let the fund performance do this for you. And don't worry as to whether they are on an incentive plan or not. Such plans don't work. Don't worry if the fund has a 1 percent redemption fee. This is too small to be concerned about.

After buying some aggressive growth funds, the following actions on a continuing basis will make you money and keep you out of trouble:

Step 1.   Set up a plot, preferably on semilog paper to keep movements proportional, and plot the price of each of your funds on at least a weekly basis. You will notice that funds in general move together, some more and some less than others. If you don't like plots, make up a table. In either case clearly mark the date you bought so that you don't inadvertently sell a day or so before a year is up.

Step 2.   Glance at your timing service each time it comes in. *If you are invested,* and if it says buy, do nothing (or add money to the fund that has gone up the most in recent months). If it says sell, (1) check your funds to see if a one-year-date is near, and if so, hold that fund until then if you have a profit in it; (2) for those funds in a sell position, write them enclosing stock powers or use the telephone switch and request a halfway redemption. If the predicted movement takes place, sell the other half in, say, two weeks. If not, hang in there until the next timing letter. Then make a new judgment. *If you are out of the market* and the timing service says sell, do nothing except smile. If it says buy, bring your plots and tables up to date, make your selection, and send money to your favored funds, or, if you are in a switch fund, call them up and ask to be moved into the stock fund. A halfway move is good again here.

Step 3.   If the up-market signal continues for several months, and your personal tax situation is not unbearable, look over the performance of each fund and sell the poorest, and either add the proceeds to your best fund or make a start in a new one. If you take two timing services and there is a conflict on the recommendations, move partway or obey the no-move signal.

The satisfactory application of the above 11 "buy" points and 3 "manage" points is really not very difficult, nor is it time-consuming. You will find that most of the work has been done for you by your advisory service.

4.10. SELECTING FUNDS TO BUY AND MANAGE FOR LONG-TERM GROWTH

Long-term investors can do very, very well in no-load funds, provided they select the right funds; namely, those whose managers have shown skill in avoiding market drops. I have belabored you with arguments that fund managers can not get their portfolios out of the market, and they can't, overnight. But if you look long enough you can come up with a selection of drop-resistant funds, and their long-term performance really supports the argument that stocks that go down 50 percent have to go up 100 percent to get even.

Table 4.11 shows the yearly and monthly performance of seven funds that have shown good to excellent growth—less than the aggressive funds, but if you are not going to trade, you belong in growth funds such as these. Although the 178 percent rise during the four "up" years was not as good as the 253 percent rise for the aggressive growth funds, the drop during the two bad years gave the aggressive growth funds a total profit of 183 percent, but the growth funds, 226 percent!

Remember that this is for one group of aggressive growth funds and one group of growth funds for one six-year period in the market, but it is typical for a cycle covering a good and a bad market. In short, if you are going to trade funds and do some switching, you can make the most in aggressive funds. If you are not, then you will make the most in well-selected growth funds. I see no reason for either income funds (which deliver most of their distributions in fully taxed dividends) or balanced funds, which, as we saw in Figure 1.5, have barely kept up with inflation and are clearly behind money market funds as well. Years ago people argued to switch from aggressive funds to balanced funds and vice versa. I see no evidence that this is a sensible procedure.

Coming back to the growth funds, although only a few avoided the violent downtrends in 1973–1974 (Mutual Shares and Janus come to mind—there might have been others), a substantial number of growth funds have resisted the falling market from mid-1981 to mid-1982. These include Fidelity Magellan and Fidelity Equity Income Funds, Value Line Leveraged Growth, Lindner, Guardian, Mutual Shares, Nicholas, Sequoia, and Janus. The remarkable thing about this list is the entirely different ways employed to beat the falling markets. Some did increase their normal cash position, and others simply invested in vehicles that resisted the decline. Figure 4.9 shows how the Lindner Fund increased its cash position (largely by not investing its cash flow) from a high 31 to 52 percent as the Amex fell from 370 to 290, decreased it from 52 to 47 percent as the Amex rose to 330; and held above 45 percent cash as the indicator fell to 270. (The S&P 500 could have been used as well in the example.) This is market timing at its best.

Table 4.11. Percent Profit Made by Seven Growth Funds

Fund	Total Assets ($ millions)	1977	1978	1979	1980	1981	1982 Estimated	October 1, 1982		
								Last month	Last 3 months	Last 6 months
G-1	105.0	+17.9	+16.7	+50.4	+32.1	−7.3	−7.9	+1.6	+5.4	+5.7
G-2	37.0	−0.1	+7.7	+39.2	+39.4	−3.5	+12.1	+2.5	+16.8	+16.9
G-3	75.0	+29.9	+22.2	+28.0	+32.6	+34.6	+12.6	+2.3	+9.3	+12.6
G-4	58.0	+20.3	+25.3	+31.0	+35.0	+8.6	+12.4	+5.7	+18.9	+19.5
G-5	140.0	+15.6	+18.4	+43.0	+19.4	+8.7	−0.1	+2.8	+6.2	+6.3
G-6	39.0	+51.5	+27.6	+26.2	+29.5	+15.9	+16.9	+3.1	+13.3	+14.6
G-7	140.0	+14.5	+31.7	+51.7	+69.9	+16.5	+13.0	+4.0	+13.0	+19.3
Average		+21.3	+21.3	+38.5	+36.7	+10.1	+8.4	+3.1	+11.8	+13.6

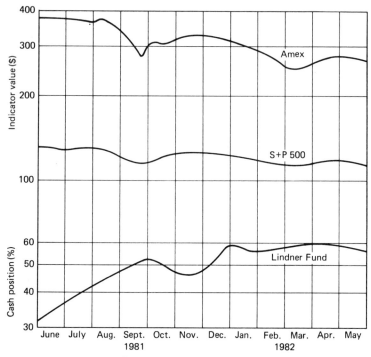

Figure 4.9.   Illustration of increasing cash position as market indices drop, for the Lindner Fund.

The point of avoiding market declines is not only the worry they cause, and the financial pain in the event that you have to sell to raise some needed money, but the enormous advantage the nondropping fund has during the next bull market through starting with a larger amount of money. Figure 4.10 has been constructed to show this and much much more. It compares the performance (all distributions reinvested) for a very aggressive growth fund (44 Wall Street); and a very well run growth fund (Mutual Shares) that meets my stringent definition of a growth fund, including resistance to market drops. Table 4.12 shows the yearly change in the per share value of both funds, and I defy you to get any nourishment from it. If you count the number of periods that one fund did better than the other, you will come out close to even. If you

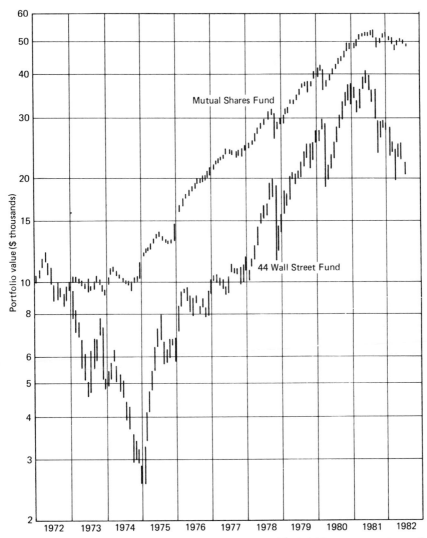

Figures 4.10. The subsequent monthly ranges of $10,000 investments made January 1, 1972, in the Mutual Shares Fund and the 44 Wall Street Fund.

Table 4.12. Performance of
44 Wall Street
and Mutual
Shares

Year	44 Wall Street (%)	Mutual Shares (%)
1972	−5.3	+0.5
1973	−36.8	−8.1
1974	−52.2	+8.1
1975	+184.1	+35.0
1976	+46.5	+55.2
1977	+16.5	+15.3
1978	+33.7	+18.1
1979	+73.4	+43.4
1980	+36.0	+19.7
1981	−24.6	+8.7
1982[a]	−21.6	−5.9

[a]Through July 1.

glance at the difference in percent in each period, you would guess that 44 Wall Street really beat Mutual Shares. In short, tables won't do the job as well as charts.

The figure must not be misinterpreted either. Although a $10,000 investment in Mutual Shares made on January 1, 1972, kept above a similar investment in 44 Wall Street for the following 10 years, you could have, with some not too difficult timing, made a lot more money in 44 Wall Street than in Mutual Shares. Admittedly, you would have been better off in Mutual Shares during the 1973–1974 decline, and much better off in 44 Wall Street during 1975 (+184 percent—a record!) and also through the bull market of 1976–1980. Let's put all this into a set of rules for comparing fund performance:

1. There is little to be learned by comparing the performance of funds from peaks to bottoms, or bottoms to

peaks. The conservative funds always win the first, and the aggressive growth funds always win the latter.

2. If you compare funds from peak to peak or bottom to bottom, you will be surprised at how small the difference is as measured by the compound growth rates.

3. The really big money is generated by being out of the market during declines, and in the aggressive growth funds during bull markets. Referring again to Figure 4.10, rather than ending up with, say, $20,000 to $50,000 for the 10-year period, reasonable timing in the 44 Wall Street Fund could have raised the initial $10,000 to close to $100,000. In short, the game is worth the candle.

4. And, of great importance, there is nothing in the world the matter with buying and holding or continuously buying into a growth fund that has good resistance to declines. The growth of Mutual Shares, for the time period shown, is a respectable 19 percent a year.

I hope the foregoing has not been too confusing. It just follows along the tenor of this book that well-selected growth funds are great investments, and you can do even better with aggressive growth funds as long as you do some timing. The rest of this chapter is devoted to helping you do all this.

Turning now to Table 4.11 to make our selections, we see the following steps are needed.

Step 1. Check your timing service and see if this is the time to put money into the market. If not, leave it in your money market funds. If it is, follow Steps 2–6.

Step 2. Check the items in Section 4.1.

Step 3. Find a service that lists a number of growth funds and their performance several years back, as well as for recent periods, and make up a table or use theirs— see Table 4.11.

Step 4. Looking over the size of the funds, none even approach our $200 million limit. (This "limit" is not as rigid for long-term growth funds as it is for aggressive growth funds.)

Step 5. Review all funds for cash flow and put a plus sign by those having the most.

Step 6. Glancing over the table, we notice that G-1 and G-2 have performance below the average of the group for 1977 and 1978, and they are not as drop resistant as the others, as shown by their performance in 1981 and 1982 (Estimated). Funds G-3, G-6, and G-7 look mighty nice for their profits in 1981, when the rest of the world went down. G-7 has a great record, right up there with the best of the aggressive funds, during the bull market years. I'd go for G-3, G-6, and G-7.

Continuing management includes the following steps:

Step 1. Glance at your timing service each month. If it says "buy", add new money to the fund in your portfolio that went up the most during the past month. If it says "long-term sell," redeem half of your investment from the two or three poorest performers and move it to a money market fund. If the trend continues down, continue to get out, but only if your funds continue down.

Step 2. If "long-term buy" continues, besides adding new money to the top performers, move some money from the poorest performers to the best, keeping an eye out for the one-year holding period.

One of the points that can be made from the two tables is that fund managers *can* achieve their aims in the sense that in a good market the aggressive growth funds do better, on the average, than do the growth funds.

4.11. SELECTING FUNDS TO BUY AND MANAGE FOR WITHDRAWAL-PLAN USERS

The withdrawal plan program is covered in Chapter 6. The general items covered in Section 4.1 also apply to withdrawal-plan users and that section should also be consulted.

Actually, I have had a great change of heart about the withdrawal plan. At first it seemed mighty nice to invest in a good conservative mutual fund and take the profits out via a withdrawal plan. To that end I used the Keogh plan of investing money earned directly—up to the limit—in just about the largest and most admired stability fund in the country. I paid into this fund from 1968 to 1977. When I retired, *I took out less money than I put in!* This was of course the period of the great slide in stock prices brought on by recession and endless government controls and regulations. But to have a continuous slide exceed the dividend intake for 10 straight years really got my attention. When you consider that the money should have at least doubled in the 10-year period, my net loss really stung. I would, therefore, stay out of stability funds and use growth funds, particularly as I have defined them as funds with good growth in bull markets and strong resistance to downtrends.

But, returning to the withdrawal plan, many funds charge a couple of dollars *per check*, and this works out to be a very large percentage of your income. You could reduce that by getting quarterly checks, or reduce it to zero by writing four times a year for a redemption. Since I am often moving my money to keep in the best performing funds, I just don't reinvest the total I move and use some for added living expenses. This may or may not suit you, but it sure works for me.

I also had a worrisome period when a fund salesman talked an elderly friend of mine into using that withdrawal plan with a 10 percent a year withdrawal, just when stocks started to slide in 1968. She was 75 at the time, and the rate wiped out the account. So think a lot about withdrawal plans after you have read Sections 6.1 through 6.5.

4.12. SELECTING FUNDS TO BUY AND MANAGE FOR PRESERVISTS

Preservists are investors who, for reasons of their own, place preservation of their capital above all. This really doesn't preserve buying power in an inflationary economy, but it makes sense for the very, very wealthy to whom income is secondary or just because somebody wants to. Until interest rates settle down and the bond market once again becomes a haven for capital preservation, preservists should most certainly invest in a selection of money market funds, and if they want to go the extra mile, pick those with a federal portfolio. I believe it would also be useful to subscribe to an advisory service that covers bond funds to make sure their yield is not moving too far away from the money markets, as bonds may someday.

4.13. SELECTING MONEY MARKET FUNDS

In view of the high safety of the money market funds, though they are not insured, I am satisfied to select those managed by the larger financial houses such as Dreyfus, Fidelity, and Value Line. The needed data—current yield and days to maturity— are given each Monday in the *Wall Street Journal* for about 150 money market funds, so the choice is adequate. Most funds have days to maturity of from 20 to 40, which is safe and keeps the yield close to market conditions. It would make sense to check the fund's safety ratings in either of the services mentioned in Section 1.13, item 16.

The following checklist will enable you to select a high yield and convenient fund:

1. High yield.
2. Low or no monthly charge.
3. Satisfactory starting amount (usually from $1,000 to $5,000).
4. Satisfactory small check limit (usually from $250 to $500).

5. Satisfactory minimum for additional investments (usually $100).
6. Telephone switch to bank available.
7. Telephone switch to mutual fund available.
8. No delay in reinvesting after switch.
9. No limit to number of switches per quarter.

As I said in Section 1.13, don't gloss over a couple of percent difference in yield. You might as well have the extra money.

If you are really concerned that the financial world is about to collapse, then put your money into the money market funds with federal portfolios. They are supersafe.

4.14.   SELECTING BOND FUNDS

There are, in my opinion, two reasons to buy bond funds:

1. You believe interest rates will come down and hence bond prices will go up. Your best chance to profit thereby is to be in high-grade, discounted bond funds. The no-load feature and the complete liquidity are very valuable.
2. You are in a very high tax bracket and lazy and want tax-free yields and somebody else to do the selecting for you. Any of a number of municipal bond funds would be suitable.

Refer to Section 1.13, item 15, for reasons *not* to buy bond funds.

5

<hr>

Behind the Scenes

In Chapter 1 we looked at mutual funds as entities. In this chapter we will see how they get started and the main subdivisions of fund operations:

1. The fund management corporation, with its president, board of directors, and staff.
2. The fund, with its own president, board of directors, and shareholders.
3. The custodian bank.
4. The watchdog SEC.

The management corporation and the fund itself often have common directors, but the custodian bank must, by law, be separate. The SEC has federal responsibility to see that the fund and the fund management corporation abide by the laws for mutual funds, or, as they call them, *regulated investment companies.*

5.1. STARTING A FUND

No-load funds arise from two different sources:

1. A broker or a financial adviser already managing a number of accounts wants to combine them into one

in order to simplify his work, be less subject to flak from his clients, and obtain more money on which he can earn a fee.

2.   The managers of a load fund sense that many people don't want to pay sales commissions and it would be advantageous to change to a no-load.

The motive for managing a fund is simple: money, big money. Should a fund succeed and grow to, say, $500 million in total assets, and should the management rate be one-half of 1 percent, the fee becomes $2.5 million a year. Should the market capitalize that at a P/E of 10, the management corporation shareholders will be worth $25 million.

Assuming that "our" fund is starting from scratch, the first step is to form a management corporation, and to locate people who will put up an aggregate of $100,000 or more, which is necessary to get the fund large enough to be licensed; some people, possibly out of the management group, to be the fund officers; and some people, not connected with the management group or the fund industry, to complete the fund board of directors. The last are known as "disinterested directors," not because they don't care, but because, not being on the payroll of the management corporation, they have a freer chance to represent the shareholders, which is what all of the fund directors are supposed to do. Application is then made to the SEC for licensing, and a fee of about $700 is paid. Typically, all this takes a lawyer (probably in Washington) to keep the paperwork moving and implement changes as requested by the SEC. After the fund has permission to go ahead, it must be licensed in each state in which it plans to sell shares. These licenses cost from $25 to $300 per state, sometimes depending on how many shares the fund expects to sell in the state; sometimes $50 a dealer plus $10 a broker. It is not unusual for some states to be arbitrarily excluded because they have regulations (such as not licensing funds whose managers can make more than 1 percent per year of the total assets) that the management group does not want to agree to. Some states require photographs and personal histories of the officers; some do not.

While this is going on, portfolio managers who will make the actual buy and sell decisions are being lined up, and a trader, the man who makes the deals, is hired. The portfolio managers receive a salary from the management corporation, sometimes with a bonus arrangement if they beat selected market averages. The trader will also be salaried, and he might get a bonus if his trades average better than the market. The sales of shares for no-load funds is done by the management group. They should be ready to go as soon as state licenses are received. This whole process may well take a year, and, depending on the situation, cost anywhere from $25,000 to $1 million.

The continuing money for all this—other than the starting expenses, which must be borne by the fund management corporation in the hope of recovering them later—will come from the management fees allotted to the management corporation, and certain other items that may be charged to the fund, meaning you as a shareholder. (These "others" might average about 1 percent per year.)

In the case of a load fund, an additional group composed of the distributors and its wholesalers must be set up. These will all be paid from the fraction of the sales commission kept by them.

A fund management corporation that desires to start a new fund in order to cover what is for it a new area or method of investing has of course an easier time than a beginner. They have been through the mill and possibly have lawyers skilled in the field. They may also have the finances to start up several funds and only go public with ones that have a fortuitous record.

How big is the market that the management corporations are looking at? There are some 30 million accounts at all the stockbrokers' offices, and some 6 million mutual fund accounts with about half of them in no-loads. How many investors this represents, nobody knows. A good guess would be about 10 million individuals. A larger number will be in the market one way or another, should our economy pick up.

5.2. *THE FUND MANAGEMENT CORPORATION*

The fund management corporation is responsible for the maintenance of the fund as an entity, for which it gets a fee, usually one-half of 1 percent of the total assets of the fund per year, paid monthly on the average total assets figured daily. Although duties and pay vary from fund to fund, in general the management corporation is responsible for the following:

1. Office space, and all office facilities, equipment, utilities, and supplies.
2. Supplying and paying the fund managers, who may be on salary from the management corporation or hired as an outside group.
3. Handling federal and state regulations including filing all necessary registrations.
4. Accounting services and bookkeeping, including preparation of financial statements and federal, state, and local tax returns.
5. Preparation and filing of the N-1R and N-1Q reports for the SEC or other agencies. These cover all the financial and personnel changes during the past year.
6. Preparing and distributing prospectuses, various sales material, reports and newsletters, quarterly reports, and miscellaneous other documents to shareholders.
7. Providing transfer services (this means the buying and selling of shares by shareholders).
8. Payments for auditors, bonding, and insurance as needed.
9. Paying salary of trader, if any.
10. Payment for computer.

The fund itself pays the following:

1. The fund management fee.
2. Registration fees.

3. Expenses for fund shareholders' meetings.
4. Fees for custodian bank and transfer agent if different.
5. Fees and travel expenses for the fund board of directors.
6. Interest and taxes.
7. Brokerage commissions and expenses.
8. Extraordinary expenses not included in the agreement with the management group.

This works out to about 1 percent of the total assets of the fund each year.

The management corporation's fee of about one-half percent of the total assets is the subject of much misunderstanding both as to rate and total amount. If you remember that the fee is taken out of the dividends before they are distributed, and if, you will recall, that dividends (less $100) are fully taxed, then you realize that you would pay part of the managers' fee *as taxes* if you received the money instead of them. Possibly you would save about 3/8 of 1 percent if the managers were free. You couldn't save the whole one-half percent because part of this money goes to the management corporation. As for the total amount, for small funds it clearly isn't enough. Until a fund reaches $50 million in total assets (fee $250,000 per year) the management fee probably doesn't pay the costs of a top adviser, staff, clerical staff, and the other expenses. As long as it doesn't, the fund management corporation must come up with the deficit each year, or be sold out to someone who can bring the operation into the black, or settle for part of a manager's time. When the fund reaches $1 billion (fee $5 million a year) the one-half percent per year is probably too high. Management groups that get in this enviable position frequently either voluntarily or under fire from the shareholders reduce their rates.

In a few instances, the fee may be adjusted according to how well the fund does relative to, say, the Dow Jones industrial average. This could result in fees well above one-half percent per year. Some states prohibit such incentive pay. California, for instance, has a law that if an arrangement exists such that the managers of a fund can ever make more than 1 percent of the total asset value of a fund per year, then California investors must buy at least $20,000 initially, or $10,000 if their portfolio is $100,000 or more including the proposed shares.

Both the management and the shareholders seek a larger fund; the management because it gets a percentage of the assets, and the shareholders because they benefit from the cash flow that makes the fund larger, and possibly a fee rate reduction as size increases.

5.3. THE PORTFOLIO MANAGER

The portfolio manager is the one who makes the day-by-day and hour-by-hour buy and sell decisions. The "manager" usually consists of a team of research and analysis people under a senior manager, and may be part of the fund management group, or entirely separate from it and manage the fund as a portion of their management of other funds or pension monies. A separate manager is preferred, as it is then easier to change managers if need be. If the manager owns the management corporation, it is just about impossible to make a change.

When a fund is successful, it is the manager who gets all the credit, although it is a basic tenet of this book that he is only super successful while he has a high percentage flow of new money. In the next few pages I am going to be very critical of managers, and this takes a lot of gall because many—probably most—are a lot richer than I. But this doesn't mean that a lot of us don't wonder what managers really accomplish. Let me use the words of Daniel Seligman in *Fortune* magazine (October 1970, page 169): "One thing nobody explains which seems in the end to be most in need of explanation is the continuing failure of Wall Street's professionals to demonstrate that they have any edge at all over dart throwers. In the wake of this elaborate new study, that failure may be taken as an established fact." The "new study" referred to was by the 20th Century Fund and a Merrill Lynch grant in 1970. If you will look up the *Fortune* reference you will believe even more that Chapter 2— the effect of cash flow—makes sense. And now on to managers.

Managers have two facets to their job: keeping track of seven housekeeping accounts, and making the buy and sell decisions. Here are the accounts:

1.   **Cash in hand account.**   This is the sum of the monies received from the sale of stocks and the sale of new shares less the cost of purchases of new stocks and the monies paid out to shareholders for the redemption of their shares. The net amount comes from the custodian bank shortly after the close of the market each day.

The cash account is a managed account. As soon as redemptions are closed out Friday afternoon the money is loaned out for the weekend or until it is needed. When the managers feel that the time is not right for investing in the market, it may be put into short-term paper or, more likely, a money market fund. A fund has seven days to pay for the stocks it buys, and smart managers earn a little extra interest by lending the allocated money until it is actually needed.

The size of the cash account varies according to whether the fund managers think the market is going up or down. An "up" market means a full or nearly full investment. A "down" market might justify a 15 to 50 percent cash reserve, if the manager is smart enough to so act.

2.   **Accumulated dividend account.**   This account records the sum of the dividends accumulated from the various stocks held by the fund. These monies are normally reinvested as received (less the amount used for managers' fees) and paid to shareholders once a year.

3.   **Accumulated short-term capital gain account.**   This is the sum of the profits minus the losses from stocks held less than 12 months, plus the net of profits and losses from any "short sales" (provided the fund is allowed to make them). These monies are also distributed to the shareholders once or twice a year; they in turn must report the money received as ordinary income. Funds in general try to avoid short-term gains to save their shareholders tax expense.

4.   **Accumulated long-term capital gains.**   This is the net of profits and losses from the sale of stocks held more than 12

months. This must be distributed to shareholders during the year they are accumulated in order for the fund to avoid paying income taxes itself.

5. **Office account.** This is the simple business expense account covering the housekeeping expenses. Shareholders should make it a point to visit the offices of their funds to see how things are being handled. Most fund offices are very busy places and hence not as cleaned up as a lot of other offices.

6. **A list of the stocks held.** This is not complicated, but must be kept up to date, including close track of stock splits and stock dividends. By law the stock splits may be kept, but the stock dividends must be sold and the money passed on to the shareholders.

7. **Reports to the SEC on all transactions made for the fund.** It used to be that the SEC was satisfied with the quarterly listing of the stocks held by the fund as listed in the reports sent to all shareholders. Recently a change was made and now *all* transactions must be reported. The manager must show that of all profits made by the fund, at least 90 percent were made in stocks held more than 90 days. The reports to the SEC are the most vexing of the manager's jobs.

As far as describing the portfolio manager's job, there is no such thing as a typical manager. All have their computers, favorite analysts, favorite sources, and sometimes favorite brokers. And all of the managers of active funds probably work as hard at their jobs as does anybody in the country. Besides the brain straining analysis, there are endless plant visits to be made and the worry that some unseen force will negate all the study in the world. A conservative manager will rely mostly on long-term data, earnings and the like. But an aggressive fund manager will trade wildly, sometimes trading a dollar value equal to four times the total assets of the fund each year, holding tight to the winners and trying others time and again. The maneuvers the manager can use that are not within the reach of the usual individual investor are wildcatting, buying letter stock, waiting for results before going public, help from big brother, bootstrapping, churning, and going on margin. Here's what these terms mean:

1. Wildcatting. The term *wildcatting* means buying stocks with large risks in the hope of large gains. During the bull market of the late 1970s new issues frequently pushed up in the first days of their lives and enormous profits in a few days were quite normal. Managers engaging in wildcatting are not *investing* in the proper sense of the word, but they sometimes make good profits. Another form of wildcatting consists of buying stocks in very small companies in the hope that some will "hit" and yield big profits. Wildcatting in new issues cannot be discovered by reading the quarterly reports because the new issues are usually held only a few days. Wildcatting with the smaller companies may be discovered by noting what percentage of a fund's portfolio consists of over-the-counter stocks. More than, say, 30 percent shows a high-risk portfolio.*

2. Investing in letter stock. Most corporations have unissued shares, either not distributed after a stock split, or authorized but never sold; or the shares may be privately held and never registered. To get those shares to market, the closed corporation must reveal a lot of information they might like to hold back. They also may face delays in getting SEC approval, and may have to pay an underwriter substantial fees. On the other hand, these unregistered shares may be sold directly to an investor provided he agrees in writing (hence the name *letter*) that he is buying the shares as an investment, and not merely using this route to avoid registration problems. To get the immediate cash for the stock the seller usually agrees to accept a price 25 percent or more below the current market price of the shares (if there is one) or an even larger discount if the corporation has never gone public. This gives the buyer an almost certain profit, and in order to make sure he will be able to sell his unregistered shares some day he usually demands a "letter" from the seller that the shares will be registered on some agreed-upon date.

Now let us tie this in to our mutual fund manager and suppose he has bought some shares that will be registered in two years, and that he has paid $20 a share for shares currently

---

*Bank and insurance stocks are sold over the counter but are often high quality. They're a special case.

selling at $30. How does he treat these shares when he lists them in his portfolio? He has all sorts of choices. They range from listing the shares at zero (which no manager would ever do) because the investment has no immediate market value, to showing an instant profit by listing the shares at $30. Most of the time the managers like to mark the shares up gradually, taking some pains to use the markup to make the fund show a profit on a down market day when most of the others are showing a loss. This gets a little free advertising. Now I do not propose to get into an argument about how a manager *should* treat letter stock; I'm simply pointing out that a phony profit may be hidden in his statistics. The SEC rules now prohibit a fund's holding more than 10 percent of its assets in restricted securities, so this is not a big point—it used to be a smasher for some funds. On the other hand, it is big enough that some shareholders have sued funds for "inflating" their worth, and thus redeeming the shares for others at amounts above their real value.

If you want to avoid all this, read the fund's prospectus and see whether it says, "We will not invest in letter stock or other restricted securities." Or write them; most fund managers are cured of letter stock.

3. **Waiting for results.**   Many fund buffs have noticed that some funds have a great record before they go public. A little thought will show that it is possible to start a number of funds, and then only go public on the best performers. This enables brokers to say, "This fund is up 15 percent so far this year," or such, and it then becomes much easier to sell shares. Have you ever been surprised that a new fund had such a nice record? Now you know.

4. **Help from big brother.**   Anytime a big fund (say $400 million) starts a new fund (say $200,000) it is possible for the big fund to buy the same stocks the little one buys, only later. Thus a 10 percent cash flow for the big one ($40 million a year) could really bolster earlier investments made by the small one. Nothing illegal or immoral about this; it just gives new funds in an old family an edge over others.

5.   Bootstrapping.   It is possible, as long as a good cash flow continues, to buy the shares of small corporations repeatedly and thus drive the price up—lift yourself by your bootstraps. This is an exceedingly risky procedure. It will be difficult to sell the shares without beating their price down as much as the continuous buying raised them up. Having a large percentage of a fund's portfolio in one or a few stocks defeats the principle of diversification and should be avoided by all but the most aggressive managers (and shareholders).

Bootstrapping is the single largest contributor to the fantastic profits of the high-cash-flow funds. Let's look at part of the portfolio of one as shown in Table 5.1. The process of "trying" a number of stocks that should go up, dumping those that don't, and plowing more money into those that do is standard for an aggressive manager, and usually quite successful. It can hardly hurt the performance of a stock to have customers buying it in 10,000-share lots. However, bootstrapping has led to serious declines in some mutual funds because of the "to whom" factor.

6.   Churning.   Churning is excessive buying and selling. If a fund sold a third of its stocks and bought something else in a year, this would be a turnover of 33 percent. This is about the average figure, although the range may be all the way from

Table 5.1.   Portfolio Changes of a Fund Having a Substantial Cash Flow

	Shares Held	
Corporation	12/31/79	12/31/81
Communications Industries	4,000	30,000
Kennington	15,300	30,400
Maryland Cup	12,500	41,300
Western Financial	3,900	39,000
MGIC	19,000	25,200
Acme United	12,466	46,232
Valleylab	8,500	20,200

zero to several hundred percent. The turnover does not concern itself with the number of different stocks sold. Holding 9 out of 10 and selling the last one 10 times gives a 100 percent turnover. There is no set number, but probably more than 100 percent turnover would be considered churning. Almost always, the more conservative the fund, the lower its turnover rate. Still further, a large turnover rate could mean that a not-so-honest manager was paying off a friendly broker.

7.   **Going on margin.**   A fund manager is under no obligation to keep all of the monies in the fund, fully invested in the stock market. Typically he holds out a few percent to pay any redemptions without having to sell some stock to raise cash at what might be a poor time. One would hope he would be fully invested when the market is going up, and much less than fully invested when the market is headed down. This is a facet of timing, and more is said on the subject in Section 4.5.

A manager can do much more than simply maneuver his cash balance. He may take some of the certificates in the portfolio to a bank or to a broker and borrow some fraction of their value (the maximum fraction is set by the Federal Reserve Board), which he then uses to buy more stock. This is called going on margin. An example is the best way to see its effect.

Example 5.1   A $10 million fund making a 4 percent dividend borrows 30 percent of the value of the fund ($3 million) and invests it in the portfolio. How will the 30 percent margin affect the dividend and the profit and loss for a 25 percent rise and a 25 percent fall?

1.   The fund still has 1 million shares, but now the dividend, previously 4 percent, $400,000, is increased to $520,000. Since the cost of the loan at 10 percent is $300,000, there is $220,000 less for a dividend.

2.   If the fund goes up 25 percent, instead of being worth $1.25 \times $10 million = $12 million, it will be worth $16.5 million, which even when the $3 million is shown as a debt on the balance sheet leaves $13.5 million or an effective rise of 35 percent for a 25 percent rise in the market.

3. On a 25 percent fall, instead of a $2.5 million drop in value there is a $3.25 million drop to $9.75 million or $6.75 million when the debt is shown. Thus instead of a share being worth 75¢, it would be worth only 67.5¢. Thus margin makes the fund more volatile, and an astute manager on margin endeavors to get off when the market drops, and return to margin when it goes up.

Fund managers work hard. They live in the glare of the spotlight and have their mistakes exposed to all the world. Yet not one of them would prefer to manage individual portfolios over managing a fund. The reason is that they have more freedom with the fund's money. If they desire they may take a position in a stock because they think it will go up, sell it an hour later if it doesn't and buy it back again for a second try. This "churning" would bring screams of anguish from somebody whose portfolio they were managing because they would be accused of trading to make somebody some commissions. On the other hand, individuals have little chance to compare the peformance of their account managers, while the fund's performance is published for all to see. Until recently, churning didn't have to be reported—just the stocks held at the end of each quarter. Those bought and sold during a quarter never showed. But the SEC ruled that *all* transactions must be reported, and shareholders can, with some effort, learn about every trade.

The period 1973–1974 produced some near-psychotic fund managers. Some went from a gunslinging 100 percent profit in a year to a fall of 40 percent in 1973 and another 40 in 1974, leaving 36 percent of the pre-market-drop value. Almost a 200 percent rise was needed to "get well." Picking up 200 percent in the stock market is no easy task, even in five years. On top of the immensity of the job, the poor manager is hamstrung by a collapsed confidence in himself. He may get so scared he cannot commit a dime. So things are bad for a manager with a greatly depressed fund, and it makes a lot of sense for shareholders to switch to another fund that is climbing out well. Not only do they get some tax relief, but they get rid of a frantic manager. Admittedly they lose the losses the first fund accumulated, but in many cases the new fund has as many.

A few years back, incentive plans appeared for managers wherein they would get paid extra for exceeding some market average, and get docked if they did worse. Arguments for and against such plans run far and wide. Proponents say such a plan spurs managers to do better; opponents say they are paid to do their best anyhow, and a sliding scale leads to taking extra risks. Proponents say the possibility attracts new people; opponents say managers participate anyhow since good performance attracts more investors and they are paid a percentage.

So, right or wrong, about 20 percent of the no-load managers are on an incentive basis. And how have they done? The SEC and others studying the situation cannot find the difference. And all this fits in with the thesis of this book, that it is cash flow that makes a fund successful and all managers of the same type funds do pretty much alike.

No discussion of mutual fund managers would be complete without noting that it is not necessary to have one. A very few funds, of which the load-type Founders Fund is an outstanding example, were started with a selected group of stocks and *have made no changes in the portfolio over the years.* Founders, for instance, was started in 1938 with the selection of 40 stocks, and since then no changes have been made in its portfolio. New money is simply split among the 40 issues and invested each month, the essence of dollar cost averaging. Founders has performed above average for many periods, an action that must give little comfort to fund managers who have been outperformed by a secretary who sends a check to the custodian bank each day.

Did the dollar cost averaging work? Elsewhere I remarked that the effect would be negligibly small, if any exists. To be fair, Founders Fund never really got a chance to dollar cost average. It didn't get the same amount of money each month, and shareholders redeemed shares at market bottoms and bought extra at market tops, the exact opposite of what should be done. So nothing was learned, except that high-quality stocks do well.

There is one area of managing that I might as well be frank about, namely, poorly performing funds. Many studies were discussed in Chapter 1 showing that random (dart-board) portfolios or simple market averages beat a substantial fraction of the mutual funds. True, the dart-board winner appears most frequently during a roaring bull market, and the market averages are typically winners during market declines. Even so, long-term performance figures for many funds are not outstanding, but their managers are still receiving perhaps a million dollars a year for below average management. Something to think about.

Management groups are pretty hard on their managers, and those who have bad luck on their decisions are often fired. This means that the management groups always have a list of future managers in case one or more is needed. These possible managers flood the groups with their sample portfolios, and hope when it comes time for a change, they will be hired from their records. Well, this was the case with one fund whose president I knew, and we went over the sample portfolios of several aspirants one day, only to discover that the *most successful one* was from a chap who suggested that the fund buy every third stock on the American Stock Exchange! The president was distraught. "Alan," he said, "I couldn't hire this guy. They'd laugh me out of the business."

Fund managers like to see the fund grow in total assets because their pay is on this basis. Second, they like to see it perform well because that makes it easier to sell shares, and they then make more money. Given the choice of a rise in total assets, either from the sale of $10 million worth of new shares or a rise in the value of the portfolio, they would pick the latter because it makes them look better. Fund managers of load funds usually may buy shares at the net asset value, without paying a sales commission.

5.4. THE TRADER

The trader is the one who actually negotiates the buy and sell decisions of the manager. Traders are selected for their ability in trading large blocks of stocks. They have three possible sources: "block salespeople" who specialize in moving large blocks of stocks; other mutual funds; and ordinary buying through regular brokers. Lists of block salespeople and the stocks in which they specialize are available. Sometimes traders give a block salesperson a few hours exclusive right to make a deal, or, depending on the circumstances, they may move on to other sources. Going to other funds directly is frowned upon, because the moment it becomes known that one fund wants to buy or sell, the price rapidly adjusts in the "wrong" direction. Sales between funds are not inherently bad. The market is made through differences of opinion, and one fund may need a stock to balance its portfolio while another seeks to sell for the same reason.

Should the trader decide to buy in the open market, the decision as to which broker to use must be made. Many funds state openly that they give business to brokers who help sell their shares. This is reasonable, since the broker makes no commission on the sale.

The trader's day consists of calls from managers directing buy and sell actions and giving prices that must not be exceeded, or target prices, or orders to execute regardless of the price. Return calls come in from brokers stating they have or have not been able to execute orders as requested or asking for more time to call other sources. Frequently market news is obtained to be passed back to the managers.

Traders can be very busy. Their skill makes itself felt in their judgment of what the market can stand, and where they might get the best price. Thus, a trader with 5,000 shares to sell may elect to test the market by putting out 1,000, and, if they go well, part of the rest or the total. Even though the people the trader is dealing with know how many shares the fund holds of each stock, they do not know whether the fund is just "lightening up" or completely liquidating.

The movement of enormous blocks of stocks held by some of the larger funds may take days or even weeks, to avoid saturating the market and hurting the price.

After a deal is consummated, the trader makes a note of the price agreed upon and who made the trade and sends it to the accounting department. Later it will be compared with the statement from the broker, and if the records agree, authority will be given the custodian bank to make (or accept) the payment. Disagreements are usually errors of a fraction of a point that must be arbitrated.

Through modern communications, the trader can keep abreast of all New York American stock exchange trades, (and some of the over-the-counter trades) and not infrequently sees an order make an impact on the market. The trader has an advantage over the manager in that once the market closes, work is over. Managers can worry 24 hours a day and most do.

The trader is a member of and is paid by the management group, receiving a salary and sometimes a bonus determined by how much his or her trades average better than the market.

5.5. THE FUND OFFICERS

The fund officers are the president, vice-president, treasurer, and board of directors. These are almost never full-time employees paid by the fund, but the president, vice-president, and treasurer may be full-time employees of the management corporation, and some members of the board of directors may be members of the management corporation board as well. Members of the board who are not employees receive a fee (usually a yearly amount plus pay for each board meeting attended); the board members who are employees may or may not get an extra fee for attending board meetings. The fund officers and board members act for the shareholders, suggesting changes that will be in their behalf. These could be changes in policies, custodian banks, even managers, and in practice most changes comes from the management corporation president, who, of course, really runs the show.

The fund officers have expenses, but not money in the bank. Anything they spend is a "fund expense" and is paid by the custodian bank after authorization by the fund president. Expenses might include salaries of the officers, if any, or meeting fees, rent, secretaries' salaries, miscellaneous office expenses, and, rarely, travel. Office expense includes mailing out quarterly and other statements to shareholders. (If the distributors of a load fund want more literature for advertising, they usually must pay for the extras.) Fund officers may nearly always buy shares of load funds at the net asset values, that is, without commissions.

Fund officers like to see their fund perform well because (1) they usually own stock in the management company, and good performance helps it grow, and (2) they usually have some money of their own in the fund.

5.6. THE CUSTODIAN BANK

When a mutual fund is first started, the officers select a custodian bank because by law the assets of a mutual fund (cash and stock certificates) must be held in trust by a custodian bank and released only to pay fund expenses, or to distribute certificates or cash to shareholders upon request. Thus it is not possible for a fund officer, manager, or anybody else to order out cash or negotiable securities and depart for Rio de Janeiro. They can't because they don't have access to the cash or securities. The custodian bank would be worth its pay if security was all it offered, but it does much more. It receives the certificates of new acquisitions, holds those already bought, and surrenders certificates of stocks sold when directed to do so by the fund managers. The custodian also accepts dividends and payments from sales, and stock dividends when they occur. It makes payments for fund expenses. The computer tab run that it furnishes each day has an alert signal so that the fund portfolio managers are notified when a proposed investment will exceed its constitutional limit of, say, 5 percent for one corporation, or would if the managers bought any more.

(It is permissible for a fund to exceed a limit by appreciation of an investment.)

The custodian bank is quick to point out that it has no part in the portfolio managers' decisions and hence no responsibility for fund performance or lack of thereof. It acts solely as custodian and financial agent. Typically it is paid a flat $6 per account-year for stock funds and $15 per account-year for money market funds. Often the custodian fees are graded downward as the fund grows larger. The custodian also gets paid for each certificate it receives or delivers (say $10); for each check issued for payment of the various expenses authorized by the managers; and for each check issued to shareholders for dividends or capital gains distributions (say 50¢).

The total cost of the custodian to you will be around one-tenth of 1 percent per year, say $1 per $1,000 value. This is not much for the peace of mind it brings, nor is it significant when compared to the general administrative expenses and the management corporation fee. The custodian fee is included in the "expenses" described earlier.

The custodian may withdraw its services with proper notice to the fund officers and the managers. This is a rare step, if it has ever been taken, and might occur either because the custodian has failed to negotiate a contract change, or because in the custodian's opinion proper authorizations are not coming through from the managers so that it cannot properly discharge its duties. A fund may also change its custodian bank when it feels a change would be advantageous.

Once again, as a shareholder you send new money to the custodian bank, not to the fund office, ordinarily using the preaddressed envelopes furnished by the bank.

It comes as a surprise to learn that most of the custodial business for the nation's 790 mutual funds is handled by a total of less than 20 banks who have specialized in this facet of banking. Indeed, the State Street Bank of Boston handles nearly 30 percent of all mutual funds.

Who buys the loss if a criminal act occurs? The insurance company. All of the employees who handle money are bonded.

5.7. *FOLLOWING THE ROUTINE*

There is really no reason why you have to know the details of how your money is handled at the fund office or at the custodian bank. However, how the hundreds or thousands of checks totaling possibly $1 million a day are safely processed was always a deep secret to me, until I became associated with a fund and walked a payment through the system, so I have included the process. I have a hunch that you are about to learn more than you want to know about the details, but here goes.

Your letter, along with several hundred others, comes in each day by mail, and a machine in the mail room slices a sixteenth of an inch off the long edge to open it. (Does it ever slice your letter? Yep. It gets taped back together.) The mail clerks (they work in pairs for security) know that your letter (once advertisements and nonfinancial mail are separated out) will request one of four things: (1) Buy me some shares; (2) switch some or all of my money from one fund to another; (3) transfer some shares to somebody else; or (4) redeem some shares and send me a check. We'll deal with switches, transfers, and redemptions in a minute. Only purchases have a check in them. Out comes your check and it is immediately stamped "For deposit only."

Envelope, check, and fund slip go to a "mail verification clerk," who verifies that (1) the account number is enclosed—if it isn't she puts it on the check—and (2) the amount is above the minimum purchase allowed. If the account is a new one, she so notes and underscores needed data to help the entry clerk. If you have asked for a certificate, she makes a note.

At intervals the checks, clipped to their account slips, go to the data entry room. Here an entry clerk punches in your account number and the display shows it and your name. He compares the name against the check. The computer says "Type of procedure?" This could be a purchase, switch, transfer, or redemption. The purchase code is given (we'll deal with the others later) and the computer says "Type of purchase?" This could be (1) accounts receivable, (2) automatic, (3) reinvestment, or (4) a new account. The code for reinvestment is punched and the computer says "How much?" The entry clerk puts in the amount and the date of receipt.

The *accounts receivable* code would tell the computer that this money is to cover a "telephone buy" order. *Automatic* means that you have signed a draft order form such that the fund can write a draft on your bank, savings and loan, or credit union for some specific amount on a day selected by you each month. (The advantage of this is that the amount in an automatic plan can usually be less than the minimum purchase stated in the prospectus.) A daily notice of the automatic accounts is brought up by the computer a few days early, and the draft along with an account slip joins the incoming mail on the proper day. If the purchase is a new account, the computer assigns it an account number, and asks for registration name, address, Social Security number, and whether distributions will be reinvested or taken in cash. It kicks out a starting amount below that required by the fund, and a shareholders' representative would then call you and explain the problem.

Typically there are a number of shareholders' representatives, each of whom has a sequence of numbered accounts (about 3,000). This procedure makes clarification calls or letters more coherent. After the entries are made into the holding computer, the checks and account slips are dropped into as many boxes as there are representatives. Filing these and getting the checks to the bank are the daily work load. The shareholders' representatives total their checks and put the account slips into each shareholder's file. The totals of all the shareholders' reps must equal the total shown by the computer entries. Since it has separate accounts for each rep, errors are found without going through the whole day's receipts. When the reconciliation is complete, the bank clerk makes out a deposit slip and takes the checks to the bank. (Almost nobody sends cash. When this occurs a receipt is made out by the mail clerk, the cash is verified, and an immediate deposit is made. Cash is not wanted around the office.)

Nothing has been said so far about how many shares you get for your money. That's because the share price has not yet been determined.* At the close of the market, the custodian bank gets the closing prices of all stocks and bonds. These are given to the computer, which discards data on stocks and bonds not held by the fund, enters those that are, and whacks out today's closing value of the shares held by the fund. It adds the cash already being held and the amount phoned in from the fund office. It divides this by the total number of shares outstanding and gets a "Today's closing price per share." The records computer uses this price to compute how many shares you got for your payments, and overnight it prints out the up-to-date statement you will get in a few days, a copy of which is of course added to your file in the fund office.

Getting a little ahead of ourselves, this new total, less redemptions, and the plus-or-minus value of switches, is also figured and given to the portfolio manager, who then knows how much he has to spend on new stocks if he wishes, or how much he must sell to raise the money needed to cover redemptions.

Now let's go back and pick up what happens in case your letter said "switch" or "transfer" or "redeem." A switch, if not already in dollars, is converted into dollars, and the dollar value is taken from the losing fund and used to buy new shares in the gaining fund. Since accounts are filed by number and not by name, you probably will have one rep who handles your money market account and another who handles your growth fund.

A transfer may be a gift to a new or already established account, or it may be into a trust or other account in case of death. In the latter case, copies of the death certificate, authority for the personal representative, and a signature guarantee must be included. A redemption request follows the same path, except the mail verification clerk sends it first to a shareholders' representative who checks your latest statement to see if you have the shares or dollar value you seek to redeem in your

---

*This infuriates some buyers who are used to a firm quote for a stock. As noted earlier, the share price is not available until the close of the market, 4 PM eastern standard time.

account, and *how long you have had them*. The former is
checked because though you may own enough shares for the
redemption, you may have received some of them as certificates, and a check can't be issued until you send them in. The
latter is to cut off a would-be crook who might have sent in a
bogus check for, say, $50,000 and a couple of days later, before
the check has time to bounce, asks for a $40,000 redemption
check. It's been tried. If you do have the shares or dollar value
you request for redemption in your account, your letter goes to
the computer entry clerk to be entered for the records computer
to handle. The computer would kick back the request if you
didn't have enough. In that case you would get a letter or a
phone call from your representative and the matter would get
settled. If all is well, when the statements come back from the
records computer, a check is written and mailed to you, or if
the fund wants to make a little interest, it can hold the money
for seven days according to the SEC regulations.

To pick up a few missing threads, here is how some other
facets are handled:

1. **Request for a certificate.** Less than 10 percent of
    shareholders ask for certificates. If you do, when you
    send in money, it is noted on the account slip, and then
    the statement from the records computer shows (a) shares
    owned, (b) shares held by shareholder, and (c) shares
    held by custodian bank. Obviously, (b) + (c) should equal
    (a). Physically, the unissued certificates are in a safe
    under the auspices of a certificate clerk. The mail verifi-
    cation clerk calls her and is given a record number of
    the next certificate. This goes to the entry room and on
    to the record computer where the number of shares
    purchased is computed and noted on the statement. Since
    certificates are only issued for a digital number of shares,
    the remnant dollars will be returned to you. Nobody knows
    why certificates aren't issued in fractions of a share (since
    the accounts are so managed), but they aren't.

2. **Big money.** Whereas you and I would send a check,
    sometimes registering the mail, big money (define it

yourself) usually is wired directly from the shareholder's bank to the custodian bank. It in turn phones the transfer agent, who then sends it through the system already described.

3.   **IRA and Keogh plan payments.**   IRA and/or Keogh plan accounts are separate from fund accounts and may be administered by entirely separate banks. At any rate, if the account is separate such payments are returned to the sender for proper remailing.

What's the biggest source of error? A tired mail clerk failing to notice that a check is to pay for a telephone order. This results in the customer getting more shares than he wants, and being dunned a few days later to pay for the telephone buy. Other continual sources of trouble are the bad checks and failure to pay for telephone orders. Failures to pay are kicked out by the computer after seven days have gone by and the order is canceled if the shareholders' representative can't get satisfaction from a call. Pay failures occur when a client calls in a telephone order and notices a day or so later that the share price has dropped. So he doesn't send the check. (When this happens in a broker's office, the broker gets to make the purchase and sale of the stock ordered and *he* eats the loss. He also doesn't do any more business with a client whose word is worthless.) Sometimes checks are sent, but come back stamped "insufficient funds." Both of these retroactive procedures must be backed out of the system, including being taken out of the commission payments figured each day for the management corporation. Handling the paperwork is a very serious and difficult task. I have had mistakes made in my accounts, but in every case they have been satisfactorily remedied.

The degree to which the mutual fund industry (and the whole stock market as well) is run on trust would certainly belie the stupid and unthinking remarks about business "being crooked," often made by people whose own finances are in such poor shape you would think they had been getting advice from the government. Millions of dollars change hands each day on no more than the spoken word, and untold billions are in escrow without any certificates being issued. It would surprise me if there is any business on earth more honestly run, proportionately, than the stock markets.

5.8. DISTRIBUTORS AND WHOLESALERS

There is a vast sales organization needed by the load-type funds, but of course it is not a part of the no-load setup. You should know about all this and get a feel for what you are not paying as a no-load investor. The organization includes the distributors with their wholesalers and dealers with their brokers. This section covers the first two.

We have already seen how a no-load fund can be several entirely separate corporations: the fund officers elected by the shareholders; the fund management group, which may hire outside managers; the custodian bank; and still another bank to handle Keogh and IRA plan investors. (See Chapter 7.) Load funds have, in addition, a distributor, which may or may not be an entirely separate corporation (it usually is), and possibly hundreds of dealers and brokers who actually make the sales. The distributor corporation buys shares from the fund at net asset value and sells them to dealers at the net asset value plus a commission. The distributor corporation usually consists of a home office and possibly a half-dozen wholesalers. The wholesalers are the people who travel a great deal visiting the dealers, trying to get them to sell more shares of their funds. They furnish their dealers with sales aids, information about changes in the fund portfolio, policy, and personnel and on occasion invite them back to headquarters to meet with the fund managers and hear more sales pitch.

Most of the sales commissions go to the dealers selling the fund, who in turn pay a part of what they receive to the sales people making the sale. On an 8.5 percent commission it would not be unusual for the distributor corporation to get 1.5 percent. For those funds that charge a commission on dividends reinvested, the distributor also gets a share. Table 5.2 gives a

Table 5.2   Sample Distribution of Commission for
Distributor, Dealer, and Broker

Amount of Sale ($)			Total Commission (%)	Distribution (%)		
				Distributor	Dealer	Broker[a]
Less than		10,000	8.5	1.5	7.0	3.0
10,000	to	25,000	7.5	1.3	6.2	2.7
25,000	to	50,000	5.5	1.0	4.5	2.0
50,000	to	100,000	4.0	0.7	3.3	1.4
100,000	to	500,000	2.5	0.5	2.0	1.0
500,000	or	more.	1.0	0.2	0.8	0.5

[a]The broker's share comes out of the dealer's share.

possible breakdown for the commissions that go to distributor, dealer, and broker.

The wholesaler, particularly of a fund that is currently performing poorly, has a tough job trying to convince sales-people to sell the fund he represents, and ingenious are the methods used to show a fund's superiority. Wholesalers like to see their fund perform well because that makes it easier to sell shares, and they are paid only on what they sell.

Sales for no-load funds are accomplished solely through ads paid for by the management firm and by good words put forth by the various no-load advisory services.

5.9.   DEALERS AND BROKERS

The ultimate sale of load-type mutual fund shares are made by brokers who may be in stock brokerage houses full time, sell-ing mutual funds because the customer wants them or because the particular broker believes they are the best investment; or, they may work in houses that sell only mutual funds. The stock market is a very complex market, and I would recom-mend that if you want to buy load funds seek a broker who is strongly interested in funds, or perhaps handles them only.

Funds make up a complex market. Many dealers combine fund sales with other types of estate advice, possibly including insurance. These people can be especially helpful.

As I mentioned earlier, of the typical 8.5 percent commission, the distributor gets about 1.5 percent. The remaining 7 percent goes to the dealers, who pay from 3 to 5 percent to the brokers. Sometimes bonuses for outstanding sales are also paid, either by the distributors or by the dealers.

Apropos nothing, the employee benefits available for brokers are far behind those available for salaried people and labor in other industries. The same could probably be said for salespeople in other industries.

Brokers like to see a fund perform well because they have sold it to customers who will come back if they are pleased with their investment. No-load investors do *not* have the distributors, wholesalers, dealers, and brokers on their payroll.

5.10. SHAREHOLDERS

Now we come to the lowest one on the totem pole . . . you, the shareholder. All you have done is furnish the money to pay the officers, managers, and custodian banks (and distributors, wholesalers, dealers, and brokers, if you own a load fund). For this you get (1) some profit, (2) a number of services covered elsewhere in this book, (3) the opportunity to make a few choices about how your distributions should be handled, and (4) the opportunity to vote on items that concern the fund and its officers, managers, and custodian banks.

When you do get the chance to vote, ballot counting is different than when you elect a mayor. In mutual fund voting you get as many votes as you have shares, and you may put all your votes on one person or item, or spread your votes around. A little thought will reveal that this is both fair and the easiest to check.

You have one more big vote: redemption. If you do not like anything about the fund, vote yourself out.

5.11.   FUND EXPENSES

The previous sections have described the many jobs that must be handled in order to have a viable fund, and obviously the people who do them must be paid. This section covers both how big the expenses are and what they cover, and I have also elected to include as an expense of sorts the extra money you might have to come up with to pay the taxes that arise if the fund makes money and you have all your profits reinvested.

1. **Management fees.**   These run from 0.5 to 2 percent per year of the total value of your shares. They are subtracted from dividends before they are paid to you or reinvested for you. Management fees and what they cover were handled in Section 5.2.

2. **Other fund expenses.** In addition to the management fees, fund expenses run from about 0.4 percent to 1.2 percent of the total value of the fund per year. These monies are subtracted from the dividends that the fund receives before the remainder is passed on to you as a shareholder.

   If the sum of the management fee and the fund expenses is greater than the dividends received, additional monies are taken from the fund. Settlement is usually on a monthly basis. See Table 5.3 for a list of fund expenses.

3. **Taxes.**   In addition to expenses, mutual funds usually generate taxes of two types for their shareholders:

   a. **Taxes on dividends, interest received, and short-term capital gains.**   These vary according to how much you receive and your income tax rate, and you must pay them whether you elect to receive them or have them reinvested. To get some sort of a number we will assume that dividends and so forth amount to 3 percent per year, and the average shareholder has a 33 percent income tax rate. He will then have to scratch up 1 percent of the value of his shares each year for taxes.

Table 5.3. Items Usually Listed as Fund Expenses and Paid Directly out of the Fund

1. Salaries of fund officers (president, vice-president, and secretary, if any)	9. Cost of annual meetings
	10. Insurance
	11. State registration fees
	12. Custodian bank
2. Taxes	13. Directors' travel and fees
3. Legal and accounting fees	14. Cost of quarterly and annual reports and prospectuses
4. Transfer fees	
5. Interest on money borrowed	
	15. Rent for office and equipment
6. Proxies	
7. Commission on stock sales and purchases	16. Cost of sending out distributions
8. Cost of fund certificates	17. Special meetings

   b. **Taxes on capital gains.** These vary according to how much you receive in capital gains and your income tax rate, and you must pay them whether you elect to receive them in cash or have them reinvested. To come up with some sort of a number here we will assume 7.5 percent for the yearly capital gain distribution, and again a tax rate of 33 percent. Thus you will need to scratch up 1.0 percent of the total value of your shares each year to pay the taxes on your profits. (This is pretty wild bit of averaging, as some years you will have a loss, and some years gains bigger than 7.5 percent.)

4. **Redemption fees.** A fair number of no-load funds charge a 1 percent redemption fee, sometimes waived if the shares are held more than, say, six months, and sometimes limited to a maximum of $100. Some people feel this is a sneaky way to collect a commission, but it is not. It is paid *to the fund*; you as a shareholder get a little bit more when somebody else leaves, and of course, a little bit less if you leave. The purpose of this is to discourage trading.

Table 5.4.   Yearly Expenses Incurred When Owning a
No-Load Fund

Item	Expense (%)
Commission to buy	0
Management fee	0.3 to 2.0
Fund expenses	0.4 to 1.2
Taxes on dividends, etc., received by the fund	1.0
Taxes on capital gains	1.0
Redemption fee (maybe)	1.0
Total	2.7 to 5.2

Table 5.4 shows what a no-load fund will cost to buy and keep. As you can see, your visible and hidden expenses are from 2.7 to 5.2 percent per year, plus maybe a 1 percent redemption fee. The first two are hidden because they are taken out of dividends before you ever see them. (If the dividends don't cover them, and this is not at all unusual, some stocks are sold to make up the remainder.) The taxes on dividends and capital gains would be the same wherever you made the money, so don't run around saying "Pope says no-load mutual funds cost from 2.7 to 5.2 percent per year." They really cost from 0.7 to 3.2 percent per year, and I am certain you'd pay that and more in commissions if you bought stocks directly.

Expenses for no-load funds average a little higher than for the load funds, by about one quarter percent per year. This might be because they are usually smaller, and the fixed expenses show up as a larger percentage. It isn't large enough to be important.

Now let's see what the load fund buyer pays in expenses. First and foremost is the sales commission. As we have seen, it is typically 8 to 8.5 percent up to $10,000; less for larger amounts. This could be amortized over several years, depending on how long you hold the fund, but the profit no-load owners might make on the commission money is lost forever. So there's a big difference between the loads and the no-loads.

Second, though none of the load funds charge a commission on reinvesting profits made through capital gains, some charge one when they reinvest dividends. You may forget this if you wish.

Dividends might be, say, 3 percent per year, and the commission of 8 percent of 3 percent is about one-quarter of 1 percent. This is clearly too small to argue about, but I will for two reasons. First, a stockbroker doesn't get a commission when you get a dividend from a stock he sold you, and there is no reason for him to do so with mutual funds. Second, most funds *will not reinvest capital gains without reinvesting dividends too*, so if you own one of the funds that charges a commission on dividends reinvested, you will get a check for *both* if you demand a check for one. You will end up spending more on the reinvestment than you would have on the dividends alone.

6

Income Programs

There are two ways in which you might want to receive money from your no-load investments: (1) soon (define that any way you wish) and (2) much later. The "soon" programs cannot benefit from the several tax-deferred programs that are so useful for later retirement, hence they require a different treatment. Chapter 7 deals with retirement plans.

Mutual funds are unique in having ways to get income to you without disturbing your portfolio and without forcing the sale of a large investment and then paying substantial capital gains taxes because it cannot be sold piecemeal. This income is often derived from capital gains that have not been taken and hence have not been taxed. Taxes only come when capital gains are used little by little. There are three mechanisms that will provide income: (1) the withdrawal plan, (2) living off distributions, and (3) the extremely simple redeeming system.

6.1. THE WITHDRAWAL PLAN

The withdrawal plan is a program whereby mutual fund shareholders may, if their accounts meet certain conditions, have the fund send them monthly (or quarterly) checks for whatever amount they specify. If the specified amount exceeds the income from dividends during the period, the fund will sell as many shares as is necessary to make up the payment. The purpose of the plan is threefold: It enables a shareholder to receive a monthly income; the amount of the income may be larger than it would be if generated only by dividends or interest; and, finally, the money is composed mostly of long-term capital gains, which are taxed at less than the dividend rate. There are currently several hundred thousand withdrawal plans in action. Using part of your capital gains for income is a relatively new procedure in the field of investing. It assumes that investors can count on making some profits over the years and so are justified in using some fraction of these profits along with their dividends to live on. The market collapse of 1973–1974 cast some doubt on this procedure, as withdrawing, say, 10 percent from a fund that is down 50 percent greatly hurts its recovery. However, dips such as in 1981–1982 of a few percent can be taken in stride.

In the preceding paragraph I used the word *income* in a manner that would make many investment counselors and bankers get red in the face and scream "Profits aren't *income!*" I guess a financial dictionary would prove them right. But hear me out. The long-term record of growth-stock mutual funds, except for the 20-year periods ending in 1973 and 1974, has been such that owning a group of several funds would, without exception, have yielded profits of 10 percent and more likely 12 percent over the years. Thus it does make sense to augment the 2 or 3 percent per year dividends with a few percent of the expected capital gains. Many examples exist in the various fund record books where the remaining growth has been sufficient to permit frequent and large increases in dollars for the monthly withdrawal checks. If you as an investor own common stocks directly, and they go up in price, you may or may not get any more income from dividends. In short, a rise in the value of your investments can't be of benefit to you unless you sell off some stock to realize the profits.* On the other hand, a rise in the value of your mutual funds thoroughly justifies your

---

*This is not practicable unless you sell thousands of dollars worth each time, as the commissions on small sales become too expensive.

asking the fund to send you a larger check each month than they have been sending.

Let's be frank. There will be poor market years when the value of your funds will go down and you may squirm a bit at adding to the annihilation of your estate by withdrawing capital from it, but the long-term record shows that things will balance if you haven't been too greedy in what you have taken out. Think of your mutual fund investment as water in a rain barrel. The "rain" that tends to increase the amount of water in the barrel corresponds to the dividends, interest, and capital gains earned by the Fund. The withdrawal corresponds to a spigot at the bottom of the barrel. If you open the spigot to, say, 6 to 8 percent a year, while it rains 10 to 15 percent, then the level of the barrel will rise, even while you get more income after taxes than you could through dividends.

You will find references that talk about accumulating an estate through the use of growth-stock mutual funds and then switching to an income fund when retirement time comes. The idea is that an income fund will have more "income" than a growth fund, and hence the investor will have more to live on. This philosophy is only remotely connected with the real world. Ample statistics exist to prove that growth funds in general make more total money per year than do income funds, and holding growth funds and living off their dividends *plus* a part of their profits really give the investor the greatest amount of usable money to spend. It may be called "income" or "using one's capital," but the statement still stands.

So let's sum up the main point: Investors needing a certain percentage of their portfolios to live on will on the average come out ahead if they get this percentage from growth-stock funds using a small fraction of their capital gains to live on than if they get it all from dividends from an income fund.

And now, let's get back to the withdrawal-plan discussion. Most funds have the following features regarding withdrawal plans:

1. A lower limit to the value of the holdings of a person before a withdrawal plan is permitted. A fairly typical

amount is $10,000 for those desiring a monthly check; the amount is sometimes $5,000 for quarterly withdrawals and sometimes $5,000 for monthly withdrawals.

2. A lower limit on the amount withdrawn. Typically this is $25 per withdrawal; sometime $50. Sometimes a charge of 25¢ to $1 is made per check, or perhaps a percentage, say, 1 percent.

3. A few load funds permit "refilling" the account without charge. Thus if you have withdrawn $2,000 in payments and come by some money, which you wish to put back in, it will be accepted without a fee up to $2,000. This may be desirable if one inherits a withdrawal account, and owns load funds.

6.2. GETTING READY FOR THE WITHDRAWAL PLAN

Although I certainly think that investors should have their objectives before them during all phases of investment, somewhere around five to eight years before retirement, some soul-searching should be done as to how active one plans to be after retirement, and a look should be taken at the amounts in each fund in relation to the withdrawal-plan minimum when retirement comes around. If you plan to stay in a few growth funds, you should add enough to get them to the minimum withdrawal amount by retirement time. Appendix B can be used to make a rough growth estimate according to the number of years you have to go and the amounts you now have. Allow for a market drop of, say, 25 percent "at the wrong time" so you have some cushion.

6.3. SELECTING FUNDS TO BUY FOR THE WITHDRAWAL PLAN

Retirees face three problems in making their move toward a withdrawal plan:

1. Which funds to buy and when to buy them.
2. The withdrawal rate to select (see Section 6.4).
3. What their income will be after taxes.

If you have invested in a few good growth funds selected to be very defensive during market dips, by all means stay with them. The chances are that you have some capital gains and taking them will incur taxes. Not taking them means you will get their growth and use some of it for living expenses with very small taxes. If you have not invested, don't make this a period of trauma. Take the following steps:

1. Get your portfolio in order by putting it all in three or four places. Chances are you have a couple of savings accounts, probably some stocks, and a bond or two. Take a hard look at everything and get most of it into a money fund or two.
2. Subscribe to a couple of the advisory services mentioned in Section 4.2, and if the time is not right to go into some growth funds, leave your money in the money market funds, and use the time to study which growth funds have good growth in bull markets and are defensive in bear markets. Consider Linder, Mutual Shares, Magellan, Janus, Equity Income, and others.
3. When your services say the time is right, move gradually into a growth fund, getting your withdrawal plan going before you start another. Work toward four funds unless the number has to be reduced in order to meet the minimums.
4. Keep track of your investments, and once a year or so sell the poorest performing and either add to the best or start in a new one whose record looks good.

6.4. SETTING THE WITHDRAWAL RATE

I spoke earlier about not making the withdrawal rate so high that your account is drawn down, and a starting rate of 6 percent with changes as you go along makes sense. You do have several choices:

1. You may request an even dollar amount each month or each quarter, usually $50 or more, in increments of $10.
2. You may request that a specified number of shares be sold each month and a check sent to you.
3. You may request that 5, 6, 7, 8, 9, 10 or whatever percent of your total assets be sent to you yearly, monthly, or quarterly. In this case the computer will read your total assets and take the appropriate percentage. I like this best of all, in that a rising check tells you that your investment is doing well, and a falling one alerts you to cut back on the percentage until the market turns around.

Although a starting amount of around 6 percent a year may seem low, and currently you can probably do much better than that via bond or bond funds, as I said this is a *starting* amount, which may be well above dividends currently paid by most common stocks. Remember, the amount is under your control and if you can get along now with a modest withdrawal, experience tells us that later on your income will be much larger indeed, possibly 100 percent larger or more.

6.5. THE MECHANICS OF THE PLAN

To participate in a withdrawal plan one first obtains a special form from the fund in question directed to the custodian bank. It must be filled out requesting periodic withdrawals and stating the amount. *If you have not been reinvesting capital gains and dividends, this procedure will be initiated.* You must also deposit shares to meet the minimum amount. It may well be desirable to hold some back for use as collateral from time to time since shares in a withdrawal plan may not be pledged.

After a short time needed to get the plan started, you will begin to receive checks as requested. Two different plans are in effect by which the funds obtain the money for the checks:

1. Most funds, load or no-load, reinvest all capital gains and dividends as they become available and derive all monies needed for withdrawal checks by selling the proper number of shares.

2. The few load funds that charge a commission for reinvesting dividends set up a special account in which dividends are collected. These monies are used first, and augmented by sales of shares if need be. This procedure saves the shareholder the commission cost of reinvesting the dividends. Insignificant amounts of profits are lost since the time involved is short. This plan does not concern no-load investors.

Regardless of the mechanism used by the fund, when shares are sold the price you will get will be the asset value per share on a day about 10 days before the check arrives—the lag is needed for paperwork. Some funds send a statement with each check, stating how many shares were sold, the price, and how many you have left. Other funds give a statement once a year. You cannot have the check endorsable by two people—like "Payable to John H. or Mary K. Smith." It has to be only one. This is because the fund would have no way of finding out if one should die, and the survivor could then continue to receive income without the estate going through probate and estate taxes.

6.6. WITHDRAWAL-PLAN TAXES

The proper payment of taxes on withdrawal-plan checks is so sticky that one finds the following on many withdrawal plan forms: "Neither the custodian bank nor the fund assumes any obligation to furnish information to the investor for tax purposes." Here is how the problem arises: Suppose that to get the money for a monthly payment, the custodian bank must sell 4.186 shares. Which shares are these? The ones bought in 1936 at $18.12 a share, or those bought in 1965 at $7.40 a share after a split; or shares bought last week from capital gains invested the week before (i.e., short-term capital gains)? The answer is that the choice is up to you. You may elect last in, first out (the shares most recently acquired are the first sold); see the example in Section 3.1. Or, you may match up shares sold with shares bought starting at the beginning of your history with the fund. *In any case records are essential.* You must be able to prove that you bought shares on the day you claim and at the price you claim. To examine the logic a bit more, each year any shareholder normally receives some long-term capital gains that are reinvested and some dividends that are reinvested. Taxes must be paid each year on this income. After taxes have been paid, the shares purchased with the money become part of the capital invested and if sold at the same price would generate no new taxes. (If sold at a higher or lower price, appropriate reporting and taxes must be considered.)

Once again, the fund or custodian bank will not accept the responsibility for furnishing the needed data to you. It is imperative that each shareholder keeps his or her own records.

6.7. AN ALTERNATIVE TO A FORMAL WITHDRAWAL PLAN

Curiously enough, investors are normally very reluctant to sell shares to obtain money to live on, feeling that they should be living on their "income" and not on their "capital." The withdrawal plan, by supplying a monthly or quarterly check, sort of fools investors into thinking they are receiving income, and the sale of shares becomes more palatable. Actually, though the withdrawal plan is fairly new, there never has been any restriction on selling a few shares each month or quarter—running your own "withdrawal plan," as it were. (This would not be possible with stocks owned directly—the commissions would be too large.) Three advantages result:

1. There are usually no handling charges, which can run a fairly large percentage of a monthly check.
2. You need not tie up your shares by depositing them with the custodian bank, as must be done when a withdrawal plan is started.
3. You can continue to manage your portfolio more easily.

The first advantage is probably minor compared to the nuisance of having to write each time you want money. It probably only becomes meaningful when your fund charges you, say, 50¢ a check and you are withdrawing $25 a month. This comes to 2 percent of your income and is a little steep for the convenience. You should change to larger, less frequent checks.

The second point has more substance to it. Availability of certificates for collateral when borrowing to cover emergencies is a substantial advantage, and prompts restating that one should never deposit all one's shares if it is not necessary to meet the withdrawal minimum. Keep some for use as needed. Running your own withdrawal plan also gives you the opportunity to take your shares to the bank, borrow on them, and buy more shares with the money. This probably isn't practical with the current high interest rates, but when they come down it will be.

The third point, continuing to manage your portfolio, depends on your temperament. It absolutely destroys some investors to "dip into their capital" (the withdrawal plan hides this beautifully); others, particularly after a long market slide such as happened in 1973–1974, realize that getting in and out of the market is a big step toward the preservation of capital. They don't mind it at all.

6.8. OTHER RETIREMENT INCOME PROGRAMS

Cycles in the market change the attractiveness of various types of investments as time passes, and there is no reason to be fixed on the idea that mutual funds, either using or not using a withdrawal plan, are the optimum. Examining bonds and mutual funds for (1) current income after taxes, (2) safety, and (3) future growth to beat inflation may reveal alternatives that have become attractive. "Safety" has a different meaning for retirees: As long as the income continues, oscillations in the market price are secondary. As I have said before, it means little to a retiree if a stock he owns doubles in price while the dividend stays constant.

When interest rates soared in 1981, bond prices tumbled until the then current yield of bonds matched them. This resulted in many bonds selling for half of their face value with their current yields of 10 to 13 percent and yields to maturity of 13 to 16 percent. These rates have tapered off as interest rates have come down, but some are still very attractive. Bond yields should clearly be checked as an investor seeks income. As a matter of interest, while funds get their safety (admittedly greatly influenced by market conditions) from diversification, bonds get theirs from their nature: If the corporation survives, the bond interest wil be paid.

6.9. LIVING ON DISTRIBUTIONS

A number of funds have a steady record of large distributions, and since you are going to pay taxes on them anyhow, there is no reason, if you are looking for income, why you cannot have all distributions sent to you in cash. I do this myself (being retired) and as I said earlier this has the secondary benefit of awakening you to setting some money aside for taxes and—if you don't need the money right now—putting it in another place. There is another advantage and it is big. The whole distribution is a purchase at a single price per share, and with it comes a statement of how much is stock dividends, how much capital gains, and how much interest. This brings the nearly insoluble problem of computing income taxes right under foot. To repeat what I said earlier, funds often take a *month* to send you your distribution check if you take the distribution in cash, and during this time you make no money on it. The answer is to tell the fund to reinvest all distributions, and the day you get the notice of the purchase of more shares, call the fund and telephone switch the money into your bank account or money market fund. In this way you will only lose the income for a few days.

Funds differ widely in their investment philosophy, even those of a similar type. If you want to make immediate use of the distributions, obviously you would like a fund that makes them both large and regular. The distribution record of two growth funds is shown in Table 6.1, where a vast difference is shown in distribution policies. This information is hard to find and could require gathering a number of prospectuses, or getting your advisory service to do it for you. Funds that have a record of making more than one distribution each year include Acorn, Boston Capital Appreciation, Fidelity Equity Income Fund, Guardian, Lindner, Mutual Shares, Sequoia, and Value Line Income Fund; I am sure there are many more.

Of the different ways of getting money to live on out of your no-load fund, I much prefer using distributions. It really isn't

Table 6.1. Distributions Made by Two Growth Funds (in percent)[a]

Year	Scudder Development	Lindner
1972	2.6	—
1973	0.0	18.2
1974	0.0	11.6
1975	2.1	12.7
1976	2.6	8.7
1977	4.5	20.0
1978	2.4	15.2
1979	1.9	22.8
1980	1.6	22.5
1981	10.2	11.8

[a]Based on the average price during the year involved.

much different from ordering redemptions when you need money, but it *seems* different. Letting a fund grow for a year and then making *all* income capital gains by a series of redemptions makes the most sense of all, but I never heard of anybody doing it. Some of us, it turns out, are pretty lazy.

7

Retirement Programs

It is quite proper to dream of retiring and "doing things you want to do," and to have the money to do them. Toward this end employers, the government, and you yourself have the choice of a number of programs:

1. Save the money you will need and pay yourself a pension.
2. Have an employer who will arrange for you to have a pension, and possibly he will ask you to help with part of the needed money.
3. Use one of the tax-free (tax-deferred, really) plans to help accumulate money.
4. Get your employer to reduce your salary and invest the money for your later use.

No-load funds can play a very important part in any or all of these programs, not only in the accumulation part, but in getting payments to you, and that's what this chapter is all about. But I want to talk to young people a moment about getting started. So if you're over 28, just go on to the next section. Or maybe you'll read this and say "I wish I had done that."

I have always had great difficulty in getting young people to pay any attention at all to financial freedom later on, and I quite understand why. Peer pressure ("The Browns have a new car") and perfectly real and normal expenses for a family make saving almost a dream. But there are a couple of slick ways to change this. The first is to agree on what you need to purchase this month, and put it off a month. That frees a few dollars for the accumulation pot. Put that money in your credit union, or wherever you can get the highest interst with high safety. Next month buy the gadget and put off something else. You can sow the seeds of a fortune by simply living a month behind. Just $50 a month will get you free of time payments for appliances and such in a year (you borrow from yourself, and not at 18 percent or so). You will be free of high car payments in three or four years, and will feel comfortable with your nest egg in six.

The long-term implications of getting started *now* are tremendous. One hundred dollars a month at 12.3 percent for 40 years is *$1 million.* Tables 7.3 and 7.4 list other interest rates and time periods. The basic idea is to set some money aside right now. Very soon financial matters will help and not hinder your marriage and working life.

Another way to make the "set aside" as painless as possible is to fill out the forms so that your employer sends $100 a month to your credit union. A third method would be to continue any time payments you are now saddled with after the items are paid off, and put that money into investments. Practice a little plastic surgery and cut your credit cards in two. Don't I ever use credit cards? All the time. But I never ever pay inter-est—I pay the whole bill when presented. They lend me money, interest free. I love them. And do not get caught up in the new car syndrome. Why not buy a three-year-old car for half the price of a new one, half the license fee, and two-thirds the insurance? I built my estate with used cars.

Also stay clear of recreational vehicles, boats, airplanes, beach cottages, and the like. If you won't use it at least 15 percent of the time, find a partner and share the cost. Two suggestions if you do this: Let one of the partners own more than an equal share and let that partner make the decisions (new sails, new tires, new roof). If you do not like the decisions, sell out. Write an agreement and pay a lawyer to check it so that everything is clear. I have been in partnerships and had my troubles with them, but nothing like the whole expense of buying a new crankcase for an airplane engine ($3,000).

After you get a tight rein on yourself and have financial matters in hand, what are you going to do with the money? For many years I urged young people to find a way to own a home. Now I have to hedge that. It is still a good idea in most areas, but in California homes are so high that renting makes more sense. If you can rent for less than 1 percent of the value of the house per month, rent. You'll do better. Elsewhere in the country, look at the population growth rates before you buy. The way things are going, it will be mighty hard to find some-one to buy your home in the northern states, but probably no problem in the south. If you decide to buy, give preference to a house so arranged that rooms can be added later on. And, if you can, buy a new house. Putting in the lawn, trees, and garden is work, but it's fun and adds to the value of the house. You can also save by buying a house before it is built, like when a contractor is going to build many. He likes a down payment and the knowledge that the house is sold.

So, anyhow, when you get these things in order, then this book and no-load funds are for you. First, set up a regular accumulation program of growth funds because you may need to borrow against the certificates from time to time, and then, as soon as you can, start an IRA because your money will accumulate without taxes.

7.1. RETIREMENT

As a retiree, I have quite a bit of sympathy for the 82-year-old retiree I met recently who said, "College and my job taught me everything I needed to know about working, but nothing about not working." He gave up, bought a business, and will work until he can work no more. That might suit him, or be neces-sary for him, but for the vast majority of us it doesn't constitute retirement. In my opinion, people approaching retirement should pay almost as much attention to what they plan to do to stay busy, effective, contributive, and happy as they do to having the money they will need. This isn't a book on how to be happy in retirement, so I'll quit this subject by saying that it really is easy: There are so many, many organizations needing help that any person willing to put out a little effort to locate them will have no problem being busy and happy. But I can't imagine anybody being happy in retirement without sufficient money, and that *is* the subject of this book, so I'll get on with it.

Believe it or not, you have been living on about 65 percent of your pay; Social Security, workmen's compensation, insurance, medical and dental, possibly part of your retirement, and many other things make up the "deducts," which usually come out at about 35 percent. *You will not need as much as you have been taking home to live comfortably in retirement.* If your income totals 50 percent of your final base pay, you will make it all right; and 65 percent is very comfortable indeed. This assumes few or no debts, the house paid for, and the kids off the payroll. (I'm not sure that last is achievable, but that's what we're here for.)

For those of us who do not see hitting those targets, then take a hard look at Tables 7.3 and 7.4 and make whatever drastic changes are needed. Old age without a decent income is no fun at all. The next section wil help clear up how much you will need in dollars.

7.2. PENSIONS

Pensions seem to have a lot of mystery about them, and almost nobody I have ever talked to knew what his or her pension would be. It's easy to figure, at least roughly. An annuity of $100 a month costs about $12,000 at retirement, with minor variances between men and women. A modest additional amount is needed if a spouse is also covered. You can understand the $12,000 figure by assuming that it earns 9 percent which works out at $90 a month. The portion taken out of the $12,000 based on life expectancies pays the remaining $10 a month and covers the costs of administration. So if you must supply your own pension, figure out how much you will need per month in hundred dollar bills and multiply the number by $12,000. If you are employed the company uses the money with your name on it in the pension fund to buy an annuity. There would be little reason for you to do this on your own— you can just live on the income and still have your estate intact when you die.

The usual way for the pension to be set up is to plan such that the employee will receive as a pension about 1.35 percent of the number of years worked times the average pay for the last five years. Civil service retirees get a much higher pension; 2 percent instead of 1.35 or about 48 percent higher than industry. You had better be ready to run if you complain about this to civil servants. "We pay for our pensions!" They will say, and to a surprising degree they are right. To understand why they get more than you, during periods of low inflation it takes about 12 percent of a person's pay to end up with enough money to make the 1.35 percent retirement figure, so we could reasonably conclude that the employer could have paid his employees 12 percent more and not provided them with any pension. Since civil service retirees get 48 percent more retirement money for the same salary and number of years worked, in effect the government is holding back 18 percent of their employees' pay. Had they no pension, they would not have to pay 7 percent on one, and they would in addition receive 18 percent more spendible pay.

So on an equal basis, industrial workers getting $1,000 a month are really getting 12 percent more, or $1,120 a month. Civil service employees getting $1,000 a month are really getting 18 percent more, or $1,180 a month, less the 7 percent they have to pay, netting them $1,110 a month. Thus the two systems are remarkably alike: Industrial workers pay nothing toward their pensions and get the 1.35 percent figure, whereas government workers pay 7 percent and get a 2 percent coefficient.

I do not propose to get into arguments about whether civil service salaries are high or low—in my experience they are higher than in industry for low-paid workers and lower than in industry for executives—but whatever the truth, there is not a whole lot of difference about how much more could be paid to them if they had no pensions at all. Where the whole discussion blows apart is that when inflation is included, the civil service retirees are indexed, but the industrial retirees are not. The total indexing from 1970 to 1980 is close to 100 percent. Thus civil service retirees who have been out 10 years receive about *double* the pensions of industrial retirees, and the same holds true for the legislators who wrote the federal pension bill. So though arguments can be made that civil service pensions are a shade higher (or lower) than those of industry, when indexing is added in, civil service pensions are far, far above those of industrial workers. And what do the civil service retirees say about all this? "Well, it's not my fault!" Of course it isn't. But I can't imagine a properly funded pension program that would furnish an indexed pension, and in case anybody asks if I think one segment should be protected against inflation, I don't. And I can't think of a savings plan that could be protected against double-digit inflation, either.

Many working people are not covered by a retirement plan. Perhaps they run their own businesses, or did not work long enough to become vested with any one plan. For them, and for those who feel their pensions will not be large enough, the government has set up a number of savings plans. I will discuss these in some depth in the sections to follow.

7.3. SOCIAL SECURITY

The Social Security program is another part of your pension income. Originally set up as a supplement to what you and your employer could come up with, the program is, as I write, in jeopardy because of (1) the benefit payments added to the original program without additional contributions, (2) being indexed against inflation, while the salaries that contribute the money are not, and (3) the larger-than-predicted number of old folks who live longer than they used to. I both hope and believe that the program can be brought back into fiscal balance through a combination of changes.

As for answering the question of whether Social Security pays enough or too much for what people pay into it, it depends on each situation. Some get more than they paid, and some get less.

Since Social Security is indexed, it is impossible to figure what you will get at retirement. For a first cut you might call the local office and find out what you would get now at age 65. You will get an amount to provide the same buying power later on.

7.4. TAX REDUCTIONS FOR INDIVIDUALS

The Tax Relief Act of 1981 includes seven major tax changes that benefit individuals and in turn will make it easier to find the money needed to put into the selected savings and accumulation plans:

1. There are tax reductions of 5 percent (on a yearly basis) effective October 1, 1981, and additional reductions of 10 percent effective July 1, 1982, and 10 percent more on July 1, 1983. Since the first reduction was actually only for a quarter year, it ended up being 1.25 percent, and was scarcely noticed, as Social Security taxes were increased at the same time. The other tax reductions work out to 19 percent in 1983 and 23 percent in 1984. Estimates are that the bill would cut tax receipts by $2.1 billion in 1981, $37.2 billion in fiscal 1982, $93.7 billion in fiscal 1983, $149.5 billion in fiscal 1984, and $191.9 billion in fiscal 1985. These cuts, unless offset by reductions in federal spending or by increases in tax receipts through a higher level of business, would quite obviously put our federal deficits over the $100 billion mark. Furthermore, they

would have the government pull in, according to whose estimate you use, about 85 percent of *all* the loan money in the country, unless the decision was made to monetize part or all of the deficit, which would be the cause of higher inflation.

2. The top tax rate on investment income was lowered from 70 to 50 percent, a change that could affect a number of no-load investors.

3. The maximum rate of taxes on capital gains was lowered to 20 percent, again important to investors.

4. The tax tables will be indexed in reverse so that income increases due to inflation will no longer push a person into a higher bracket, beginning in 1985.

5. There will be some relief to the "marriage tax penalty" in the form of a 5 percent deduction of the lower income up to $1,500 in 1982 and a 10 percent deduction up to $3,000 in 1983 and thereafter.

6. Provisions were made for un-itemized tax deductions for charitable gifts. These seem unrelated to the subject of this book and will not be covered.

7. The gain on selling a house with a replacement home purchased within two years will be tax free up to $125,000. This is a possible source of investment money.

7.5. SAVINGS PROVISIONS

Four changes in the previous tax approach to savings were included in the Tax Relief Act of 1981, as follows:

1. Individuals were given $1,000 lifetime exclusions ($2,000 for joint returns) for interest received on certain qualified tax-exempt savings certificates issued after September 1, 1981, and before January 1, 1983. These certificates were to be issued by banks, savings and

loans, and credit unions with specific provisos for the money to be used for residential and agricultural loans.

2. Beginning in 1985, individuals can exclude annually 15 percent of the difference between interest income and interest deductions, ignoring deductions for interest paid on home loans.

3. The 1981 $200 ($400 on a joint return) dividend and interest exclusion was repealed January 1, 1982 with half of those amounts continuing thereafter. The rationale for this was that investors could buy All Savers certificates and exclude $1,000.

4. The IRA (Individual Retirement Account) was increased from the lesser of $1,500 or 15 percent of your pay to the lesser of $2,000 or 100 percent of your pay. Married couples with one spouse working have a $2,250 limit and working couples may shelter $2,000 each in separate accounts. These changes are very, very big and will be discussed in a later section.

7.6.   THE KEOGH PLAN

The Keogh plan was set up to permit self-employed workers to accumulate a retirement fund without taxes in a manner similar to that of salaried employees whose employers provide a pension plan. Those eligible for a Keogh plan include:

Accountants	Chiropractors	Ministers
Architects	Dentists	Plumbers
Artists	Doctors	Restaurant owners
Authors	Farmers	Store owners
Carpenters	Grocers	Veterinarians
Consultants	Housepainters	

and many others who are self-employed. Keogh plans may also be set up for income from moonlighting of a direct personal service type (writing, yard work, playing in a band, etc.)

The Keogh plan (also known as HR-10) has been substantially improved by the Tax Relief Act of 1981:

1. The amount a person can shelter is still 15 percent of what he or she earns, but with increased limits of $15,000 in 1982, $20,000 in 1983, and a 20 percent rate to a maximum of $30,000 in 1984.

2. You may add an additional 10 percent of self-employment income up to $2,500 if you have at least one employee in a plan.

3. If you do not have a total of $100,000 in self-employment income (which would qualify you for the maximum $15,000 tax-free amount, you may deposit 100 per cent of the first $750 earned in a Keogh account. (This is a big winner for part-time moonlighters.)

4. The time during which you can send money earned in any one year has been extended to the day you file your income tax.

Keogh money may be subtracted from income—taken off the top, as they say in Las Vegas—without any payment of taxes and invested in certain vehicles whose earnings are also tax free until the gross is finally used. These vehicles include mutual funds, trusts, endowments, annuities, face amount securities, or government bonds. During the period of growth the monies are in escrow and are not available for use or collateral, nor may they be garnisheed. However, and this is exceedingly important, if they are invested in a switch fund, they may be switched from the stock fund to the cash haven fund at will. This means that your retirement monies do not have to ride a poor market down.

Nor are you locked into a poor fund. Should you desire to change the fund you have selected for your Keogh plan, you may move to another fund, incurring new commissions if it is a load fund, but not any taxes, even if there are profits. The new commissions may be avoided if there is another fund in the same family to which a switch is possible, or if the money is moved to a no-load fund. Movement of a Keogh plan is a difficult procedure, and it might well help to enlist the help of a friendly broker. The process takes several weeks and should not be attempted at the end of the year when you may want to add additional funds to the account, as this is a busy time for Keogh plan people.

The Keogh monies may be first used at age 59½ and must be withdrawn by age 70½.* Thus any time after reaching 59½, you may:

1. Request the return of all of your contributions and profits and use the total to buy an annuity, or put it into a mutual fund withdrawal plan. This is called a *rollover*.

2. Continue your Keogh plan even if you have retired from your salaried position. This ends at age 70½.

3. Receive the total amount in a lump sum. If you do this, use 10-year averaging when you figure your taxes.

The retirement plans, which may or may not be managed by the custodian bank, are charged about $10 a year for the extra services. The funds usually make three minor concessions to their normal modus operandi:

1. If the fund has a required starting amount, it is almost always reduced or waived entirely.

2. If the fund has a minimum amount for subsequent payments, this is waived too.

---

*No, I don't know where the one-half came from.

3. If the fund charges for reinvesting dividends, this is also waived.

Going back to "skimming off the top" and excluding taxes during growth, these features are *big*. The effects are illustrated in Example 7.1 and Table 7.1.

Example 7.1. Compare the difference in accumulation for one year, assuming an investment of $1,000 at a 12 percent rate of profit and a 32 percent tax rate, with and without taxes.

	With Taxes	Without Taxes
Gross amount	$1,000.00	$1,000.00
Less 32% tax	−320.00	0.00
Net	$ 680.00	$1,000.00
12% earnings	76.16	120.00
Less taxes	−12.18	0.00
Net at year's end	$ 743.98	$1,120.00

For these particular circumstances, not paying taxes saves 50.5 percent. The combination of no taxes and withdrawing over a 10-year period while a 10 percent profit rate continues on the remainder is particularly impressive. The payouts shown

Table 7.1.   Results from Investing $1,000 per Year in a Tax-Free Plan Growing at 10% a Year[a]

	5 Years	10 Years	15 Years	20 Years
Contributions	$ 5,000	$10,000	$15,000	$ 20,000
10% growth	1,716	7,535	19,960	43,024
Lump sum payout	6,716	17,535	34,960	63,024
10-year payout rate	1,093	2,854	5,690	10,260
Total payout	10,930	28,540	56,900	102,600

[a]Payments are withdrawn over a 10-year period while the growth continues at 10 percent per year.

in Table 7.1 run from 50 to 100 percent more than a taxed investment program, depending on the tax rate.

About 70,000 people use no-load funds as their Keogh vehicle.

Almost every fund has a Keogh plan arrangement. There is a little paperwork needed for you as an individual to get one into operation, as follows. First, you will have to fill out a federal form stating the source of your income (investments do not qualify) and then get permission to have a Keogh plan. Then during any calendar year you may invest up to 15 percent of your service income to maximums given earlier and subtract that amount from your taxable income. Should you hold the Keogh plan until you have reached 59½, you may use the withdrawal plan to receive a steady income. Should you withdraw the money earlier, the amount you withdraw must be added to the current year's income and taxes paid on it.

Note the word *service* in the preceding paragraph. Thousands of moonlighters who make extra money by doing something for somebody else are eligible for the Keogh plan if the extra money is not already covered by a retirement plan. Those who run a business may not set up a plan for themselves unless their employees are included.

As for the mechanics of setting up a plan, Step 1 is the rather obvious one of ascertaining that the proposed fund will handle a Keogh plan. Step 2 is the filling out of the forms furnished by the fund. The first is an agreement with the fund accepting their terms. The second is a request to a custodian bank (not necessarily the same as the fund's custodian bank) to implement the agreement with the fund and naming a beneficiary in case you die before the retirement money is used. The third is an Internal Revenue Form 3673 which must be sent in duplicate to the local office of the IRS for their concurrence that you have income that qualifies under the Keogh plan. Your no-load fund will have the IRS forms. After the IRS approves your plan (this only takes a few days), it will return one of the 3673 forms to you. For the last step, you may then start sending money using the retirement forms provided by the fund. This money is entirely separate from any other account you may have with the fund.

Most of the foregoing has been written for individuals. Employers may use the Keogh plan if they bring their employees in, as mentioned before, and an added benefit for the employees is that they may keep the retirement plan if they change jobs, a situation which is sometimes not possible under the usual retirement plans. The plans may also be continued if the business acquires a new owner, and he or she agrees to continue it.

7.7. INCOME TAXES ON KEOGH PLANS

The monies in a Keogh plan when used may be taken over a period of years or as a lump sum. For the delayed payments, all contributions except those on which taxes have already been paid are treated as straight income and taxed accordingly. If taken in a lump sum, there is a special tax computation, which seems so advantageous that one can hardly decide against it. Basically it permits capital gains on the monies received before January 1, 1974, and income averaging on those received after that date. The procedure is a masterpiece even for the IRS and is best followed ("understood" would be the wrong word) via an example.

Example 7.2.   Assume Mr. Smith received a lump sum Keogh or IRA payment in 1975 of $65,000, which was $40,000 cash and $25,000 in stocks that originally cost $10,000. He has been in the *non-contributive* plan 10 years. How should the taxes be figured?

1. The total taxable amount is the lump sum less personal contributions (none in this case) and less paper profits (in this case $25,000 − $10,000 = $15,000). Thus the total taxable amount is $65,000 − $15,000 = $50,000.

2. The *minimum distribution allowance* (MDA) is the smaller of $10,000 or one-half of the total taxable

amount. Since the latter is ½ × $50,000 − $25,000, the MDA is $10,000. The *net* MDA is $10,000 less 0.2 ($50,000 − $20,000) = $4,000.

3. The *effective tax amount* is the total less the net MDA or $50,000 − $4,000 = $46,000.

4. The initial tax on the effective amount is obtained by reading the single person's tax for one-tenth of the effective tax amount, and multiplying it by 10. From the single person's table the tax for $4,600 is $816. The initial tax is then 10 × $816 = $8,160.

5. The capital gains monies are based on the fraction of the retirement plan years before January 1, 1974. In this example this is 8/10 × $50,000 = $40,000. This amount is subject to capital gains treatment and income averaging from Schedule G.

6. The ordinary income monies are based on the fraction of the retirement plan years after January 1, 1974, or 2/10 × $50,000 = $10,000.

7. The *separate tax* is based on the fraction of retirement plan years after January 1, 1974, and the initial tax. This is 2/10 × $8,160 = $1,632.

8. The income tax for the year is finally based on IRS Form 4782 and Schedule G to average the last year's salary and the capital gains, and then the separate tax of $1,632 is added in.

The important part of this is realizing that it results in a large reduction of taxes that could arise through a lump sum payment, and no special treatment.

For a "bad news" closing, many states do not permit you to skim off the top for a retirement plan, regardless of what Uncle Sam says, and you will have to pay state income taxes on the full income. You will have to check your own state to find out.

7.8. INDIVIDUAL RETIREMENT ACCOUNTS (IRA)

The original Individual Retirement Account act was intended to fill a gap in retirement plans: self-employed people had been able to use the Keogh plan, many workers had employer-paid pensions, and the old IRA permitted those workers whose employers did not have a pension plan to build one for themselves.

The new IRA has three different plans:

1. **Accumulation IRA.** Any wage earner under the age of 70½ can set up an accumulation IRA. He or she may contribute 100 percent of earned income, up to $2,000 annually. If both husband and wife work, each can establish a separate IRA of up to $2,000 a year.

2. **Spousal IRA.** Anybody who is eligible for an accumulation plan may also contribute to an IRA for his or her spouse. The maximum contribution is then 100 percent of earned income up to $2,250, split in any way between the two accounts, except neither may receive more than $2,000 a year.

3. **Rollover IRA.** Any person who has received a lump-sum distribution from a qualified retirement plan may roll over this money within 60 days into a number of new investments for his or her retirement.

I'll discuss the accumulation and spousal IRAs together. Rollovers are discussed in Sections 7.10 and 8.3.

The advantages that result from the rules of the new IRA accumulation plan are so cogent that every working person should really strive to start one. If necessary start one with less than the maximum allowed, but start one. In essence you may invest up to certain limits tax free for now, in a number of different investments. Making a payment into your IRA saves on this year's taxes, as shown in Table 7.2.

Table 7.2   Taxes Deferred by Using an IRA Accumulation Account

| Tax Bracket (%) | Taxes Deferred ($) | | |
	$1,000 Deposit/Year	$2,000 Deposit/Year	$4,000 Deposit/Year
20	200	400	800
30	300	600	1,200
40	400	800	1,600
50	500	1,000	2,000

Your IRA investments, whatever they may be, will grow faster than investments that don't use the IRA plan because (1) you can afford to put more in them (no taxes are taken out of the $2,000) and (2) no taxes are paid, and as the nest eggs earn money, it is all reinvested.

For an example of how much the tax-free-profits angle contributes, consider an individual in the 50 percent bracket who invests $2,000 for 25 years at a low 9 percent. Over the years she would accumulate $184,000. Had she paid taxes at her 50 percent rate on the profits, the total would have turned out to be only $46,000. Quite a difference.

You may put the money into your investment in any way you prefer that is acceptable to the custodian, up to the time you send in your taxes by April 15 the following year. Of course, the sooner you get the money invested the sooner it starts making money for you. You do not have to agree to put in a fixed amount each month or year, but note that the sooner the money gets invested and earns, say, 15 percent a year tax free (for now), the faster the account will grow. The results of investing the maximum of $167 a month are shown in Table 7.3, and for investing $100 a month in Table 7.4. The $100-a-month table is included so that you may easily figure smaller amounts, such as $50 or $25 a month, which will yield half or a quarter of the amounts in Table 7.4.

One cannot help but be impressed by the enormous amounts of money that accumulate under a steady investment program

Table 7.3.   Amounts Accumulated Through Putting $167 a Month into an IRA Account

Number of Years	Amount ($) at Yearly Rate of Return of				
	5%	10%	15%	20%	25%
5	11,600	13,400	15,500	17,800	20,500
10	26,400	35,000	46,700	62,300	83,100
15	45,300	69,000	109,400	172,800	274,200
20	69,400	126,000	253,000	448,000	857,300
25	100,200	216,300	489,400	1,132,700	2,636,900

at interest rates in line with what no-load mutual funds have been earning.

Another way to use Table 7.4 is to suppose IRA had started earlier and you had been putting $50 a month into a mutual fund account for 10 years at 15 percent. Your account would now be worth $14,000. Now go to Appendix A and see what $14,000 would be worth 20 years later, when you retire, at the same rate of 15 percent, supposing you never put another dime into your IRA. It comes out to $228,200.

One would be hard put to argue that an IRA investment is not essential for nearly every working person, at least until other sources (pensions, Social Security, other investments)

Table 7.4.   Amounts Accumulated Through Putting $100 a Month Into an IRA Account

Number of Years	Amount ($) at Yearly Rate of Return of				
	5%	10%	15%	20%	25%
5	7,000	8,000	9,300	10,700	12,300
10	15,800	21,000	28,000	37,400	49,800
15	27,200	41,900	65,600	103,600	164,000
20	41,600	75,600	141,000	269,000	514,000
25	60,000	129,800	293,000	680,000	1,570,000

will clearly provide adequate retirement monies. On the other hand, this is not an investment for a home or a child's schooling. The tax-free $2,000 or whatever is put into the account is effectively gone for a long, long time. But it's yours. You can't lose it by being fired or moving before you are vested. It's a portable pension.

An IRA may not be used for collateral, nor can it be attached by creditors. Nor is it a short-term vehicle as it turns what might be capital gains into fully taxed income. A good guess would be that those having less than five years before they reach the age of 70½ would not benefit by an IRA accumulation plan, even if they continued working.

Only part of one's savings should be put into an IRA. Save some for emergencies.

It is misleading to think about an IRA as "an account." It can and should be a series of accounts: bonds or bond funds to nail down high interest rates when they are available, growth mutual funds when there is a bull market, money market funds when there is a bear market, or other investments listed subsequently. Thus you will have a continuous requirement to make investment decisions and whether to move money already invested. There are six permissible investments for IRAs: U.S. retirement bonds; banks and S&Ls; credit unions; self-directed brokerage plans; insurance companies; and mutual funds. You may not employ municipal bonds, U.S. government bonds, real estate, precious metals, diamonds, or other collectibles for an IRA. Those permitted are discussed here:

1.   **U.S. individual retirement bonds.**   These bonds have been created especially for IRA accounts and are the only investment that you may make directly by yourself. The bonds pay 9 percent compounded semiannually and the interest rate is guaranteed until you reach 70½. You may buy these in person or by mail from the Federal Reserve banks. Safety in these bonds is superb.

2.   **Banks and S&Ls.**   Banks and S&Ls offer investments that pay a guaranteed rate of interest, usually for a few years, and a significantly lower rate should the money be withdrawn

or switched before the time period is up. These vehicles are insured for up to $100,000.

3. **Credit unions.**   If you are a member of a credit union you may buy its three-year certificates of deposit. This yield usually surpasses that of banks and S&Ls, but is for a short period only.

4. **Self-directed plans.**   Your broker will help you set up a self-directed IRA wherein you say what you want to invest in and he handles the investments and the IRA paperwork. Fees for this should be looked at, as they are often quite high. As you know by now, I don't recommend that you endeavor to run a stock and bond portfolio for your IRA program. Your chances of success aren't very good.

5. **Insurance companies.**   Deferred annuities (those which start paying later) are the vehicles most often offered for IRA accounts by insurance companies. There is usually a sales charge of several percent.

6. **Mutual funds.**   The continuity of mutual funds and their successful record of profit making surely make them top contenders for IRA monies. Add in a telephone switch arrangement and it seems to me that funds, particularly no-load funds, offer the very best of all vehicles for long-term continuous investing, recognizing that it would be continuous only in the sense that one fund group would be involved even though several funds might be used as the occasion demands. To that end there are about a dozen families of no-load funds—you may identify them in your daily paper, and essentially all have telephone switches for IRA accounts. This sounds like I am saying that you have to stay with one fund group. Of course that is not so. You may use any number you want. Each will be continuously available. Since profits are tax free while in an IRA savings plan, new no-load funds are coming on the market whose managers are free to take short-term capital gains. This has been an advantage for offshore funds; we will have to see how it works out here.

Selecting no-load funds for your IRA, you will probably end up with a group of about six funds of the growth type, plus maybe a bond fund, or bonds bought directly through a broker IRA account.

Income received from the investment is tax free provided it is left in the account, which is not available for borrowing from or pledging for a loan except in extraordinary instances. Withdrawal may start at age 59½ and all monies withdrawn are taxed at the full income rate. You must start withdrawing at age 70½, when the total may be used to buy a lifetime annuity or withdrawals may be at the life expectancy rate of the owner, or the life expectancies for husband and wife.

It is simple to open an IRA account:

1. For the U.S. retirement bonds, go to your bank or the nearest Federal Reserve bank and fill out the forms and pay as directed.

2. For banks, savings and loans, and credit unions, go to your choice and learn of their different vehicles and make your selection.

3. To set up a self-directed plan, go to any broker and have him explain how he can set up a separate account for your IRA and how you can use it to buy and sell stocks or bonds.

4. To use an insurance company for your IRA, visit your choice and discuss their programs.

5. For using no-load mutual funds for your IRA, write a number of funds, preferably in a fund family that permits telephone switches, and ask for the forms needed to set up an IRA. The forms are quite easy to handle. They ask for your name, address, Social Security number, home and work telephone numbers, date of birth, name of spouse, spouse's Social Security number and name of your primary beneficiary. The usual starting amount is waived and another ($25 to $250) replaces it. There may be a starting fee of, say, $5, a yearly charge of $2 to $12, and a charge for each check they send to you later on. In most cases the account will be held by the custodian bank of the fund concerned.

Deciding where to invest your IRA monies is not a one-time thing, nor is it permanent. You will be investing up to $167 per month or borrowing some money to make the $2,000 investment in one crack, and you may be doing this for a long, long time. You may take the money out of any or all IRA accounts,

hold it for up to 60 days, and put it back in once each year—
this is called a rollover—or you may switch any or all accounts
without having the money come to you, as many times as you
wish. Thus each year or even more often you must make the
decision as to which investment is best at the particular time
the money is to be put in, which in turn may be any time
during the taxable year, and whether to switch what you have.
It would not make sense to invest in money market funds during
the work year and then put the money into one of your IRA
accounts, because there would be taxes due on the profits.

Bonds should be looked at, as it may be possible to lock in a
high interest rate for many years. It probably would not be
possible to use the exact dollars and come out even with a bond
purchase, a problem that could be avoided by using a bond
fund, or putting some money in bonds and adding the leftover
funds to another account.

7.9. WITHDRAWING FROM YOUR IRA ACCOUNT

There are three time periods that are significant to IRA accounts:
(1) the years before you become 59½; (2) the years from then
until you become 70½; and (3) the years after you become
70½.

1. You may withdraw any or all of the money in your IRA
before the year when you become 59½, and unless you can
justify the need for the money as urgent—extreme illness, death
of wage earner, or such—you will be taxed on the whole amount
withdrawn, and in addition there will be a 10 percent tax on
the amount withdrawn. Don't take a quick look at that statement and say, "Well, I'll just put my money in, and if I need it,
I'll take it out and pay the 10 percent." You may well end up
paying more than if you never had an IRA account. The reason
is that after a few years a large part of your account may have
been due to long-term capital gains, and the IRA requirement
turns this into income and so taxes it. When you add the 10
percent penalty for early withdrawal, there is a good chance

that you would have been better off without your IRA. You might work out a hypothetical example using your tax rate and some estimated rate of gain. For the examples I have worked, using an IRA or not using one does not make a lot of difference for those 65 or older, but the IRA owner does not have the opportunity to use his or her investment as collateral for loans, or have easy access to the money.

2.   Between 59½ and 70½ you may withdraw any or all of your money at whatever rate suits you. Again, you will pay taxes on whatever you withdraw at the regular income tax rate. The more you leave in, the more it will grow.

3.   Before the year when you become 70½ you *must* tell the custodians of your IRA accounts that you want to start withdrawing your money, and which of the two choices you plan to use:

a.   Use the money to purchase an annuity that will guarantee payments for the rest of your life, or for the life of you and your spouse.

b.   Have the custodian spread payments over a fixed number of years not to exceed your life expectancy or that of your spouse. At age 70½ this is 12 years for males, 15 for females. However, either spouse may be considerably younger than the other, and payments may then be spread out over a long, long time. Jill Bittner in the *Wall Street Journal* gave an example of a $100,000 account earning 12 percent a year that was paid out over 25 years. The account actually paid out $635,542.

I prefer spreading payments over buying an annuity in order to save the commissions.

Nearly all advertisements for "Use our plan for your IRA" make the point that although your IRA money will be fully taxed, you will get it at a time when your income is down and your tax rate is low. If you do have a pension, a modest collection of other investments, and a couple of hundred thousand dollars that must be taken over a period of a relatively few years, your tax rate may be anything but low. I don't think you will get a lot of sympathy for this, but I would keep watch on my IRA account, and as soon as your prediction shows you will meet your retirement aims, there is no sense putting more money in the account. Spend it.*

As for avoiding taxes, since the 10-year averaging is not available for IRA accumulation plans, one could take a lump sum and use the five-year averaging for special aberrations in income. Or you could conveniently die, and run the corpus of the investment through your estate as discussed in the next chapter. There really isn't much you can do to reduce your taxes on a large income. I don't think it's a big worry for now. By the way, don't play with just not withdrawing it. Failure to take out monies as prescribed can result in 50 percent penalties on the difference between what you took out and what you should have taken out.

7.10. ROLLOVERS

Often a person receives a lump sum from a qualified retirement plan and is faced with a jump in that year's income along with concomitant taxes. He or she may use 10-year averaging to reduce the lump sum taxes, or may roll it over within 60 days into an IRA. Once it is in the IRA, the lump sum can grow, tax free, until the year when the investor reaches 70½. As covered in Section 7.8, there are ways in which IRA monies can escape estate taxes.

The fact that an IRA account has a rollover in it does not affect the right of the account owner to add each year up to the limits given heretofore.

7.11. CHOICES FOR BENEFICIARIES

If the owner of an IRA account dies and has only one beneficiary, he or she has several options:

*That's a heck of a thing for an investment adviser to tell a client: "Spend your money." And I have a hard time getting me to take my own advice.

1. The beneficiary may continue to treat the account as an IRA of the deceased, but the money wil have to be withdrawn from the account within five years.
2. The beneficiary could roll over the assets and buy a lifetime annuity, paying taxes as payments are received.
3. The beneficiary could treat the account as his or hers and withdraw as described from age 59½ to age 70½. The beneficiary could even add to the account if he or she is a wage earner.
4. Distributions to beneficiaries will not be subjected to estate taxes if they are made in regular payments for a period of at least 36 months.

7.12.   *SALARY-REDUCTION PLANS*

Advertised as "better than an IRA," salary-reduction plans have been around for a long, long time. Usually they were called *deferred compensation plans* and many movie stars and TV personalities had part of their pay held back and paid later to reduce the high bracket they were in. With the renaissance of the concept of saving for one's retirement via the plans discussed previously, new interest has been kindled in deferred compensation at all levels of pay.

Here is a summary of the deferred payment plan features:

1. Deferred payment plans can permit withholding up to 25 percent of a person's salary (the average cannot be more than 15 percent for all employees) as opposed to the $2,000 per person for the IRA plan.
2. Payments into a deferred payment plan never pass through the employee's hands and hence are not subjected to Social Security taxes, which for many people are more than income taxes. (With IRA all of one's salary is taxed for Social Security payments.)
3. Money in deferred payment plans can be withdrawn under fairly lenient "hardship" rules. (With IRA with-

drawal without substantial penalty payments is only for disability or death.)

4. When money in a deferred payment plan is finally used, it may be 10-year averaged with a subsequent reduction in taxes. (IRA monies are taxed as income.)

5. Your employer may contribute additional monies to your deferred payment plan. This cannot be done for an IRA.

6. You may borrow from your salary reduction plan, but not from your IRA.

On the fairly negative side are the following:

1. The employer arranges for management of the money held back. (With an IRA you can direct and switch your money.)

2. You can't have a deferred payment plan unless your employer sets one up. Setting up an IRA is up to you.

Possibly the biggest problem with a deferred payment plan is the question of who manages the money. For instance the state of Louisiana, with the best of intentions, set up a deferred compensation plan a few years ago and the organization that was hired invested the money in a program that paid it a 20 percent commission! If that weren't enough, the program included a 50 percent penalty if the money was withdrawn early. (This is in court at the present time.) Other examples can be found that are just as sad. It is hard to see why hiring a special manager is necessary when so many mutual funds have excellent public records. If you do elect to use a deferred payment plan, make sure you know what happens to the money should you leave the company, and that there are no big withdrawal penalties.

7.13.   403 (b) TAX-SHELTERED RETIREMENT PLAN

A third type of tax shelter plan that should be included in this chapter is the 403(b) plan offered only to employees of nonprofit and tax-exempt institutions. This plan also allows contributions to be deducted from pre-tax salary. It permits up to 20 percent of the earned income to be squirreled away without being taxed, and in some cases the amount is even larger. Money placed in a 403(b) investment plan may be withdrawn if you leave your present employer (and taxes paid at that time), or it may be withdrawn if you encounter "financial hardship." You cannot set up a 403(b) plan on your own; your employer must approve the plan you select.

8

Mutual Funds and Estates

Looking back at my estate and that of various friends and acquaintances, it seems to me that there are four stages in accumulation and management:

1. In early life, age 20 to 30, the overwhelming aim of an estate is to provide a reasonable living standard for your family. Often this is not possible at the time, and most of the direct effort is aimed at creating an instant estate with insurance.

2. In the next period, 30 to 55, it becomes possible to hold back on increasing one's standard of living, and some monies are invested, aimed toward more income now or later. This is a fine time for no-load funds.

3. The third period, 55 to 65, is spent getting ready for retirement—finishing up time payments on whatever, and rearranging investment to provide income. Possibly insurance should be cashed out.

4. The fourth period, from 65 on, is the time to think about the second and third generation, and how to make the assets last as long as possible, while suffering as little as possible from the tax collector.

If things have gone well, the period from 55 on can be one of agonizing over whether you should make your kids wait for their inheritances, or whether you should pass out some money each year to help them along. Watch out for this one. I have seen friends ruin their children's lives by making them independent. A free fortune can make a person lazy—why work for $20,000 or $30,000 a year when you have $100,000 coming in besides? My suggestion is to keep the gifts light and the support when they need it heavy; and—who knows—one kid may need it all.

Anyhow, mutual funds are being used more and more in estate planning as time goes by. The reasons are that they furnish the following:

1. Acceptability in financial and legal circles.
2. Continuous management for as long as needed.
3. Very long term performance records.
4. Safety.
5. Suitability for trusts.

So whether or not your estate is already in mutual funds, there may be circumstances where you or your "personal representative" will direct that mutual funds be employed. The Tax Relief Act of 1981 greatly reduced estate taxes, and for those with estates below several hundred thousand dollars only a simple will is needed to make sure the estate goes where you wish it to go and is protected from incompetence as needed. This chapter thus serves to inform you of the many ways mutual funds can help achieve your desires. Surely an accountant will be needed with all but the smallest estates.

There are really three regimes to be considered when passing your estate on to your loved ones:

1. The year after your death during which the executor may pass out some living expenses, but in general the estate is stagnant.
2. The support of your spouse during his or her lifetime.
3. Passing as much of the estate as possible down to the children, possibly with controls such that a divorce does not send it to an ex-family member.

If your shares have been registered jointly with right of survivorship (see Section 3.6), they may be immediately transferred to the survivor and withdrawal-plan payments may continue uninterrupted. The mechanics of this are quite simple. Your executor will send your state succession tax office a request to transfer the shares to your spouse's name. The state succession tax office then issues an "Authorization and Consent to Transfer," and sends it to your executor, who sends it to the fund's custodian bank. It usually makes the change in a week or so. As a matter of interest, there could be claims against this money, but that's not the worry of the state succession office. It's the worry of the executor.

Shares not held in trust for your spouse or not registered jointly with right of survivorship go into the general estate and await the final disposition as requested in your will. This is one time that all concerned will appreciate owning mutual funds, as the money will continue to be managed, even though it is essentially in escrow.

8.1. THE TAX RELIEF ACT OF 1981

The new tax relief act made profound changes in estate taxes. Under the previous law you could leave one-half of your estate to your spouse tax free, but now you may leave it all. By setting up a trust, you will be able to ensure that your spouse will have an income from the estate as long as she or he lives, and that your children will receive whatever is left after your spouse dies. Should you be unmarried at the time of death, the amount of your estate exempt from estate taxes will gradually increase, as shown in Table 8.1.

Thus for most of us (it has been estimated that the number is 98 percent), estate taxes will not be a problem. Should you have an estate above the exemptions in Table 8.1, and should most of the property be in your name, transfer appropriate amounts to your spouse as a gift—there are no limits on this. This will make use of the higher exemptions available. For example, should your estate be $1.2 million, the split will enable

Table 8.1.   Estate Tax Exemptions and Rates

Year	Amount Exempt from Estate Taxes ($)	Maximum Estate Tax Rate (%)
1983	275,000	60
1984	325,000	55
1985	400,000	50
1986	500,000	50
1987	600,000	50

either of you to leave his or her part to the children with income to the survivor sans estate taxes.

The new tax law also enables you as the donor to have greater control over the trust, as you can now get the income to your spouse and not permit your spouse to change the beneficiaries should a second marriage or other changes occur.

8.2. GIFTS

No-load funds make excellent gifts, because often the recipient is not a skilled investor, and management of the money involved ensures its security. Currently gifts up to $10,000 a year ($20,000 for a couple) are tax free, and can be made to as many individuals as the bankroll can afford. Gifts move the owner-ship of the funds from the donor to the recipient, whose tax bracket would certainly be less, and of course there is a concomitant reduction in the donor's estate. If there is a choice, give funds that are close in current value to their actual cost, leaving capital gains to the donor's use. The total of all the gifts has no effect on exemptions from estate taxes.

Someday the recipient of the gifts will want to sell them, and it happens that tax treatment is different according to whether the sale encompasses a profit or a loss. For examples, suppose a child receives a fund worth $5,000, but which cost only $2,000 some years back. If sold for $9,000 some time later, taxes would be owed on $7,000—the original cost being the basis. Had the shares been sold at a loss for $4,000, only $1,000 could be claimed; the basis this time is the value at transfer.

While we are on the subject of gift taxes, here's one that's hard to explain. If the same shares that cost $2,000 when they were bought were *willed* to your child, and were worth $5,000 on the day you died, the $5,000 figure would apply for both future profits and losses. Nope, I don't know why it's so different from gifts.

Gifts of mutual fund shares to minor children should be made as early as possible so that any capital gains will be in the child's estate and taxed at his or her rate, not yours.

Gifts of appreciated property such as mutual funds that have gained in value over the years, made to a charitable public tax-exempt organization, are fully tax deductible, and you do not have to prove when you purchased them or for how much. If you normally make gifts of this kind in cash, consider giving a few shares of a Fund.

8.3. ROLLOVERS

Many readers are participants in profit-sharing, reduced-salary, or savings plans that will result in a large distribution in the event of work termination, retirement, or death. Such funds may be rolled over into IRA or other types of investments described subsequently. These investments can result in very large tax savings, if handled properly. Since they are part of an estate, be sure you have named only one beneficiary. Should you name two or more, upon your death the monies will be taxed as ordinary income and not eligible for the 10-year averaging described later. (You may name your estate as beneficiary.) You will have 60 days to make up your mind and act, and if you find yourself not ready to move when the 60 days expires, open an IRA rollover account and deposit the funds within the time limit. The monies can be withdrawn any time up to when you file your income tax for the year, which in effect gives you an extension of the thinking time. Getting caught making a rollover after 60 days can result in a series of fines that will ruin your day, week, month, and year. There is a 6 percent excess contribution penalty for each year and a 10 percent premature withdrawal penalty; the entire amount becomes ordinary income, and you can get a one-half percent per month penalty due to failure to pay when due. It could be the largest tax rate you have ever heard of.

Should your spouse as a beneficiary receive a lump sum from your protected plan, within 60 days he or she may open an IRA rollover account, keeping all funds tax sheltered and compounding tax free. The IRA rules explained in Chapter 7 apply. Withdrawals cannot be taken before the year in which your spouse becomes 59½, and all payments will be considered ordinary income. The lump sum is in this case not considered as part of your estate.

If you use an IRA rollover for a lump sum distribution, any monies remaining in the account at your death must be distributed to your beneficiary within five years. The distributions are excluded from your estate if they are paid within three years.

Here are the choices:

1. Do nothing and accept the sum for whatever purpose you wish. It will be taxed as ordinary income. In short, you probably should do something.

2. Convert the money to an annuity and pay taxes on the money as you receive it for use. There will be a sales fee of several percent when the annuity is bought.

3. Take payments from the plan over a period of time and pay taxes on the money as received. This would be taxed as ordinary income.

4. Take a lump sum payment, and since the plan was started after December 31, 1973, use the 10-year averaging program to reduce the tax burden.

5. Put the money in an IRA rollover account. This cancels the possibility of income averaging on a 10-year basis, but it permits you to keep full control of the money under IRA rules until you start withdrawing it during

the year in which you become 70½. If you select a large mutual fund family for your IRA, you will have a wide selection of funds between which you can telephone switch or even use broker services for buying stocks and bonds.

6. Give the money to a trust to perform whatever you select within the current regulation, which the trustee will explain to you.

8.4. *USING MUTUAL FUNDS IN TRUSTS*

Mutual funds are particularly suitable for use in trusts because this action makes it possible to separate the trustee, who is expert in legal matters, from the money manager, who is expert in financial matters. For an example of why this procedure is necessary, let me tell you of my adventures seeking a trustee for my estate. If I wanted to feel sorry for anyone in the investing game, I would select bank trust officers during the past decade. Following hallowed procedures of buying government bonds for their trusts, they had to sit by and watch interest rates rise and the value of their trusts fall miserably. It was a very embarrassing and tragic era. But I'm really not all *that* sorry, since I visited one at my bank. He would, he assured me, make no effort at all to make my estate grow. His only aim in life was to keep it at the same value it had when it came into the trust department. All of the monies would be put into government bonds, which were then yielding 6 percent a year, and for his efforts he would charge the estate 0.75 percent a year. This works out to 12.5 percent of what would have been my wife's income, and it didn't thrill me then and it doesn't thrill me now. As we now know, interest rates went up, the value of the bonds went down, but the income would have held, and some day the bonds would have matured at their face value. So I guess it is clear why I don't recommend simply making your bank the trustee of your estate; law firms or younger informed relatives suit me better.

Coming back to trusts, there are two basic types: *testamen-*

tary trusts, which become effective upon your death, and *living* or inter vivos (between the living) trusts, which are effective for whatever period you so decide. Trusts require four parties: the *trustee*, who carries out the instructions of the trust; the person who makes the trust, called the *settlor* or *grantor;* the person who receives the income from the trust, called the *income beneficiary,* the *present beneficiary,* or if he or she gets the income for life, the *life beneficiary;* and the person who gets what's left of the trust when it terminates, called the *remainderman* or the *principal beneficiary.*

If you don't mind my stretching a point, all mutual funds are trusts in principle: You, the grantor, send money to them, the trustees, with the instructions to make some money for you, possibly send you, the income beneficiary, the dividends, and by acting as a trustee for your spouse you create a remainderman.

There are many types of testamentary trusts, but in general they are used in connection with mutual fund shares by leaving the shares to a bank, or other trustee to be held in trust for your children with the income to go to your spouse for life. To save arguments, have your lawyer spell out that the capital gains distributions are to be considered as income (if you wish) and are not to be reinvested in the fund. Or, if you wish, let the income be a withdrawal plan, and set the withdrawal rate yourself. You may also arrange for emergency use of the basic shares.

There are two types of living trusts: *revocable* and *irrevocable.* They mean what they say; you may revoke a revocable trust, but the irrevocable one is permanently as you set it. For an example of a revocable trust, it is probable that you would buy all your shares with yourself as trustee holding the mutual fund shares in trust for your spouse. Should you die, the shares are still in your estate for tax purposes, but they do not come under probate. This saves about 3 to 5 percent and is worth doing. After your death the certificates are simply rewritten in your spouse's name. Should your spouse die first or should you change your mind, a letter to the custodian bank (properly notarized) will dissolve the trust.

Clifford, or short-term irrevocable trusts, must be set up for 10 years and a day or more, and for $10,000 or more. For the term you must specify that a certain percentage be used for a particular purpose, such as providing income for a person not your social responsibility, or for your child to be used for items not your legal responsibility. For instance, instead of giving a daughter $100 a month out of your income, you could set up a trust of $12,000 and set the $100 rate, which is 10 percent a year. When the corpus is returned to you after the 10 years of investment in a successful mutual fund you should receive well over $12,000. You cannot have your daughter or other beneficiary return any of the income to you, and with her exemptions she will not have to pay any taxes herself, while you still get the $1,000 exemption for a child.

Here are a few more examples to pique your interest should your estate be of a type needing extra help. The six situations are all amenable to using no-load funds:

1. Widow Smith had $100,000 in bank certificates of deposit, and though not an experienced investor, she could see that her spending allowance through income taxes and no growth of principal was not keeping up with inflation. A lawyer skilled in trust work explained that she could create a revocable trust using mutual fund shares, held by a mutual fund group having a variety of funds including growth and tax-free yields. She could direct switching if she was so advised, and as beneficiaries of her estate, her children could too, later on. Should she become ill, the trustee could make additional funds available, and upon her death, probate time and costs would be avoided, and the fund shares could continue in further trusts for her children and grandchildren. Widow Smith also has the pleasure of watching the value of her trust in the daily paper, knowing she has constant professional management.

2. Engineer Jones could see that his estate would not take care of his children and his wife. Using both an IRA and monies above the IRA limits for direct investing in no-load funds, he bought additional life insurance and arranged for the proceeds to go into a mutual fund trust for his family's benefit.

3.   Executive Maydew collected a bundle of stock in the company he served, and upon retirement he realized that all of his eggs were in one basket, and that he might not be around to watch the basket for his wife. If he and his wife, who have no children, wish to leave the remainder to their favorite charity, it is possible for him to set up a charity trust to accept the shares, sell them without any capital gains taxes, and reinvest the money to provide the couple with more and diversified income during their lifetimes than they would have received from the stock. As they receive payments from the mutual fund trust they would have taxes for the so far untaxed capital gains spread out over the years. Provided their withdrawal rate is not too high, it is entirely possible that their mutual fund would grow fast enough to provide more income later on. At the death of the survivor the charity would receive a large tax-free gift.

4.   Mrs. Wilson has over the years set aside $25,000 to be used for her daughter's education. Because she is in a 50 percent tax bracket, the earnings from the account aren't making the fund grow very fast. She learns that she can set up an irrevocable living trust and use the $25,000 for an interest-free loan to the trustee. He would then invest the money in mutual funds and the profits would be taxed at her daughter's rate. Because the loan is interest free it adds nothing to her income, and she has the right to call back the loan at any time should she so wish.

5.   Wealthy Frank Nichols was distressed that his daughter Edith just couldn't handle money, and when she inherited her share of his estate it would be gone in no time. He talked this over with her, and she agreed that when the day came she would put her inheritance into a mutual fund trust to be managed by a trusted friend. She would receive all the income and could revoke the trust only with the approval of the trustee. Emily had to sign this agreement.

6.   Old Mr. Donahue, 88, found that he actually wasn't doing things he thought he had done, and he suspected that one day he would become incompetent to run his own affairs. Having his estate taken over while he was still living would require a sanity hearing, embarrassing to all. He found that he could set

up a trust whereby competent people would run his affairs for his benefit, simply on the statement of his physician that he could no longer do it—again an opportunity to separate the financial know-how of fund managers and the legal know-how of lawyers through the use of mutual funds.

As mentioned before, the purpose of this section is to acquaint you with some of the many things mutual fund shares can do for you besides, in all probability, making you a profit. Your lawyer can handle any of the foregoing procedures.

8.5. THE FUTURE OF MUTUAL FUNDS

The future of mutual funds is clearly tied in with the future of American industry, and one can be very optimistic about industry because at long last the people of the country understand that printing money is no solution to growth; in the final analysis all *that* does is require more and more of our tax money to go for nonproductive interest payments.

The growth of the no-load mutual fund industry has been phenomenal, and is surely due to the many advantages fund investing has over other types. Funds now own about 6 percent of the total market, with no-load stock funds about 1 percent of the total. The current proper emphasis on saving and investing is estimated to bring $20 billion a year into IRA plans, with a third of that going to the no-load funds. Surely this influx will ensure a strong and productive era.

8.6. FINALE

I hope that this book has been both educational and entertaining, and that you will want to keep it on your shelf for future reference, or even better lend it to your friends. To summarize my story, I have tried to make five points:

1. Mutual funds offer continuous management of your

money, absolutely essential in a changing world, and when business, death, or other personal matters don't give you time to do the job yourself.

2. Profits from the *right* mutual funds are outstanding. Your profit-to-risk ratio is higher with their wide diversification.

3. Managers are helped when they have a large percentage cash flow.

4. Besides being a good investment, funds offer many special features (use in trusts, custodian, Keogh, IRA, and withdrawal plans, etc.) that would make them attractive even if they cost money instead of making it.

5. Since no-load funds do as well as load funds, there is little reason for a person willing to do a little investment work not to pay himself the difference.

Good luck, and good investing.

Appendixes

APPENDIX A
VALUE OF $10,000 INVESTED FOR 1 TO 20 YEARS AT
COMPOUND GROWTH RATES OF 1 TO 40 PERCENT PER
YEAR

This table was constructed to cover higher interest rates than
are generally shown in conventional tables.

1. For investments less than $10,000, simply reduce the
    value in the tables according to the investment; $5,000,
    for instance, would yield half the amounts shown.

2. Examples:

    a. An investment of $10,000 grew to $14,146 in 6
        years. What was the average compound growth
        rate? *Answer:* Follow the 6-year line until you read
        that a 5.5 percent rate yields $13,790 and a 6
        percent rate yields $14,180. Since $14,146 is quite
        close to $14,180, we estimate the answer to be
        5.9 percent (Actual answer is 5.94 percent.)

    b. The per share value of an investment grew from
        $5.76 to $16.17 in 10 years. What was the aver-
        age compound growth rate? *Answer:* Divide
        16.17 by 5.76 to get the growth ratio, in this case
        2.80. Multiply 2.80 by $10,000 to match up with
        the table, which is based on a starting amount of
        $10,000. We see that 10.5 percent for 10 years

yields $27,140 and 11 percent yields $28,390. We then estimate 10.8 percent for $28,000. (Actual value is 10.83 percent.)

c. How many years will it take to increase $43,000 to $100,000 if a growth rate of 10 percent can be maintained? *Answer:* Divide $100,000 by $43,000 to get the growth ratio needed, which is 2.32. Next follow down the 10 percent column, seeking $23,200 (2.32 × $10,000). The best we can do is $21,440 for 8 years and $23,580 for 9 years. Estimate about 8.8 years. (Actual value is 8.83 years.)

Growth Rates

Number or Years	1%	1.5%	2%	2.5%	3%	3.5%	4%	4.5%
1	$10,100	$10,150	$10,200	$10,250	$10,300	$10,350	$10,400	$10,450
2	10,200	10,300	10,400	10,510	10,610	10,710	10,820	10,920
3	10,300	10,460	10,610	10,770	10,930	11,090	11,250	11,410
4	10,410	10,610	10,820	11,040	11,260	11,470	11,700	11,920
5	10,510	10,770	11,040	11,310	11,590	11,880	12,170	12,460
6	10,620	10,930	11,260	11,600	11,940	12,290	12,650	13,020
7	10,720	11,100	11,490	11,890	12,300	12,720	13,160	13,610
8	10,830	11,260	11,720	12,180	12,670	13,170	13,690	14,220
9	10,940	11,430	11,950	12,490	13,050	13,630	14,230	14,860
10	11,050	11,600	12,190	12,800	13,440	14,110	14,800	15,530
11	11,160	11,780	12,430	13,120	13,840	14,600	15,390	16,230
12	11,270	11,960	12,680	13,450	14,280	15,110	16,010	16,960
13	11,380	12,140	12,940	13,790	14,690	15,640	16,670	17,720
14	11,500	12,320	13,190	14,130	15,130	16,190	17,320	18,520
15	11,610	12,500	13,460	14,480	15,580	16,750	18,010	19,350
16	11,730	12,690	13,730	14,850	16,050	17,340	18,730	20,220
17	11,840	12,880	14,000	15,220	16,530	17,950	19,480	21,130
18	11,960	13,070	14,280	15,600	17,030	18,570	20,260	22,080
19	12,080	13,270	14,570	16,000	17,530	19,220	21,070	23,080
20	12,200	13,470	14,860	16,390	18,060	19,900	21,910	24,120

Growth Rates

Number of Years	5%	5.5%	6%	6.5%	7%	7.5%	8%	8.5%
1	$10,500	$10,550	$10,600	$10,650	$10,700	$10,750	$10,800	$10,850
2	11,020	11,130	11,240	11,340	11,450	11,560	11,660	11,770
3	11,580	11,740	11,910	12,080	12,250	12,420	12,600	12,770
4	12,150	12,390	12,620	12,860	13,110	13,350	13,600	13,860
5	12,760	13,070	13,380	13,700	14,030	14,360	14,690	15,040
6	13,400	13,790	14,180	14,590	15,010	15,430	15,870	16,320
7	14,070	14,550	15,040	15,540	16,060	16,590	17,140	17,700
8	14,770	15,350	15,940	16,550	17,180	17,840	18,510	19,210
9	15,510	16,190	16,890	17,620	18,380	19,170	19,990	20,840
10	16,290	17,080	17,910	18,770	19,670	20,610	21,590	22,610
11	17,100	18,020	18,980	19,990	21,050	22,160	23,310	24,530
12	17,960	19,010	20,120	21,290	22,520	23,820	25,180	26,620
13	18,860	20,010	21,330	22,670	24,100	25,610	27,190	28,880
14	19,800	21,160	22,610	24,150	25,780	27,530	29,370	31,340
15	20,790	22,320	23,970	25,720	27,590	29,590	31,720	34,000
16	21,830	23,550	25,400	27,390	29,520	31,810	34,260	36,890
17	22,920	24,850	26,930	29,170	31,590	34,190	37,000	40,030
18	24,070	26,210	28,540	31,060	33,799	36,760	39,960	43,430
19	25,270	27,660	30,260	33,080	36,160	39,520	43,150	47,120
20	26,530	29,180	32,070	35,230	38,700	42,480	46,610	51,120

					Growth Rates			
Number of Years	9%	9.5%	10%	10.5%	11%	11.5%	12%	12.5%
1	$10,900	$10,950	$11,000	$11,050	$11,100	$11,150	$11,200	$11,250
2	11,880	11,990	12,100	12,210	12,320	12,430	12,540	12,660
3	12,950	13,130	13,310	13,490	13,680	13,860	14,050	14,240
4	14,120	14,380	14,640	14,910	15,180	15,460	15,730	16,020
5	15,390	15,740	16,100	16,470	16,850	17,230	17,620	18,020
6	16,770	17,240	17,720	18,200	18,700	19,210	19,740	20,270
7	18,280	18,870	19,490	20,110	20,760	21,420	22,110	22,810
8	19,920	20,670	21,440	22,230	23,040	23,890	24,760	25,660
9	21,720	22,630	23,580	24,560	25,580	26,640	27,730	28,860
10	23,670	24,780	25,940	27,140	28,390	29,700	31,060	32,470
11	25,800	27,130	28,530	29,990	31,520	33,110	34,790	36,530
12	28,120	29,710	31,380	33,140	34,980	36,920	38,960	41,100
13	30,650	32,540	34,520	36,620	38,830	41,170	43,630	46,240
14	33,410	35,630	37,980	40,460	43,100	45,900	48,870	52,020
15	36,420	39,010	41,770	44,710	47,840	51,180	54,740	58,520
16	39,700	42,720	45,950	49,410	53,110	57,070	61,300	65,830
17	43,270	46,780	50,550	54,600	58,950	63,630	68,660	74,060
18	47,166	51,220	55,600	60,330	65,430	70,947	76,900	83,320
19	51,410	56,090	61,160	66,660	72,630	79,110	86,130	93,740
20	56,040	61,410	67,280	73,660	80,620	88,200	96,460	105,500

Growth Rates

Number of Years	13%	13.5%	14%	14.5%	15%	15.5%	16%	16.5%
1	$ 11,300	$ 11,350	$ 11,400	$ 11,450	$ 11,500	$ 11,550	$ 11,600	$ 11,650
2	12,770	12,880	13,000	13,110	13,220	13,340	13,460	13,570
3	14,430	14,620	14,810	15,010	15,210	15,410	15,610	15,810
4	16,300	16,590	16,890	17,190	17,490	17,800	18,110	18,420
5	18,420	18,830	19,250	19,680	20,110	20,550	21,000	21,460
6	20,816	21,380	21,950	22,530	23,130	23,740	24,360	25,000
7	23,520	24,260	25,020	25,800	26,600	27,420	28,260	29,120
8	26,580	27,540	28,570	29,540	30,590	31,670	32,780	33,930
9	30,040	31,260	32,520	33,830	35,180	36,580	38,030	39,530
10	33,940	35,480	37,070	38,730	40,460	42,250	44,110	46,050
11	38,360	40,270	42,260	44,350	46,530	48,800	51,170	53,650
12	43,340	45,700	48,170	50,780	53,500	56,360	59,360	62,500
13	48,980	51,870	54,920	58,140	61,530	65,100	66,850	72,820
14	55,340	58,880	62,610	66,570	70,760	75,190	79,870	84,830
15	62,540	66,820	71,370	76,220	81,370	86,840	92,650	98,830
16	70,670	75,850	81,370	87,270	93,580	100,300	107,500	115,100
17	79,860	86,080	92,760	99,930	107,600	115,800	124,600	134,100
18	90,240	97,710	105,700	114,400	123,800	133,800	144,600	156,260
19	102,000	110,900	120,500	131,000	142,300	154,500	167,800	182,000
20	115,200	125,700	137,400	150,000	163,700	178,500	194,600	212,100

Number of Years	17%	17.5%	18%	18.5%	19%	19.5%	20%	20.5%
				Growth Rates				
1	$ 11,700	$ 11,750	$ 11,800	$ 11,850	$ 11,900	$ 11,950	$ 12,00	$ 12,050
2	13,690	13,810	13,920	14,040	14,160	14,280	14,400	14,520
3	16,020	16,220	16,430	16,640	16,850	17,060	17,280	17,500
4	18,740	19,060	19,390	19,720	20,050	20,390	20,740	21,080
5	21,920	22,400	22,880	23,360	23,860	24,370	24,880	25,410
6	25,650	26,320	27,000	27,680	28,400	29,120	29,860	30,610
7	30,010	30,920	31,850	32,800	33,790	34,800	35,830	36,890
8	35,110	36,330	37,590	38,870	40,210	41,590	43,000	44,450
9	41,080	42,690	44,350	46,060	47,860	49,700	51,600	53,560
10	48,070	50,160	52,340	54,580	56,950	59,390	61,920	64,550
11	56,240	58,940	61,760	64,680	67,820	70,970	74,300	77,780
12	65,800	69,250	72,870	76,640	80,700	84,810	89,160	93,720
13	76,990	81,370	85,990	90,820	96,030	101,300	107,000	112,900
14	90,080	95,610	101,500	107,600	114,300	121,100	128,400	136,100
15	105,400	112,300	119,700	127,500	136,000	144,700	154,100	164,000
16	123,300	132,000	141,300	151,100	161,800	172,900	184,900	197,600
17	144,300	155,100	166,700	179,100	192,600	206,700	221,900	238,100
18	168,800	182,200	196,700	212,200	229,200	247,000	266,200	286,900
19	197,500	241,100	232,100	251,500	272,700	295,100	319,500	345,700
20	231,100	251,600	273,900	298,000	324,500	352,700	383,400	416,600

Growth Rates

Number of Years	21%	21.5%	22%	22.5%	23%	23.5%	24%	24.5%
1	$ 12,100	$ 12,150	$ 12,200	$ 12,250	$ 12,300	$ 12,350	$ 12,400	$ 12,450
2	14,640	14,760	14,880	15,010	15,130	15,250	15,380	15,500
3	17,720	17,940	18,160	18,380	18,610	18,840	19,070	19,300
4	21,440	21,790	22,150	22,520	22,890	23,260	23,640	24,030
5	25,940	26,480	27,030	27,580	28,150	28,730	29,310	29,910
6	31,380	32,170	32,970	33,790	34,630	35,480	36,350	37,240
7	37,980	39,090	40,230	41,390	42,590	43,820	45,070	46,360
8	45,950	47,490	49,080	50,710	52,390	54,110	55,890	57,720
9	55,600	57,700	59,870	62,120	64,440	66,830	69,310	71,870
10	67,280	70,100	73,040	76,100	79,260	82,540	85,940	89,470
11	81,400	85,180	89,110	93,220	97,490	101,900	106,600	111,400
12	98,500	103,500	108,700	114,200	119,900	125,900	132,100	138,700
13	119,200	125,700	132,600	139,900	147,500	155,500	163,900	172,700
14	144,200	152,800	161,800	171,400	181,400	192,000	203,200	215,000
15	174,500	185,600	197,400	209,900	223,100	237,100	251,900	267,600
16	211,100	225,500	240,800	257,100	274,500	292,800	312,400	333,200
17	255,500	274,000	293,800	315,000	337,600	361,700	387,400	414,800
18	309,100	332,900	358,500	385,900	415,200	446,700	480,300	516,500
19	374,100	404,500	437,300	472,700	510,700	551,600	595,600	643,000
20	452,600	491,500	533,600	579,100	628,200	681,300	738,600	800,500

Number of Years				Growth Rates				
	25%	25.5%	26%	26.5%	27%	27.5%	28%	28.5
1	$ 12,500	$ 12,550	$ 12,600	$ 12,650	$ 12,700	$ 12,750	$ 12,800	$ 12,850
2	15,620	15,750	15,880	16,000	16,130	16,260	16,380	16,510
3	19,530	19,770	20,000	20,240	20,480	20,730	20,970	21,220
4	24,410	24,810	25,200	25,610	26,010	26,430	26,840	27,260
5	30,520	31,130	31,760	32,390	33,040	33,690	34,360	35,040
6	38,150	39,070	40,010	40,980	41,960	42,960	43,980	45,020
7	47,680	49,030	50,420	51,830	53,280	54,770	56,300	57,850
8	59,610	61,530	63,530	65,570	67,670	69,840	72,060	74,340
9	74,510	77,230	80,040	82,950	85,940	89,040	92,240	95,530
10	93,130	96,920	100,900	104,900	109,100	113,500	118,100	122,800
11	116,400	121,600	127,100	132,700	138,600	144,700	151,100	157,700
12	145,500	152,600	160,100	167,900	176,000	184,600	193,400	202,700
13	181,900	191,600	201,800	212,400	223,600	235,300	247,600	260,500
14	227,400	240,400	254,200	268,700	283,900	300,000	316,900	334,700
15	284,200	301,700	320,300	339,900	360,600	382,500	405,700	429,700
16	355,300	378,700	403,600	431,000	458,000	487,700	519,200	552,100
17	444,100	475,200	508,500	543,900	581,600	621,900	664,600	709,500
18	555,100	596,400	640,700	688,000	738,700	792,800	850,700	911,700
19	693,900	748,500	807,300	870,400	938,100	1,011,000	1,089,000	1,172,000
20	867,400	939,400	1,017,000	1,101,000	1,191,000	1,289,000	1,394,000	1,505,000

Growth Rates

Number of Years	29%	29.5%	30%	30.5%	31%	31.5%	32%	32.5%
1	$ 12,900	$ 12,950	$ 13,000	$ 13,050	$ 13,100	$ 13,150	$ 13,200	$ 13,250
2	16,640	16,770	16,900	17,030	17,160	17,290	17,420	17,560
3	21,470	21,720	21,970	22,220	22,480	22,740	23,000	23,260
4	27,690	28,120	28,560	29,000	29,450	29,900	30,360	30,820
5	35,720	36,420	37,130	37,850	38,580	39,320	40,070	40,840
6	46,080	47,160	48,270	49,390	50,540	51,710	52,900	54,110
7	59,440	61,080	62,750	64,460	66,210	28,000	69,830	71,700
8	76,680	79,100	81,570	84,120	86,730	89,410	92,170	95,000
9	98,920	102,400	106,000	109,800	113,600	117,600	121,700	125,900
10	127,600	132,600	137,800	143,300	148,800	154,600	160,600	166,800
11	164,600	171,800	179,200	186,900	195,000	203,300	212,000	221,000
12	212,400	222,500	233,000	244,000	255,400	267,400	279,800	292,800
13	273,900	288,100	302,900	318,400	334,600	351,600	369,400	388,000
14	353,400	373,100	393,700	415,500	438,300	462,300	487,600	514,100
15	455,900	483,100	511,800	542,200	574,200	608,000	643,600	681,100
16	588,100	625,600	665,400	707,600	752,200	799,500	849,500	902,500
17	758,600	810,200	865,000	923,400	985,400	1,051,000	1,121,000	1,196,000
18	978,600	1,049,000	1,124,000	1,205,000	1,291,000	1,382,000	1,480,000	1,584,000
19	1,262,000	1,359,000	1,462,000	1,573,000	1,691,000	1,818,000	1,954,000	2,099,000
20	1,628,000	1,760,000	1,900,000	2,052,000	2,215,000	2,391,000	2,579,000	2,782,000

Growth Rates

Number of Years	33%	33.5%	34%	34.5%	35%	35.5%	36%	36.5%
1	$ 13,300	$ 13,350	$ 13,400	$ 13,450	$ 13,500	$ 13,550	$ 13,600	$ 13,650
2	17,690	17,820	17,960	18,090	18,220	18,360	18,500	18,630
3	23,530	23,790	24,060	24,330	24,600	24,880	25,150	25,430
4	31,290	31,760	32,240	32,720	33,210	33,710	34,210	34,720
5	41,620	42,400	43,200	44,010	44,840	45,680	46,530	47,390
6	55,350	56,610	57,890	59,200	60,530	61,890	63,270	64,680
7	73,610	75,570	77,580	79,620	81,720	83,860	86,050	88,290
8	97,910	100,900	104,000	107,000	110,300	113,600	117,000	120,500
9	130,200	134,700	139,300	144,000	148,900	154,000	159,200	164,500
10	173,200	179,800	186,700	193,700	201,100	208,600	216,500	224,600
11	230,300	240,000	250,100	260,600	271,400	282,700	294,400	306,500
12	306,400	320,400	335,200	350,500	366,400	383,100	400,400	418,400
13	407,400	427,800	449,100	471,400	494,700	519,100	544,500	571,100
14	541,900	571,100	601,800	634,000	667,800	703,300	740,500	779,600
15	720,700	762,400	806,400	852,700	901,600	953,000	1,077,000	1,064,000
16	958,600	1,018,000	1,081,000	1,147,000	1,217,000	1,291,000	1,370,000	1,452,000
17	1,275,000	1,359,000	1,448,000	1,543,000	1,643,000	1,750,000	1,863,000	1,983,000
18	1,696,000	1,814,000	1,940,000	2,075,000	2,218,000	2,371,000	2,533,000	2,706,000
19	2,255,000	2,422,000	2,600,000	2,791,000	2,995,000	3,213,00	3,445,000	3,694,000
20	2,999,000	3,233,000	3,484,000	3,753,000	4,043,000	4,353,000	4,686,000	5,042,000

Number of Years	Growth Rates						
	37%	37.5%	38%	38.5%	39%	39.5%	40%
1	$ 13,700	$ 13,750	$ 13,800	$ 13,850	$ 13,900	$ 13,950	$ 14,000
2	18,770	18,910	19,040	19,180	19,320	19,460	19,600
3	25,710	26,000	26,280	26,570	26,860	27,150	27,440
4	35,230	35,740	36,270	36,790	37,330	37,870	38,420
5	48,260	49,150	50,050	50,960	51,890	52,830	53,780
6	66,120	67,580	69,070	70,580	72,130	73,700	75,290
7	90,580	92,920	95,310	97,750	100,300	102,800	105,400
8	124,100	127,800	131,500	135,400	139,400	143,400	147,600
9	170,000	175,700	181,500	187,500	193,700	200,100	206,600
10	232,900	241,600	250,500	259,700	269,200	279,100	289,300
11	319,100	332,100	345,700	359,700	374,300	289,300	405,000
12	437,100	456,700	477,000	498,200	520,200	543,100	566,900
13	598,900	628,000	658,300	690,000	723,100	757,600	793,700
14	820,500	863,500	908,500	955,600	1,005,000	1,057,000	1,111,000
15	1,124,000	1,187,000	1,254,000	1,324,000	1,397,000	1,474,000	1,556,000
16	1,540,000	1,632,000	1,730,000	1,833,000	1,942,000	2,057,000	2,178,000
17	2,110,000	2,245,000	2,387,000	2,539,000	2,699,000	2,869,000	3,049,000
18	2,890,000	3,086,000	3,295,000	3,516,000	3,752,000	4,003,000	4,269,000
19	3,960,000	4,244,000	4,547,000	4,870,000	5,215,000	5,584,000	5,976,000
20	5,425,000	5,835,000	6,275,000	6,745,000	7,249,000	7,789,000	8,367,000

VALUE OF $300 INITIAL PAYMENT PLUS $100 PER MONTH INVESTED FROM 1 TO 40 YEARS AT COMPOUND GROWTH RATES OF 1 TO 20 PERCENT PER YEAR.

This table was constructed on the assumption that the growth only applies to the amount invested at the start of the year, and not to the additional monthly payments. Including the growth made during the year, either monthly or using average values, would result in end values slightly higher than shown.

Most funds require a starting amount of $250 to $1,000. A starting value of $300 was selected for this table. The starting amount becomes insignificant when compared to $100 per month over the years. Accordingly, the values shown may be directly proportioned for payments of other than $100 a month—doubled for $200 a month, and so on. If you do need a more accurate figure for, say, starting with a down payment of $1,000, just use Appendix A for $700 ($1,000 − $300) and add the result to that from Appendix B.

Growth Rates

Number of Years	1%	2%	3%	4%	5%	6%	7%	8%	9%	10%
1	$ 1.503	$ 1.506	$ 1.509	$ 1.512	$ 1.515	$ 1.518	$ 1.521	$ 1.524	$ 1.527	$ 1.530
2	2.720	2.740	2.750	2.770	2.790	2.810	2.830	2.850	2.860	2.880
3	3.950	3.990	4.040	4.080	4.130	4.180	4.320	4.270	4.320	4.370
4	5.180	5.270	5.360	5.450	5.540	5.630	5.720	5.820	5.910	6.010
5	6.440	6.580	6.720	6.860	7.010	7.160	7.320	7.480	7.640	7.810
6	7.700	7.910	8.120	8.340	8.560	8.800	9.030	9.280	9.530	9.790
7	8.890	9.270	9.560	9.870	10.190	10.520	10.870	11.220	11.590	11.970
8	10.270	10.650	11.050	11.470	11.900	12.360	12.830	13.320	13.830	14.370
9	11.570	12.060	12.580	13.130	13.700	14.300	14.930	15.580	16.280	17.000
10	12.890	13.500	14.160	14.850	15.580	16.350	17.170	18.030	18.940	19.900
11	14.210	14.980	15.780	16.650	17.560	18.540	19.570	20.670	21.850	23.090
12	15.560	16.470	17.460	18.510	19.640	20.850	22.140	23.530	25.010	26.600
13	16.910	18.000	19.180	20.450	21.820	23.300	24.890	26.610	28.460	30.460
14	18.280	19.560	20.960	22.470	24.110	25.900	27.830	29.940	32.230	34.710
15	19.660	21.160	22.790	24.570	26.520	28.650	30.980	33.530	36.330	39.380
16	21.060	22.780	24.670	26.750	29.040	31.570	34.350	37.420	40.800	44.520
17	22.470	24.430	26.610	29.020	31.700	34.660	37.960	41.610	45.670	50.170
18	23.900	26.120	28.610	31.380	34.480	37.940	41.810	46.140	50.980	56.390
19	25.340	27.850	30.670	33.840	37.400	41.420	45.940	51.030	56.760	63.220
20	26.790	29.600	32.790	36.390	40.480	45.100	50.360	56.310	63.070	70.750
25	34.280	38.930	44.380	50.770	58.290	67.120	77.530	89.780	104.200	121.300
30	42.150	49.230	57.820	68.270	81.020	96.590	115.600	139.000	167.500	202.600
35	50.200	60.600	73.200	89.400	110.100	135.000	168.000	210.000	263.000	322.000
40	58.700	73.300	91.400	113.700	148.600	185.000	242.000	314.000	404.000	524.000

Number of Years	11%	12%	13%	14%	Growth Rates 15%	16%	17%	18%	19%	20%
1	$ 1.533	$ 1.536	$ 1.539	$ 1.542	$ 1.545	$ 1.548	$ 1.551	$ 1.554	$ 1.557	$ 1.560
2	2.900	2.920	2.940	2.960	2.980	3.000	3.010	3.030	3.050	3.070
3	4.420	4.470	4.520	4.570	4.620	4.670	4.730	4.780	4.830	4.890
4	6.110	6.210	6.310	6.410	6.520	6.620	6.730	6.840	6.950	7.060
5	7.980	8.150	8.330	8.510	8.690	8.880	9.080	9.270	9.470	9.680
6	10.060	10.330	10.610	10.900	11.200	11.500	11.820	12.140	12.470	12.810
7	12.360	12.770	13.190	13.630	14.080	14.540	15.030	15.530	16.040	16.570
8	14.920	15.500	16.110	16.740	17.390	18.070	18.780	19.520	20.290	21.090
9	17.760	18.560	19.400	20.280	21.200	22.160	23.170	24.230	25.340	26.510
10	20.920	21.990	23.120	24.320	25.580	26.910	28.310	29.800	31.360	33.010
11	24.420	25.830	27.330	28.920	30.610	32.410	34.330	36.360	38.520	40.810
12	28.300	30.130	32.080	34.170	36.410	38.800	41.360	44.100	47.040	50.170
13	32.620	34.940	37.450	40.150	43.070	46.210	49.590	53.200	57.170	61.400
14	37.410	40.340	43.520	46.980	50.730	54.800	59.220	64.020	69.240	74.890
15	42.720	46.380	50.380	54.750	59.540	64.770	70.490	76.750	83.590	91.060
16	48.620	53.140	58.130	63.620	69.670	76.330	83.680	91.770	100.700	110.500
17	55.170	60.720	66.880	73.720	81.320	89.750	99.100	109.500	121.000	133.800
18	62.440	69.210	76.780	85.250	94.720	105.300	117.200	130.400	145.200	161.700
19	70.500	78.710	87.960	98.380	110.100	123.400	138.300	155.000	174.000	195.300
20	79.460	89.360	100.600	113.400	127.800	144.300	163.000	184.200	208.200	235.500
25	141.400	165.100	193.100	226.200	265.200	311.300	365.700	430.200	505.700	595.000
30	245.700	298.600	363.600	443.400	541.600	662.100	810.200	992.100	1,215.000	1,489.000
35	420.000	531.000	676.000	860.000	1,096.000	1,396.000	1,776.000	2,276.000	2,906.000	3,700.000
40	713.000	935.000	1,240.000	1,666.000	2,226.000	2,936.000	3,896.000	5,196.000	6,910.000	9,200.000

APPENDIX C
MUTUAL FUND ADDRESSES

Able Associates Fund
174 Birch Drive
Manhasset Hills, NY 11040

Acorn Fund
120 S. La Salle Street
Chicago, IL 60603

Afuture Fund
Front and Lemon Streets
Media, PA 19063

American Investors Fund
88 Field Point Road
Greenwich, CT 06830

Analytic Optioned
   Equity Fund
222 Martin Street
Irvine, CA 92715

Babson Funds
2400 Pershing Road
Kansas City, MO 64108

Boston Company Funds
1 Boston Place
Boston, MA 02106

Capital Preservation Funds
755 Page Mill Road
Palo Alto, CA 94304

Columbia Growth Fund
621 S.W. Morrison Street
Portland, OR 97205

Constellation Growth Fund
331 Madison Avenue
New York, NY 10017

De Vegh Mutual Fund
120 Broadway
New York, NY 10271

Directors Capital
30 Broad Street
New York, NY 10004

Dodge and Cox Funds
35th Floor, One Post Street
San Francisco, CA 94104

Dreyfus Funds
600 Madison Avenue
New York, NY 10022

Energy Fund
342 Madison Avenue
New York, NY 10173

Energy and Utility Shares
P.O. Box 550
Blue Bell, PA 19422

Evergreen Funds
550 Mamaroneck Avenue
Harrison, NY 10528

Fidelity Funds
82 Devonshire Street
Boston, MA 02109

44 Wall Street Fund
150 Broadway
New York, NY 10038

Financial Industrial Fund
P.O. Box 2040
Denver, CO 80201

Founders Funds
1300 First of Denver Plaza
Denver, CO 80202

Foursquare Fund
24 Federal Street
Boston, MA 02110

Gaming, Sports, and Growth
  Fund
1700 Market Street
Philadelphia, PA 19103

Gateway Option Income Fund
1120 Carew Tower
Cincinati, OH 04520

Gintel Funds
Greenwich Office Park OP-6
Greenwich, CT 06830

Golconda Investors
11 Hanover Square
New York, NY 10005

Good and Bad Times Fund
P.O. Box 29869
San Antonio, TX 78229

GSC Performance Fund
SCN Building
Greenville, SC 29601

GT Pacific Fund
601 Montgomery Street
San Francisco, CA 94111

Hartwell Funds
50 Rockefeller Plaza
New York, NY 10020

Janus Fund
789 Sherman Street
Denver, CO 80203

Lehman Funds
55 Water Kreet
New York, NY 10041

Lexington Goldfund
P.O. Box 1515
Englewood Cliffs, NJ 07632

Lindner Funds
200 S. Bemiston Avenue
St. Louis, MO 63105

Mathers Fund, Inc.
125 S. Wacker Drive
Chicago, IL 60606

Medical Technology Fund
1107 Bethlehem Pike
Flourtown, PA 19031

Mutual Funds
26 Broadway
New York, NY 10004

National Aviation and Technology Corp.
50 Broad Street
New York, NY 10004

National Industries Fund
2130 S. Dahlia Street
Denver, CO 80222

Neuwirth Fund
120 Broadway
New York, NY 10005

Nicholas Fund
312 E. Wisconsin Avenue
Milwaukee, WI 53202

North Star Regional Fund
P.O. Box 1160
Minneapolis, MN 55440

Northeast Investment Trust
50 Congress Street
Boston, MA 02109

Northeast Investors Trust
50 Congress Street
Boston, MA 02109

Nuveen Funds
115 S. La Salle Street
Chicago, IL 60603

Omega Fund
77 Franklin Street
Boston, MA 02110

Oppenheimer Funds
2 Broadway
New York, NY 10004

Partners Fund
342 Madison Avenue
New York, NY 10173

Pax World Fund
224 State Street
Portsmouth, NH 03801

Pennsylvania Mutual Fund
1414 Avenue of the Americas
New York, NY 10019

The Reserve Fund
810 Seventh Avenue
New York, NY 10019

Rowe Price Funds
100 E. Pratt Street
Baltimore, MD 21202

Scudder Funds
345 Park Avenue
New York, NY 10154

Sequoia Fund
540 Madison Avenue
New York, NY 10022

Steadman Funds
1730 K Street
Washington, DC 20006

Stein Roe Funds
150 S. Wacker Drive
Chicago, IL 60606

Transatlantic Fund
100 Wall Street
New York, NY 10005

20th Century Funds
P.O. Box 200
Kansas City, MO 64141

United Services Gold Shares
  Fund
P.O. Box 29467
San Antonio, TX 78229

USAA Mutual Fund
9800 Fredericksburg Road
San Antonio, TX 78288

Value Line Funds
711 Third Avenue
New York, NY 10017

Vanguard Funds
P.O. Box 876
Valley Forge, PA 19482

Weingarten Equity Fund
331 Madison Avenue
New York, NY 10017

Index